World War Memoirs

of

Radar Reminiscence and Romance

by
KEN WATSON

A Comprehensive Account
of the Experiences of
an R.A.F. Radar Mechanic

JUNE 1941 – JANUARY 1947

All rights reserved.

No part of this publication may be reproduced,
stored in a retrieval system or transmitted,
in any form or by any means, electronic, mechanical,
photocopying, recording or otherwise without
the permission of the editor.

◆

Published by Printability Publishing Ltd.
on behalf of Ken Watson ©

Printed by Atkinson Print Ltd.
10/11 Lower Church Street,
Hartlepool TS24 7DJ

Tel: 01429 267849 Fax: 01429 865416
ISDN No: 01429 894231

e-mail: printability@atkinsonprint.co.uk
www.atkinsonprint.co.uk

ISBN 1 872239 42 0

Dedication

✦✦✦✦

Everyone born into this world is unique. How they co-operate with others as they grow up determines the quality of society. These memoirs are about people who left kith and kin, hearth and home, from places round the world, to defend their way of life under threat from powerful and well organised alien forces determined to destroy it. They were dark and dangerous times that tested resilience sometimes beyond breaking point.

It was my privilege to serve alongside men and women from many countries and all walks of life. It was a melting pot for the whole gamut of human attributes. Attached as I was to a succession of such cosmopolitan groups, often in tightly confined conditions, it was an opportunity to broaden my view of the world that surpassed anything a conventional university education could have offered. It was the University of Life.

Over 60 years after the events described in this book, my wife Enid and my good friend and colleague Alan White urged me to write a full account of experiences of which they had heard but snippets. "It is a tale that must be told before it is too late," they counselled. So began a project that took several months to complete. Throughout, their constant encouragement and constructive criticism sustained me.

The virtue of coming to the task so long after the events had been experienced is that all the dross had been expunged by time. Only nuggets of value had survived. People long submerged in the subconscious memory emerged with startling clarity. To a very large extent the book wrote itself, as though voices from the past were whispering in my ear as I went along.

It is to the men and women depicted in the book, against a background of momentous events, that I dedicate these memoirs. Sadly there will be few of them still alive to accept the dedication. In their stead, their children, grandchildren and great grandchildren can read of their exploits with justifiable pride, grateful for the legacy bequeathed to them by a generation that stood firm against tremendous odds to preserve a way of life for which they were prepared, if need be, to make the ultimate sacrifice.

CONTENTS

❖❖❖

Chapter		Page
1	Blackpool	1
2	Yatesbury	9
3	Marking Time in N. Ireland	12
4	Battersea Polytechnic	16
5	Yatesbury Revisited	27
6	RAF Crustan, Orkney	41
7	RAF Rodel Park, Outer Hebrides	68
8	Sennen Cove, Land's End	101
9	RAF Trimingham, Norfolk	102
10	RAF Cleadon	105
11	RAF Tilly Whim, Swanage	109
12	Into Europe	123
13	The Ardennes	128
14	Battle of the Bulge	136
15	Interlude in Mons	140
16	Advance into Germany	147
17	Bad Mergentheim	156
18	La Capelle, France	167
19	Epilogue	194

Introduction

◆◆◆

By

*Alan White, Headteacher,
Manor College of Technology, Hartlepool*

Having watched Ken Watson effortlessly engage children during school assemblies and witnessed beautifully delivered and often achingly hilarious presentations to a wide variety of audiences, I knew that he had a special gift for story telling and a tremendous command of the English language. Ken remains the only guest speaker at Manor college who routinely receives spontaneous applause from our children. Quite simply, he sprinkles stardust on each of them and they adore him for it.

I first met Ken Watson eight years ago when he was introduced to me as the Chair of Governors of Manor College of Technology in Hartlepool and throughout the intervening years he has been my closest friend, my most powerful advocate and following the death of my father, my mentor and confidant. Articulate, knowledgeable and blessed with the kind of infinite patience and understanding which comes only with age and experience, Ken is a precious gem and is one of Hartlepool's treasures.

I have spent countless, hugely enjoyable hours in the company of Ken Watson and have pressed him quite relentlessly to describe his experiences during World War II and about his seven decades of service to education in our home town of Hartlepool. Whenever Ken recounted his experiences I was astonished by the degree of clarity and the immense detail he was able to recall. It became abundantly clear that the events which have shaped Ken Watson's life had such a profound effect on him that he was able to recall them with remarkable lucidity some sixty years after they had occurred. Ken has shared with me many of his war time experiences and they are such compelling and fascinating accounts that he had to be encouraged to commit them to paper. This book is the result.

Mr. Watson, like the best educated of his generation, is a skilled wordsmith and having had the privilege of reading the unpublished manuscript, I am sure that readers will agree that it is an eminently readable and beautifully crafted work. Punctuated with many gloriously amusing anecdotes, the book is also rich in what is almost 'poetic' symmetry, dealing as it does with romance, personal hardship and tragedy within the context of world changing events.

This book will be of enormous value to military historians who are particularly interested in the development of RADAR but its special appeal is in its humanity. Ken Watson developed a close affinity with the Outer Hebrides and its people and although he hasn't shared it with me, I suspect that much of his book is dedicated to them as well as to his former brothers-in-arms, many of whom are no longer alive.

Like an artist, Ken Watson has painted vivid scenes for the reader to enjoy and his ability to recall the past is matchless in my experience. I have never visited the Western Isles but Ken's colourful descriptions of the landscape and the people are so beautifully written that I feel as though I am closely acquainted with them.

As the father of Manor College, Mr. Watson is loved and respected by the staff and the pupils and it is through working with people all of his life that he has developed the sensitivity and compassion that are the prerequisites for a special piece of work such as this. Ken Watson's book will be of real interest, not just to people who know and appreciate him, but to a much wider readership.

I am enormously fond of Mr. Watson and I am grateful that he has found the time, energy and spirit to be able to commit his memories to paper. We have them now, in perpetuity, and I am sure that readers will enjoy sharing his war-time memoirs as much as I have.

30th October, 2003.

Blackpool

The war had been a fact of life for a year and nine months when I joined the fray full time. After the first six months of what became known as the 'phoney war' events had speeded up. The major catastrophe of Dunkirk, the blitz and the Battle of Britain were behind us. The unrelenting Battle of the Atlantic was being waged. Rationing was in full swing. Churchill's great rallying speeches had sustained the nation through the darkest hours. In his words we were not yet at the beginning of the end but rather at the end of the beginning. I went to war young, idealistic and optimistic. It never crossed my mind that we could lose. Unlike the majority of servicemen at that time I had no responsibilities of a wife and family. I was embarking on a tremendously thrilling adventure. I was ready and willing to leave the old life behind.

Enniskillen, Northern Ireland, August 1941 - Aged 18.

The day of my departure was memorable. Case packed, I took leave of my parents, mother tearful, father philosophical. He told me to take care of myself, to write regularly, and to remember always the standards I had been brought up to live by. A firm warm handshake from him, a last hug and kiss from her, and I was on my way. A couple of minutes later, I remembered having left something behind and turned back. Re-entering the living room I was confronted by the sight of my father huddled in his armchair, sobbing his heart out. From the kitchen could be heard the quieter weeping of my mother. Between his sobs, and obviously devastatingly embarrassed by the situation, my father said, "I'm sorry son. I never thought I'd ever live to see any of mine have to go through what I went through all those years ago. Better hurry lad. You'll miss your bus." Quietly and quickly I took my leave. In those few minutes that separated my departures a lifetime of memories had confronted my father. He was entitled to privacy as he contended with his personal grief.

My call up instructions were to report to Recruiting Centre No. 9 at Blackpool. A travel warrant was enclosed. This was the farthest I had travelled by train and the first significant journey undertaken on my own. The carriages were full, and in the latter stages carried passengers of like aspirations. On arrival at Central Station RAF corporals awaited this new contingent of rookies with raucous shouts of "This way.

Let's be having you in straight lines. You're not sloppy civilians now." This was water off a duck's back to me, having been drilled in the Home Guard by Durham Light Infantry NCO's, but I observed the looks of startled consternation on the faces of some people for whom the niceties of military language would soon bring about a rude awakening. We were marched, or rather we stumbled, to a nearby billeting station where we were allocated accommodation for the first night. My temporary home was in a typical Blackpool bed and breakfast private house and I shared a bed with a long distance lorry driver from Preston who kept his socks on. He was not at all pleased to have been conscripted.

The following morning we were marched, along with a few hundred others, to the ballroom of the Winter Gardens for an F.F.I. (free from infection) and for kitting out. The first was an incongruous experience. Rows of men dropped their trousers and lifted their shirts on command while a succession of medical officers and orderlies peered at their genitals, occasionally using a torch. This was the first of many such indignities yet to be encountered.

The second was equally memorable. We shuffled along lines of trestle tables laden with greatcoats, tunics, trousers, groundsheets, shirts, collars, ties, underwear, boots, socks, backpacks, mess tins, water bottles and kitbags. At each stage you stated your current size, or were perfunctorily measured if you didn't know it, and finished up with a kitbag and a complete wardrobe. In view of all, you changed into uniform and packed your civilian clothes into receptacles provided, on which you stuck a label with your home address. Within under an hour I had undergone a change of identity. I was now Aircraftman Second Class Watson Kenneth, Service No. 1529826. The following day my civilian clothes were delivered by post. I am told my mother wept.

That afternoon we were rebilleted and I was placed in a medium sized boarding house with one façade facing the promenade at the South Shore end. We were to be there for the next six weeks. I remember the accommodation as being comfortable and the food adequate, though I was a regular partaker in a supplementary supper offer of three whole rounds of thick sliced white bread smothered in dripping. Blackpool sea air promotes a ravenous appetite when you're eighteen.

In keeping with fellow new recruits I strolled along the promenade in the evening and took stock. Everything was strange. Even the relationship of sun to sea was out of kilter. At home the sun shone over the sea from the east. At Blackpool it did so from the west. I had swapped one coast for another. They were on opposite sides of the country. As was to be expected, thoughts of home kept popping into my head but there was no homesickness. I was not looking backwards. All my thoughts were for tomorrow and the tomorrows after that.

My general welcome and induction to the RAF way of life continued the following day, again in the palatial Winter Gardens. This time several hundred of us were seated and subjected to a variety of lecturers. First on stage was a padre whose address was measured, sober, and delivered without any great enthusiasm. It was obviously an address he had delivered many times, and would have lost nothing in its impact had it been relayed over the loudspeaker system. The gist of it was that we were to beware of red biddy and loose women, advice that was to me utterly meaningless. Eavesdropping on the reactions of the more worldly wise around me, I gathered that red biddy was cheap booze in general and Methylated spirits in particular. Loose women were prostitutes, ladies of easy virtue, ladies of the night, harlots, tarts etc. A whole new vocabulary was opening up before me. The non-charismatic clergyman quit from one side of the stage.

From the other side bounded a large, brick-faced Medical Officer, positively oozing presence. "Now lads," he boomed, rubbing his large hands together with relish, "When you've been with these women this is what I want you to do." and proceeded to describe very graphically procedures to be taken immediately after sex, and where specifically the necessary treatment could be found. As a piece of gratuitous final advice he concluded, "Always carry a French letter in your wallet. You never know when you might strike lucky." Those around me gave him a good humoured round of applause. I was completely lost. It seemed my education had been somewhat lacking in certain aspects. Single sex schooling has its drawbacks.

The final public performer was an RAF prototype sporting a large, luxuriously twirled moustache. He looked like a parody but was real enough. He beamed enthusiastically around the theatre before delivering the following: "You've got to keep fit. I get up at six o'clock every morning, go to the window, which has been ajar throughout the night, and throw it wide open. I then take a dozen deep breaths---clears the lungs you know. I follow this with a dozen press ups on the floor---gets the muscles working. Next I strip off and plunge into a bath of cold water. A jolly good rub down with a rough towel ends the routine. After that I feel rosy all over." He paused for breath and was about to take his leave when a voice from the back floated across the theatre. "Can you tell us a bit more about Rosy?" I was beginning to get the hang of things.

Basic training proper began the following day, on the promenade at 7-30 a.m. There were about thirty in our squad and a mixed bunch we were, from various parts of the country, from an assortment of backgrounds, and with an age range from eighteen to thirty odd. I was the youngest. Our corporal was called Oldham. His introductory greeting was spectacular. "I'm here to make men of you and to teach you the meaning of discipline. For the next six weeks you will do exactly what I command. No ifs, buts, or arguments. Immediate, automatic, unquestioned obedience. Now, let's get cracking. Whatever I do, you do." He proceeded to perform a number of physical exercise movements with which we were all familiar. We followed every one unerringly. Then he executed a consummate and breathtaking backward flip, rising high, to land beautifully balanced on the balls of his feet, hands on hips. None of us followed suit. "A right bunch I've got here," he growled, "but I'll have you sorted before you leave Blackpool, make no mistake." In Civvy Street (I was learning the lingo) Oldham had been a stage acrobat and it showed. His carriage was erect, his step light, his balance superb, and he moved with a mixture of feline grace, pride and arrogance. To cap it, he had a sense of humour.

For the rest of that day we went through a repertoire of marching manoeuvres, starting from the beginning which was never "Fall in!" but "Get fell in!" The tallest man acted as marker and took up position. The rest of us took up our stations. On the order "Right dress!" we all shuffled into three ranks with perfect uniform spacing. On the order "For inspection, open order march!" the front and rear ranks stepped one pace forward and back respectively to create space for the inspecting officer to move between ranks. Oldham was a pragmatist. Having got us into this position for the first time, he barked, "While you're there I'd better bloody inspect you, though God knows what I'll find."

Starting at the tall marker, he walked down the front rank, then round its rear, down the second rank and rear, and down the third rank and rear. "Listen and learn," he bellowed. "I am going to tell you what an inspecting officer looks for." As he proceeded, repetitive comments wafted round the squad. "Cap on side of head lad, buttons just above the bridge of your nose." "Straighten that tie." "Belt buckle in line with tunic buttons, dead centre man." "Arms by your sides, fists clenched, thumbs in line with seams of trousers." "Boots I can see my face in, airman." "Get your hair cut." By the time he had finished we all knew the standards expected. He cast a weary eye over the lot of us. "If I was doing my job," he confided, "I'd have you all on a flaming charge. Do you know what a charge is?" "No corporal," we chorused as one voice. "You bloody well will if you turn out like this tomorrow," he threatened. "Now get yourselves back to your billets, and before you sit down to the sumptuous meal your lovely landlady's prepared for you, get yourselves to a barber's. I'll give you his address. Tell him I sent you and he'll know what to do. You'll get it cut price." With this he chuckled. Whether it was the pun or the commission he was hoping to make is open to conjecture. "After your meal," he continued, "plenty of bullshit. You've all got button polish protectors and brushes. Take your tunics off and polish the buttons till they sparkle. And don't forget your cap. Lastly, spit and polish on your boots, all round mind you, not just toe caps. I've got eyes like a bloody eagle's."

We all went to the barber's. All his training with scissors and comb was not called upon. A pair of hand clippers, a few runs straight up and down back and sides, and further loss of personal identity was evidenced by my former locks upon the canvas floor. I sat down that evening, slipped brass buttons into that ingenious device the button stick, and got to work with Brasso, brush, and polishing cloth. My new boots were polished, spat upon, polished again, brushed with a rough bristled, then with a soft bristled brush, and buffed with a soft cloth. I was ready to be confronted by Corporal Oldham in the morning. I very soon learned that Duraglit impregnated cotton swabs reduced the chore of button cleaning enormously, that by scrunching one's tunic up it was possible to get four buttons at once into the slit in the button stick, and that nail varnish, applied to newly polished buttons, preserved the shine for days.

As the days passed by our prowess as a squad improved noticeably, as did the sense of corporate identity. At the end of six weeks' basic training, there was to be a passing out parade with eight squads competing. Eight corporals were vying for recognition that could affect their promotion prospects. From what we observed and heard as other squads drilled up and down the promenade alongside us, various styles of leadership could be identified. Most were bullying, hectoring and threatening. I sensed in Oldham a real leader, bent on creating an ethos in which he and we shared common aspirations.

It being mid June, Blackpool was bustling with civilians on holiday and squads of airmen were being put through their paces in full view and hearing of all. The language was always rough, occasionally foul, and never suitable for those of a delicate disposition. Corporal Oldham decided to capitalise and took us into his confidence. Seated on a bench, enjoying the summer sun, were two elderly ladies of genteel appearance. Oldham marched us back and forth in front of them, to the accompaniment of asides, delivered in stentorian tones, calculated to disturb the ladies' equanimity. "You're like a lot of pregnant ducks." "Missing your mother are you?" "Were you born with two bloody left feet?" Eventually the squad was halted directly opposite the two ladies, as ordered by this loud mouthed, uncouth monster of a man. "Squad halt. Stand at ease. Stand easy." Oldham smiled ingratiatingly at the ladies, turned to the squad, and said in the politest of tones,"Gentlemen, say good afternoon to the ladies." As one we snapped to attention, placed our left hands over our belt buckles, bowed from the waist, doffing our forage caps in our right hands the while, and proclaimed in perfect unison, "Good afternoon , ladies." Replacing his own cap, Oldham yelled, "Squad-----Atten---tion. By the right----quick-----MARCH." and led us off, leaving behind two thoroughly bemused, elderly holiday makers.

My first Sunday church parade was not without incident. All troops were either Anglican (C of E), Catholic (RC), or Other Denominations (OD) and worshipped accordingly. Depending on the length of march from assembly point to each venue, denominational loyalties were flexible. I attended all three during my service, developing a healthy ecumenicalism.

On this, my initial venture, I opted for OD. Roll call completed, for attendance was compulsory, we marched off under the command of a sergeant assisted by corporals. As we halted outside the church, two of the corporals took up positions either side of the entrance portal. We were dismissed and proceeded up the stone steps leading to the church ingress. Those of us with some sense of etiquette and decorum removed our caps en route, placing them in our epaulettes. One airman didn't and the affronted voice of one of the corporals rang out "Take your f-----g cap off airman. You're entering the f-----g House of God."

During the period of basic training everyone had to do a guard duty. Oldham had observed my obvious previous aquaintanceship with military discipline and nominated me, along with three others, for the squad's first assignment, the Polish Embassy H.Q. On arrival we were warned by the guard commander that a high ranking RAF officer was in the habit of touring Blackpool at night, testing the security at various establishments. "He's a nasty bugger," he said, "and has put a few people on a charge." I drew the short straw of midnight to 2 am. Possibly 2 till 4 is worse but there's not much in it. Time never passes more slowly than when you are standing on guard, all alone, while all around are fast asleep. You hear the quarter hours chime and long to hear the hour. Just one more and you'll be tucked up in bed.

Sometime during my stint, a limousine glided up to the quite impressive gate of the embassy. A pennant flew from its bonnet. The driver alighted, went round the vehicle, and opened the front passenger door. Out stepped an officer with scrambled egg (gold braid to the uninitiated) all over the peak of his cap. "Aye, aye," I thought, "Action stations." The officer came up the path, silently, in the dark. Throwing my left foot forward, and thrusting my rifle at arms' length, I commanded, "Halt. Who goes there, friend or enemy?" Back came the reply, "Friend." "Well," I thought, "He wouldn't say 'enemy' would he?" "Advance friend and be recognised." I ordered. When he was just beyond the business end of my rifle I said sharply, "That's far enough." "Look here," he said, "Don't you recognise the uniform, man?" "I do," I replied, "but I need evidence of your identity." "And if I refuse to give it?" he queried. "CALL OUT THE GUARD," I thundered and was soon joined by sleepy headed colleagues and an apprehensive commander of the guard, who escorted the Air Commodore inside. As he departed a few minutes' later, he paused for a word. "Good show," he said, "damned good show. How long have you been in the service, airman?" he asked. I looked him straight in the eye. "Four days, sir," I replied. He considered for a moment, said nothing, and returned to his car, doubtless to test the efficiency of other establishments.

On Saturdays we were marched along the front and then on to the Derby baths for our weekly ablutions. Not all landlords' hospitality to troops extended to bathing facilities. At the height of the holiday season the traffic on the front was frequent and noisy, especially the trams as they rattled up and down. Squads marched in public with one man about five yards ahead of the main body, another a similar distance at the rear. On the Saturday in question, the lead man had completely lost it and our marching was a shambles. Corporal Oldham was a proud man and was not best pleased. "Watson," he barked, as we lined up for the return trip, "I'm putting you in the lead. Traffic will be at its busiest and noisiest. Keep the marching pace going and the squad will take it from you." We set off. It was reasonably quiet to start with, and, occasionally I picked up Oldham's orders, "left, right, left, right, left, right." We swung into the famous Blackpool front. Not only was the traffic din horrendous, but the whole of Lancashire appeared to be on holiday. The pavements were seething. Notwithstanding, I kept the rhythm going in my head. "left, right, left, right, left, right" and put on my best marching style, straight arms punching to shoulder height in front, waist height behind, torso erect, chest out, head up, and just the hint of a swagger. I was quite gratified after a while to notice that people had stopped doing whatever they were doing and watching as we marched past. Little groups were forming. Very very slowly I turned my head to check how the squad was performing. There was no squad. I was performing a solo act. What to do? Picking a spot where it was safe to do so, I locked my arms to my sides and started to mark time, parade ground fashion, thighs brought up parallel to the ground. After what seemed an age, I heard the welcome voice of Corporal Oldham, "left, right, left, right, left, right" and resumed marching. Some five minutes later, we arrived at the main entrance to F.W. Woolworth's, marched to the next corner where the order rang out, "Left wheel" followed by "Squad halt. Stand at ease. Stand easy. Dismiss."

We broke up and I approached Oldham. "What went wrong corporal?" I asked him. "What went bloody wrong?" he grinned "You got over a green light no bother. Before we could follow it changed to red. You played a blinder, son. Couldn't have handled it better myself. The whole of Blackpool was watching us. We're the talk of the town. I'll tell you something else. I've played before some audiences in my time, but I'll never beat the size of that one."

One of the good corporal's many talents was a gift for mimicry. He could do some very authentic impressions. On occasions he demonstrated his skills to the squad's approval and appreciation. The corporal of a rival squad was universally disliked, mostly of course by his own men. We had been dismissed for a short break and were stretched out on the grass when Oldham saw the other squad approaching, their corporal in the lead, five yards ahead. Waiting till their leader had just passed, and the squad was directly opposite, Oldham delivered a command in voice, pitch, timbre, and accent which was a perfect replica of his rival's. "About turn," he roared. The marching squad reacted immediately, and we were rewarded by the sight of the corporal forging ahead while his men were striding off in the opposite direction. Oldham had not finished yet. The orders "Squad halt. Right turn. Stand at ease. Stand easy. Dismiss." rang out. When the hapless corporal rejoined his squad they were stretched out on the grass.

Life was not all quite work and sleep, although there was little an airman could do on a shilling a day. The official rate was two shillings but I was allotting one shilling in my mother's name to guarantee her pension were I to be killed. The remaining shilling had to buy shaving materials, writing paper, stamps, cleaning materials, cups of tea, scones etc. Fortunately there was the occasional free theatre show. At one of them a member of our squad was on stage. He was a tiny Scots comedian who opened the show by twinkling from the wings to centre stage, twirling round, his kilt flouncing out, ending up with one forefinger under his chin, standing on tip toe and squeaking, "Och, the size of it." He concluded by racing from one side of the stage to the other, ending up in centre stage again, facing the audience, arms outstretched, palms uppermost, inviting audience participation. To a man we responded, "Och, the size of it." I had seen my first demonstration of the power of the catchphrase.

Corporal Oldham had not finished with us yet. We were marching very professionally by now, down the main street, myself in pole position, when I got the command, "Left wheel!" "He's made a mistake," I thought. The order would have taken us on to the pavement to the main F.W. Woolworth entrance. I short stepped to give him time. "Left wheel!" he snarled. I obeyed the order and he marched us up three flights of stairs to the café, across the café floor to the counter where he halted us, stood us at ease, and stood us easy. Removing his forage cap, and leaning with his elbows on the counter, he flashed a beaming smile at the waitress and placed his order, "Cuppa tea and a bun, love." He stood there, eating and drinking while we and a full house of customers looked on. When he had finished, he replaced his forage cap, gave the requisite sequence of orders and marched us back down to street level. Once outside he gave us quarter of an hour to slip back up and enjoy our own fare. "After that performance," he said, "you should get it on the house." "After that performance," commented someone; "it's a miracle the house is still standing. The silly bugger's obviously never heard of resonant frequencies."

The culmination of six weeks' intensive training was now imminent and Corporal Oldham was determined that we would claim pride of place. The night before the passing out parade he assembled us to issue final instructions. They were, to say the least, strikingly original. We were to have metal heel plates fitted to our boots, and to stamp down as hard as possible when we marched. The magazine chambers on our rifles were to be slackened just enough to make them rattle as drill was executed. "Not too slack," warned Oldham. "Don't want magazines littering the saluting area." Then came the really ingenious strategy. "The other corporals will be out in front, yelling their bloody heads off, saying 'look at me', declared Oldham with a grin. We'll be different, you and me. I'm going to be right in the middle, whispering the orders, and we'll be saying 'Look at us.' Lord Derby will be mesmerised."

Next day dawned bright and clear. The stage was set. At the appointed hour, with Lord Derby, a hugely massive man, in place on the saluting dais, the first squad began the parade. They were good and so were the six that followed. All were a tribute to six weeks of concentrated effort to transform men from civilians into a disciplined, cohesive unit.

Each drew loud applause from the hundreds watching the proceedings. Then came an apparently leaderless formation. Metal heel plates firmly stamped into the hard road surface emphasised the unison of the rhythmic progress. With no audible word of command the squad, now the centre of attraction, approached the point of salute. From the centre of our ranks, Oldham's hissed, sibilant orders reached our ears, "eft, ight.eft, ight, eft, ight. Then, in time to the beat of the echoing footfalls, "Right—lads—show—them—what—we're—bloody—made—of—eyes—right—check—turn." Rifles at the slope, every head turned to the right as if jerked by some invisible, unanimous force, coordinated precisely with every hand slapping a rifle butt that responded with a resounding rattle. of slackened magazines. Lord Derby returned the salute "eft, ight, eft, ight, eft, ight, —eyes—front—check—turn" came Oldham's exultant command. To a man, all heads turned with stunning precision, and right arms resumed their marching range and rhythm. There were mounting waves of applause from an appreciative audience. They were obviously impressed. So was Lord Derby from whom we were accorded the accolade. Oldham's 'Silent Squad' had proved its worth.

Many thousands of men have mixed memories of their square bashing days. Mine are mainly positive. I learned a lot, not least about myself. I had taken a significant step from boyhood to manhood. It was time to move on and hundreds of us assembled in Bloomfield Park, the home of Blackpool F.C. I waited over three hours before my service number, name and rank were called. I was handed rail travel warrant and other documents and told I would be picked up early the following day and delivered to RAF Yatesbury for training as a radar operator.

—— Yatesbury ——

Blackpool had been a staging post, a half way house between civilian life and the military. The semi-privacy of billeted accommodation had maintained contact with the former existence. Yatesbury was different. Situated deep in the Wiltshire countryside there were no refreshing sea breezes, bustling traffic, or hordes of holidaymakers. Entry was via heavy metal barriers, a guardhouse, and past permanently manned sentry boxes. Papers were checked and, in this initial instance, we reported to the orderly room where our accommodation was arranged.

The camp was huge, with many long wooden huts set in rows, each building housing anything up to forty men. We were marched to our hut and left to organise ourselves. Beds lined both sides of the floor. Large windows allowed plenty of daylight into the area. Electric lights hung from the ceiling. Cast iron stoves, three in total, occupied the central line of the barrack along its length. A wooden locker stood by each bed. Ablutions and toilets were through a door at the far end of the building. Welcome to communal living. A large central cookhouse and dining mess met our culinary needs.

This domestic site housed several hundred men, most of them undergoing training, so the population was constantly changing. The next day we were marched down a very long concrete path to the technical site. Very heavy security was apparent. High metal fencing surrounded the area. A guard stood on duty at the entry gate, which was deliberately narrow to restrict entry to one person only at a time. The NCO in charge of us having presented the required authorisation, we passed through into one of the nation's top security radar schools. The layout was briefly explained to us. Set apart from the main cluster of buildings was a small group with separate security fencing. Here two discrete groups worked. One comprised civilian boffins from leading universities. The other was composed of people, some RAF, some civilian, whose experience and expertise was practical. The two groups collaborated. The boffins would come up with some new idea and pass it across to see if it could be made to work. The practical team would experiment with circuitry, and when something new and potentially valuable resulted they would alert the boffins with the challenge, "When we created this combination of components this was what we got. Can you tell us why?" This was the cutting edge of evolutionary radar technology and I was about to become privy to it.

Before being introduced to our lecture rooms and instructors there was an unexpected formality to be completed. We had to take an eyesight test. It was a matter of routine for the rest. For me it was an unmitigated disaster. I failed it. I protested that, in having been failed for aircrew duties on account of eyesight, I had been advised to enlist as a radar operator, the inference being that my eyesight would be acceptable for that role. The Medical Officer was adamant. Such was the nature of the work, which he could not discuss since it was classified information, I would suffer blinding headaches and possible bouts of nausea if exposed to a radar screen. Utterly stunned, I watched my companions go through to the training section while I trudged back to the domestic site, a chit in my wallet to present to the orderly room.

The RAF has its own approach to maximising the use of manpower. I was transferred immediately to General Duties, the lowest form of animal life in the service. To rub salt into the wound, I was on sentry duty the following day, granting entry to my erstwhile companions as they gained further entry to a world now denied to me. In the next few days I was employed scrubbing out the guardroom floor, painting a pile of coal white, and guarding the main vehicular entrance to the technical site. This latter job proved to be fortuitous. I was very good at sentry duty and an officer in a room which overlooked the spot on which I was performing sent for me. After complimenting me on the smartness of my turnout and on the excellence of my guard duty standards, he asked how I came to be so occupied. I told him. He looked thunderstruck. He then drew some rudimentary circuit diagrams and asked if I recognised any of the symbols. My old Grammar School Physics master would have been proud of me. I identified all of them. "Have you thought about remustering as a radar mechanic?" queried the officer. "Nobody's suggested remustering to anything, sir." I replied. "Well, I think you should," he said and began filling in a form. When he had finished he pushed it across the table for my signature, alongside his. As I signed I read his comments. "Highly intelligent. Should prove satisfactory after training." Under his signature was his rank-----Wing Commander. "Thank you sir," I said, standing up and saluting. "The best of luck to you," he replied, returning the salute. Less than a fortnight after my arrival at Yatesbury, a signal arrived posting me to RAF Lough Erne, County Fermanagh, N. Ireland. My spirits rose again.

During my short sojourn in Wiltshire, I had continued to share the original quarters with the rest of my group, though their lives were entirely divorced from mine. While they marched as a group each day to the top-secret inner sanctum of the technical site, I went my individual way, our paths never crossing. My departure from Yatesbury was scheduled for very early morning and necessitated a 4-30 am call. So as not to wake the whole hut, arrangements were made for an individual wake up call by someone in the guardroom. He would know who to rouse, a towel being placed across the foot of the appropriate bed. I have to admit that I was tempted to place the towel on an adjoining bed, thus waking everyone in the hut in the ensuing protest. I resisted the temptation and a gentle hand on my shoulder roused me. Silently, kitbag on shoulder, I crept out of the hut and across to the cookhouse where a hot breakfast awaited. An open backed lorry took me down to Calne railway station. Alongside me were crates of sprung radar transmitting valves, cushioned against the buffeting. This was as near as I got to the mystique of the radar school.

――― ✦✦✦✦✦ ―――

Marking Time in N. Ireland

A long journey stretched ahead and I was on my own. I had to make a connection at Bristol Temple Mead, which took me to Crewe where there was an eight-hour wait. I spent this in the reading room of a nearby Church Army hostel and wrote a letter home. Crewe was a busy junction in those days and I turned up, well ahead of time, to catch the 8 pm express to Carlisle. Here I changed again, boarding the train to Stranraer. I was breaking all personal records for rail travel. Regular sea crossings took place from Stranraer to Larne in Northern Ireland. I climbed the vessel's gangway and found a comfortable seat on deck, the weather being quite pleasant. It was my first sea crossing. There were to be many more.

From Larne I took a train to Belfast where things became a little complicated. I had to change not only trains but also stations. A patrolling policeman proved to be very helpful and I was soon installed on a westward bound, rickety conveyance, destination Enniskillen in County Fermanagh. En route it became apparent why the island was known as The Emerald Isle. The grass was a deeper green than any I had seen before, and the air was soft but uplifting, so different from the enervating atmosphere of the Wiltshire countryside, or the bracing breezes of Blackpool. Arriving at Irvinestown, I alighted at the same time as an RAF corporal, lightly laden. He spotted me, fully burdened and said, "New arrival? There's only one place round here you can be looking for. I'm just back from leave. There'll be transport along shortly. Fancy a cuppa?" I did and he led the way to a little café just round the corner. He was obviously well known to the woman behind the counter and we were soon sitting down to an array of delicious home baking. I seemed to have fallen on my feet. My new found guide indicating it was time to depart, we walked a few yards to the main street where a 15 cwt. truck awaited. We boarded and, ere long, my long trek was over. It had taken about thirty six hours and I had slept surprisingly well on trains and ship. Food had been supplied courtesy of rations issued at Yatesbury and subsistence allowances in lieu. I had crossed from England to Scotland and from there to N. Ireland. My apologies to the people of Wales, but the journey was not of my choosing.

The unit seemed to be ideally sited on the shores of Lough Earne, Castle Archdale on an eminence nearby. I reported to the orderly room. The duty corporal took my papers. "I've remustered for training as a radar mechanic," I said, eager to cut short the formalities. He gave me a puzzled frown. "There's no radar training school around here," he observed, rustled through my papers, consulted others in files on his desk and announced, "You're down for radar training. You're here on General Duties until details of your course come through. Welcome to RAF Squadron 240. I'll get someone to show you to your billet." The words 'frying pan' and 'fire' flitted across my mind.

The accommodation was a step down from Yatesbury, a stark Nissen hut with bare concrete floor. Before going to bed, I had to undergo a free from infection examination at the hands of an officious medical orderly. If he'd told me I was suffering from every malady known to man he wouldn't have made me more despondent than I was. Several hundred miles and thirty six hours to find that nothing had changed. I hoped the period of waiting would be short.

The new regime began the next morning. The adjutant needed kindling for his fire, and I chopped wood all morning. Senior NCO's were taking up new quarters in Castle Archdale and I became a porter for two days, lugging heavy furniture up the steep approaches involved. Between operations, the Catalina flying boat crews slept in camp and I became their room orderly for several days. Armed with brush, shovel, and a bucket of water, I swept out their Nissen huts, sprinkling water before brushing to keep clouds of dust from rising from the concrete floors. In the course of this chore I met several of the air crew members. They were flying vast distances out across the Atlantic on long reconnaissance missions and returned grey faced and exhausted. Occasionally I swept their floors while they slept. Had I lobbed a grenade in, I doubt if it would have disturbed them Recruiting literature for aircrew depicted glamour, excitement, and adventure. The reality for these men was monotony, routine, long working hours, and the sleep of the completely knackered.

Recreation for ground staff was a Saturday evening liberty run into Enniskillen, organised by a Flight Sergeant who made something on the transport, and rather more, I suspect, from kick backs from the owners of the pubs on his itinerary. There were places on limits and many more off. You needed to be street wise in Enniskillen where the military police patrolled in pairs, with other pairs never far away.

There was a wonderful atmosphere in the places we patronised with lively music, good company, and Guinness to activate the blarney. Yet, over it all, hung that air of brooding menace that, sixty years since, lingers on.

Much building and construction work was being carried out on and around the camp. A lot of the activity was contracted out to labourers from the Irish Free State. Each week end, many of them slipped over the nearby border for a night at home, and a regular arrangement had developed whereby they would take with them any airman about to go on leave and wishing to take home presents for wives or sweethearts. In Bundoran, just across the border, silk stockings, perfume, lingerie, watches and jewellery were available at heavily discounted prices. Ever ready to seek new experience, I accompanied a small group one week end. It was a revelation. We left our uniforms behind in camp, and dressed in appropriate civilian clothes supplied by our Irish friends. The details of the journey to Bundoran and the events while there I shall leave unrecorded. It was the return trip that was newsworthy.

Every seat was occupied. Almost every passenger carried a parcel, securely tied with stout twine, a generous length of spare wrapped loosely round it. Customs officials boarded the train at the border crossing and the pantomime began. As the officials went through the coaches, which had central walk through passages, an observer on the track embankment would have witnessed an extraordinary sight. Packages of various shapes and sizes would be seen, either swinging wildly to the motion of the train, being lowered from open carriage windows, or being hauled in. The purpose of that extra generous length of stout twine was a very practical one. Parcels were paid out of the window, the widow was closed tight, and the twine now visible inside the carriage was tucked, out of sight, behind the leather strap that operated the raising and lowering of the window. As the customs men moved along the train, coach lengths of parcels were hauled back to safety. Leaving the border, and the border out of sight, the whole length of the train exhibited dancing parcels. By the time the officials had completed their tour, all parcels had vanished. I am convinced that the engine driver and guard were in on all this and remain to be persuaded that the custom officers were not.

Not having a wife or girl friend, nor expecting imminent leave, and, above all, being specifically short of cash, I did not take advantage of the opportunities offered by this regular weekly run. I did, however, benefit considerably from a spin off. A fellow traveller was the flight sergeant in charge of the equipment section who, having heard my story, said he could arrange for me to work with him, doing the clerical duties involved. Gladly I accepted the offer and was soon settled in. After a few weeks he asked me to apply for a permanent transfer to fill a vacancy in the establishment. I gave this a lot of thought. I had enlisted as a radar operator, which was classified as Grade 2. I was awaiting training as a radar mechanic, Grade 1. I was currently in general duties, Grade 5. He was offering me equipment assistant, Grade 3. If I accepted his offer I would be tied to 240 Squadron. Wherever it went I would go. As a radar mechanic there would be a choice of radar stations almost anywhere around the coastline of Britain. Then there was the matter of pay. Grade 1 scales were higher than Grade 3. I had a firm offer on the one hand, and the prospect of a training course on the other. I chose the latter on the principle of deferred gratification.

The equipment section was responsible, among other duties, for all the squadron's laundry arrangements. Every Wednesday there was a run to Londonderry to deliver one batch of dirty laundry and pick up a clean one. I accompanied the flight sergeant on these occasions. It was marvellous to escape the confines of the camp compound to travel through the verdant countryside between Enniskillen and Londonderry. I retain vivid memories of picturesque hamlets, with young children on the streets in bare feet. It was a land of small houses, large families, and little money. We had a regular coffee stop on the outward run, with a warm, hospitable welcome from owner and staff. Matching service was forthcoming on the return leg at another venue in a different location. Along the route, in both directions, we received many a wave and hearty greetings in a delightful Irish brogue. In Londonderry itself, there were fewer demonstrations of acknowledgement. Nor were there any indications of open hostility. We were advised not to venture out on our own, and I was never totally at ease when there. An hour's break while the truck was unloaded and reloaded provided opportunities to view the city. Whatever the weather, the fine architecture was eye-catching. Back in Lough Erne the adage was, "If you can't see the water it's raining. If you can it's going to." In Londonderry the same definition applied.

The wet weather, especially round the Lough, created conditions that were continually damp. Clothes hanging by the bedside overnight would feel unaired as you pulled them on, and feet had a hard time of it keeping dry as you moved around the site. It was probably these conditions which, starting with a common cold, developed into a raging temperature and fever. I was shivering uncontrollably and the flight sergeant confined me to bed. "I'll cover for you," he said, "if you go sick they'll have you in sick bay as sure as eggs are eggs." He came round that evening with a pile of blankets from the store and proceeded to cocoon me in them, layer after layer, till I felt like a trussed turkey. "We'll sweat it out of you." he promised. "No matter how uncomfortable you get don't throw anything off until tomorrow morning. You'll be swimming in perspiration but we'll have you as fit as a flea once the temperature's down. I'll bring you a warm towel and clean underclothes. Here's a couple of pills to help you sleep." As good as his word he reappeared at 8am the following morning. As predicted the fever had subsided and I was about back to normal. A regular serviceman, who had joined the RAF as a boy entrant, my friendly flight sergeant had seen it all before, and I was the recipient of his hard won experience.

Towards the end of September our association came to an end. I was summoned to the orderly room and told that my posting had come through. I was to take a week's leave and then report to Battersea Polytechnic in London for a seventeen weeks' course in radio theory and practice. My gratification had not long been deferred. I was back on track.

On the due date I collected travel warrants, rations and subsistence allowance for the journey, first to home, then onwards to King's Cross. My last memories of Northern Ireland are of groups of ragged urchins on the railway embankments as our train chugged through the misty countryside. There were a few hundred troops on board, many, like me, facing lengthy journeys. Almost to a man, we pulled down the windows several times and tossed our rations into the packs of hungry children who scrambled for them voraciously. We'd all enjoyed a cooked breakfast. By the looks of some of these human scavengers, it was doubtful whether they had eaten at all for days. Several were seen to eat as soon as they grabbed anything before a bigger, stronger child relieved them of it. Others carried bags into which they stuffed successive pickings, perhaps to feed a hungry family. Human nature being what it is, a few would be out to profit from the fruits of their enterprise.

It was now over three months since I had left home, and much had happened to change me. Nothing it seemed had changed there. The train drew in to the station. I stepped on to the platform and a gale equipped with teeth whistled through the station straight off the North Sea. Those of us brought up to it refer to it as the 'lazy wind' that blows through you because it can't be bothered to go round you. One leave is pretty much the same as another, with common greetings from whoever you meet, "Hallo, are you here again? When do you go back?" This was my first and ought to have been significant, but it wasn't. After I'd met up with family, former work colleagues, and people at church, there was nothing to hold me. The links with the civilian life had been severed. I was eager for London and further adventures.

—— Battersea Polytechnic ——

Every Englishman should visit his country's capital city sometime. It was my good fortune to do so for four months at His Majesty's expense. Doing it privately would have been expensive. The first aspect that struck me was its sheer size. We were in the suburbs twenty minutes to half an hour before we pulled into King's Cross, and that is well north of the heart of the metropolis. The concourse itself was heaving. I'd never seen so many platforms, entrances and exits, departure and destination boards. I was a solitary ant in an army of ants, scurrying hither and hither. I emerged into the bustling world outside. All around me, queues were forming for taxis. I was looking for buses, or more specifically one bus, but I didn't know which. At the centre of a junction, directing a continuous flow of traffic, I spotted a policeman. Resting my kitbag against a wall, I threaded my way through the traffic to his side. Still directing the flow, he looked down on me from an imperious height and shouted above the din. "Never leave your belongings lying about in this place, lad. Someone will nick it." I made as if to retrace my bag. "You're O.K." he barked, "I've got my eye on it. Now, where are you bound for?" I told him. "No. 73 red bus," he said instantly, "bus stop's over there by the corner. Ask to be put off at the Poly. Clippie will look after you." I thanked him, retrieved my kitbag and joined a sizeable queue. It was a common pick up point for a number of routes. A No. 73 drew up after a short wait. It was a double decker and I was mindful to ascend the spiral staircase for a better view. Negotiating such an obstacle with a kitbag was hazardous. There was a space under the stairwell already accommodating suitcases. There was just room for a kitbag. I stacked mine there, and had one foot on the first step upwards when the constable's advice echoed in my mind. I took a seat downstairs on a bench facing the luggage well. Another of life's lessons had been incorporated.

The initial journey through the heart of London was impressive, in terms of both immediate impact and imprint on the memory. I can relive the route over sixty years later. It seemed to go on, and on, and on. A helpful conductress put me off at Battersea Polytechnic. Mission accomplished. Things rarely run smoothly in service life. The Polytechnic was closed for the day and I was passed from cleaner to cleaner until the caretaker was located. "Can't do anything till tomorrow," was his comment, "I'll get you some blankets from the fire duty room and you can doss in one of the classrooms for the night. I can do you a pot of tea. There's a chippy round the corner." I didn't demur. I hadn't had fish and chips in ages. His tea was hot and strong. When you are eighteen and tired enough you'll sleep anywhere. I did----like a log.

Next morning I was directed to Lavender Hill in Clapham, where the RAF had an orderly room. Here I was handed papers relevant to the course, which was due to start on the morrow, and despatched to a house in the neighbourhood with a billeting notice. I was to report back to the orderly room at 8 am the following morning, breakfast to be served in an adjacent building. Along with other course members, I would then be marched to the Polytechnic. The rest of the day was mine.

RAF billeting procedures can be brusque. A list of suitable accommodation is prepared, and householders are informed that personnel will be allocated to them. In this instance, all that was required was a bed. There was no obligation to provide food. A standard rate of remuneration operated. I arrived at the address to which I was directed, rang the doorbell, and was confronted by an elderly lady. I explained the circumstances as congenially as I could, and, somewhat bemused, she took me in and showed me my bedroom. I put my kitbag down by the wardrobe and she said, "We'll see you this evening. We go to bed at ten. My husband starts work very early." With that she showed me the door.

I went back to the orderly room and reported, "I'm not sure this is going to work, corporal," I said. "We've found you a billet," was his rejoinder, "if you can find another yourself, we'll have a look at it. Meanwhile, you stay where you are." "Any suggestions as to where I can spend the rest of the day?" I asked. "Church Army has a place on Clapham Common," he proffered, "A lot of the lads go there. You'll meet some of the Polytechnic lot for sure." So to the Church Army I went. A very large, stone built house on the edge of the common, this was to become the centre of social life for the duration of the course. Captain Goodwill and his wife were genuine, practising Christians with a sense of vocation, and their home became a second home to me and a small circle of friends. All our weekday evenings were spent there. Of weekend activities we shall report in due course. I spent my first day there, in the warmth and comfort of the reading room, moving to the canteen in the evening for a cup of tea and a chat with other visitors. With my landlady's timetable in mind, I played it safe and rang the doorbell just after half past nine. There was a long pause. I rang again.

After quite an interval I heard shuffling, the rattle of a door chain, and a peevish man in pyjamas and bedcap appeared. "You've got me out of bed," he grumbled. I apologised, glanced at my watch and remarked, "Your wife said ten o'clock." He grunted and stepped back. I pushed past him without further conversation; he locked the door, and followed me upstairs muttering to himself. When I left the following morning, he was lugging a large suitcase into the hall. "My samples," he explained, "I sell door to door." I didn't ask him what lines he was peddling. I'd gone off him completely. I did make a quiet resolution to be in that evening by nine o'clock, even if it meant curtailing my social life.

It was perhaps a ten-minute walk down to Lavender Gardens where I enjoyed a good breakfast and met up with the thirty or so other airmen on the same course. We were then 'got fell in' by a perky little corporal called Jackson. From around the corner we could hear another group of about the same number being marshalled by another corporal, who answered to Doyle. He appeared to be a much more disagreeable type. The two squads marched off, one after the other. This was a route with which we would become familiar, down Latchmere Road, under a tunnel, then over a railway bridge, and into Battersea Park Road, and on to the Polytechnic. Crossing the bridge, which was of stout timber construction, and appeared to have been built to last, we were always ordered to 'break step', resuming marching on the far side. Corporal Oldham, of fast fading Blackpool memories, would almost certainly have marched us fearlessly across.

Our reception at the Polytechnic was a model of efficiency. I was struck by the daytime mode of hurry and scurry after my recent overnight stay in an almost empty shell. We registered and were directed to our classrooms. It was reminiscent of being back in school again, but reassuring. This was education with a specific purpose. I did not intend to fail this course. In my group I suppose there would be about twenty. I reckoned that the two squads of thirty had been split into three teaching groups. Our lecturer entered the room and introduced himself as Mr. Waverly. He said he had been called back from retirement to take on this new responsibility. I thought that perhaps he'd been resurrected. He looked positively ancient. We found out later that he had taken his science degree just after the turn of the century, before the thermionic valve had been invented. We also reckoned, very early on, that the standard RAF Manual of Wireless Telegraphy was new ground for him, and that he was valiantly trying to keep one chapter ahead of us.

In general conversation we elicited the fact that seven similar courses had preceded ours, but that we were different in one important aspect. Whereas the others had been of men who had enlisted as radar mechanics, and had come straight from initial square bashing, we were all second choice remustered men, with similar interim general duties experiences in common. This was to prove a powerful unifying force that welded us into a highly motivated team. We came from all parts of the Commonwealth and from all sorts of backgrounds. The age range was broad. During the morning, from the other side of the classroom I thought I detected a voice with an instantly recognisable accent. At break I tracked it down and was soon swapping yarns with a teacher from my hometown, Greg Smedley. We agreed it was a small world.

In the main set of buildings were the practical workshops to service a variety of trades. That to which we were allocated was equipped for metalwork and electricity. In an annexe, on the other side of the road, were additional classrooms, one of which was somewhat sparsely equipped for radio experimental work. The prospects were encouraging and I finished that first day in eager anticipation of those to follow.

That evening I installed myself in a quiet corner of the Church Army hostel and perused the contents of our RAF manual, most of which was entirely new to me. I had a nodding aquaintanceship with the introductory pages, which was a start. Having decided that the lecturer was not likely to be much inspiration, I resolved to put to good use my experience of distance learning, acquired while doing a correspondence course for Civil Service examinations that had been curtailed on the outbreak of war. I was used to working on my own. Blessed with a retentive memory, I was confident that, once I had identified the basic concepts, I could build up a system of interconnected principles that, once assimilated, would make fresh ideas and subsequent studies easier to master. This was to be the pattern of my days over the next seventeen weeks: Polytechnic by day, Church Army hostel in the evening for private study and recreation.

As previously resolved, I presented myself at my billet at nine o'clock precisely and rang the doorbell. There followed a replay of the first night's pantomime, "Right," I thought, "that's it. There's going to be no meeting of minds here." I was relating the story to classmates the following morning when one of them, known to all simply as Jock said, " There might be a place where I am. I'm just a few doors away from where you are, with a widow and her young daughter. You've seen the girl. She helps in the canteen at the hostel. I'll ask her if you like." I did like. That evening Jock introduced me to Brenda, the daughter in question, who said, " Mum would love to have you, but it would mean sharing a room with Jock. We've had a word with the lady next door but one. She has nobody at the moment and is willing to take you." I decided to approach the orderly first thing the following morning to complete the transfer. I rang the doorbell at ten thirty that night and had a strong suspicion that my landlord, though dressed for bed, had in fact been stretched out on the settee in the lounge. Be that as it may, we exchanged perfunctory greetings, embellished by my last words with him, "I am hoping to move elsewhere tomorrow. I do hope that you find my replacement more amenable to your evening curfew requirements." The next night I was sleeping in a new bed. My new hosts could not have been more different. A married couple in their sixties, they had three sons serving in the army overseas. As the wife said to me, "I hope that if they are looking for a bed for the night, someone will be kind to them." I had fallen on my feet.

Back in the Polytechnic, we were getting into the rhythm of the daily curriculum Apart from his inadequacy as far as knowledge of his subject was concerned, Mr. Waverly could very easily have experienced disciplinary troubles. We were a pretty motley crew. The factor that safeguarded him was the common determination not to fail. If need be, we would succeed in spite of him. Statistically, we were on a loser. Examinations were scheduled for the end of the eighth week, designed to weed out students unlikely to attain the standards required by the end of the course for specific radar training, which was a much more advanced study. The records of the previous seven groups were not reassuring, their failure rates having been substantial. This became an additional incentive to me to keep my head down. There is a level at which what you put into a project produces nothing extra at the output end Indeed, there is the danger of decreased returns if you push beyond that critical point. I decided that five evenings' study a week was my cut off marker. Saturdays and Sundays would be reserved for recharging the batteries.

The RAF and the Polytechnic were obviously aware of the need for organised breaks from study, and every Wednesday afternoon we were bussed to Merton Park for football practice and friendly games on an inter-tutorial basis. I enjoyed these interludes enormously. The Polytechnic had its own football team, and as a result of these Wednesday activities, I was invited to play for them on Saturday mornings. This led to Sunday afternoon fixtures, playing for the Wandsworth Police eleven, an experience of happy memories. The rest of the team were all six footers or very nearly so. I was five foot seven—eight if I stretched a bit. They insisted on my leading the team out, which emphasised the discrepancy. I think the spectators thought I was the team mascot All this healthy activity helped me to get the most out of my course.

There remained a gap in what might loosely be called the social life. Four of us decided it was almost criminal not to explore the sights of London while living there.

So developed a series of regular Saturday visits to places of interest, distance being no object. Travel by tube or bus was free for servicemen. We walked miles, soaking up the atmosphere of the very recently blitzed areas, mainly in the East End, and by contrast strolling along the major thoroughfares of the West End. Famous buildings, favourite parks, museums and commons all featured. One impression emerged from all these excursions. London seemed to have a liberal number of grassed areas and a surprising number of trees. Even in the central business, commercial and trading areas, there were green plots to be found. Then of course there was the River Thames and all those bridges. Perhaps above all there was the traffic. The heart of the city beat twenty four hours a day.

We always finished up at a Lyons Corner House, latterly in Tottenham Court Road, in the brasserie. Here, we had been adopted by a middle-aged waitress who had caught our eye. She always found us a table for four. On our first visit, she greeted us with, "Try the hors d'oeuvres. I can do you a lovely selection." We placed our orders. She delivered to each of us an enormous plateful of everything she could lay her hands on. We returned every Saturday evening after that, to the standard welcome, "If it isn't my favourite little family again. Same again, boys?"

One evening the small ensemble was providing musical accompaniment as usual. Our matronly waitress said, "Choose a piece of music and I'll ask the band to play it as a special request." I cannot recall the piece asked for—the Canadian in our quartet chose it---- but I do remember the delight of having the spotlight directed on our table when the request was announced. Lyons Corner Houses have long since gone, but for me the one in Tottenham Court Road lives on. So too, I hope, does our warm hearted waitress. I hope she is being served in peace and comfort in realms of celestial bliss.

One evening's experience outside our normal range was a visit to Richmond Ice Rink, arranged by Lulu, one of the volunteer assistants in the Church Army hostel. Whatever visions might be conjured up on contemplation of a girl with such an exotic name would fall far short of reality. Our Lulu was a bundle of bubbling, effervescent energy, vivacious, extrovert, and more often than not completely over the top. She attracted men as a flame draws in moths, but there the comparison ends. Moths withdraw involuntarily. Lulu rejected her admirers quite deliberately. She was the archetypal tease. If she ever did settle with one man, it would be of her choosing and not his. She liked to play the field, and there were always plenty in the arena. On ice skates she was transcended from her puckish, everyday self into an ethereal, gossamer, elfin creature that floated over the surface, apparently weightless, performing elaborate contortions with effortless ease. She was, of course, the centre of attraction, which was her real reason for having arranged the evening. In our party was a Canadian, brought up on snow and ice. He powered around the rink, executing manoeuvres with consummate confidence, bordering at times on arrogance. The two styles were demonstrably compatible, and they staged an impromptu exhibition of uninhibited experimentation. He escorted her home that evening with expectations at which one can but conjecture. The following evening he was seen to have reverted to the ranks of Lulu's ever-present retinue of admirers, no worthier nor less worthy than the rest. He'd had his day in close orbit. It was plain, and Lulu was making it so, that close was one thing, intimate was another. Sadly, I shall never know whether any man ever attained that status.

Ancillary to this account of that evening is that of my own initial performance on ice. Around the central spectacle of Lulu and our Canadian, children of eight, nine, and ten were playing subsidiary roles, gliding over the ice effortlessly, with ne'er a mishap. "Can't be all that difficult," I thought. Beginning by edging my way round the rink, hanging on to the barrier for support, I was soon making good progress and, so to speak, getting the hang of it. All that was needed was a modicum of confidence and self-belief. Picking a suitable vacant space some few feet away I launched out for it. Trouble embraced me immediately. My arms started flapping wildly, my feet began going in different directions, and the space I had been aiming for disappeared abruptly. I came to an undignified halt in quite spectacular fashion. Breathless and red faced, I allowed two small girls to lead me, one on either side, back to the safety of the barrier. On regaining both breath and some semblance of composure, I handed my skates in, donned my boots, and watched the experts with grudging admiration. I have never visited an ice rink since.

Meanwhile, the course was unfolding satisfactorily. Concurrently with lectures on wireless theory were sessions devoted to practical circuit building. In the annexe premises, four of us assembled a primitive transmitter on a breadboard, following instructions culled from the "Wireless World". It wasn't much, but it was ours. In the main building, another group was constructing a compatible receiver. Came the day when both projects were completed. The Polytechnic held a licence to broadcast. Not altogether confident, we switched on our tiny transmitter. We were linked to classmates in the receiver room by field telephone and rang to tell them we were about to go on air. Holding the microphone to my mouth, and speaking across it, rather than into it, I announced, "G7AR testing---G7AR testing." The field telephone rang. One of our group answered, to hear a triumphant voice at the other end reporting, "Blimey, it works. It bloody works." Tails were up that day.

The eighth week was approaching and tension was mounting. I was reasonably confident of passing, as was Greg Smedley. In the theory section, we were known as "The Terrible Twins" He always topped the list. I was usually second. In the practical work, I was competent in the main, Greg less so. In the cohort as a whole, there were some predictable under performers. Anyone still in the race after this hurdle had been jumped successfully would have to perform calamitously afterwards to be rejected. We were a bunch of contestants determined to pool all our resources for the common good.

A planning committee was formed to work out strategies and tactics and met nightly in a secluded corner of the Church Army hostel. Question 1: What was the priority need if we were to have any hope of pulling off what would be a major coup? Answer: Find out what questions were on the exam paper before the day of reckoning. Question 2: Since Waverly would almost certainly write them on the blackboard (he never handed out any typed notes or similar forms of communication), when would he do so? Only if he did it the day before, covered the blackboard up, and locked the door, could we derive any benefit. If he did it immediately before the exam we had no chance. Answer: Make a duplicate key of the classroom door in the hope that he did prepare the day before. A sudden flash of creative instinct followed. Whenever he wrote the questions up, he would do so from a master copy, almost certainly in his own handwriting. Question 3: Where would the master copy be? Answer: In his briefcase. Question 4: What if his briefcase was locked? Answer: Use duplicate keys. It began to make sense. We wouldn't need to make copies. If we could make a note of the numbers etched on his keys we could buy a set. He almost always left them on his desktop whilst lecturing. A quite clever plan was emerging.

A day or two before the exam we were in session in a classroom in the annexe. Waverly's briefcase was on the floor by his desk. During the break between lectures, we arranged for a telephone call on our field telephone. Associates manned the instrument at the other end. Our phone rang. Somebody answered it. Waverly had looked up as it rang, momentarily distracted. Our man called out, "Mr. Waverly, sir, telephone call for you." "For me," muttered the puzzled lecturer, and shuffled across to take the call. Our man at the other end read his prearranged script. "For me?" repeated Waverly, "What? Now? Urgent you say. Oh, very well, I'm come straight across." Then, addressing us, "You must excuse me, gentlemen. Apparently I am required urgently in the main building. I shall not be long." The one contingency that could have foiled us was for him to have taken his briefcase with him. We had counted on the sudden break in routine to disorientate him and it had worked. One or two participants, placed at strategic windows, reported his exit from the building, and remained to give advance warning of his return. One of us went to the briefcase. It was unlocked. A quick rummage through the contents and a stack of papers was held aloft. "Bull's eye," cried the finder. The final act was a triumph of meticulous planning. One of our number wrote shorthand, and did so as the questions were read out. It took but a matter of minutes, and we were finished long before our lecturer returned. Mission accomplished. That evening, in the Church Army hostel, the Moderating Committee convened comprising men with exam marking experience in civilian life. An assessment of realistic grades that might be expected from every entrant was drawn up, and a range of answers prepared for use by any examinee, in case of need. All were counselled against going for choice of answers beyond their allotted classification. Two or three days later, the results were posted on the Polytechnic notice board. All had passed and the scatter of grades looked authentic. Waverly was simply bursting with pride, never more so than when one of our more mischievous members, apparently speaking for all, proclaimed, "We couldn't have done it without you, sir."

Whether someone in authority began to ponder on the cohort's record breaking feat we shall never know. I doubt if anyone on the academic staff would. RAF officers, on receiving the results, may well have thought, "There's a rabbit away here." Whatever the facts of the case, only the practical examination stood between us and completion of the course. All previous practicals had involved the making of a marriage joint, i.e. the splicing of two lengths of multi-stranded, rubber coated cables. One end of each piece was stripped of its outer covering, the inner braiding was pared back, the copper strands were separated and fanned out, the fanned ends were interleaved and twisted together to form a sound joint. Strong waxed thread was laid along the length of the joint, bound tightly round it from end to end, and cut off neatly. Properly done, the union was barely visible. One of our number, Don Flintoff, was a master at marriage joints, which were sometimes done with black cable, sometimes with red. We allowed for both possibilities, appropriating lengths of cable in each colour, and commissioning Don at a shilling per piece. He could have done it with barbed wire. On the day of the practical test, we each carried in our tunics a Don Flintoff black and a Don Flintoff red marriage joint, in case our own efforts placed our future in jeopardy. You can imagine our dismay to be confronted with a circuitry job involving delicate soldering techniques. Maybe suspicions had been roused. The outcome, however, was excellent. Nobody failed. Cohort eight continued to break all records. We had every reason to anticipate final success and no return to the ranks of those committed to general duties. It had been the fear of that prospect that had spurred us on throughout the course. The dragon had been slain.

The second half of the course proved to be much more relaxing. Self confidence was high, morale was high, expectations were high. There was more time to explore new interests and activities. Our two corporals, Jackson and Doyle, had been ordered to introduce boxing into the occasional P.E. sessions conducted on Polytechnic premises. It was in this context that my initial assessment of these two was confirmed. Doyle chose for a demonstration an inoffensive, clumsy, badly coordinated member of his squad, and proceeded to humiliate him in public. It was distasteful, mean, petty, and the hallmark of a bully. Jackson, at the other end of the gym, asked me to join him. "Ever had gloves on before?" he asked. I answered, truthfully, that I hadn't. "O.K." he said, "the main point of the sport is self defence, and not to take punishment if you can avoid it. Let me demonstrate the basics. Let's start with the feet." This was the first surprise. Like everyone else present, I had thought that boxing was to do with the hands, more precisely with the fists. Jackson continued, "I'm going to move around. I want you to follow me, keeping the same distance all the time." He started. I matched every movement, inching forwards, sideways, backwards, on the balls of my feet. "Excellent," he enthused. "Now let's show you how to defend yourself. Stand sideways on facing me, left foot forward, body nicely balanced. Put your open left glove over your chin, forearm covering your upper torso, elbow screening your solar plexus That stance protects your main target body areas, and the two major knockout points of chin and solar plexus. Just hold your right arm loose with fist clenched. From that basic position, let's move on to attack. Push your left arm forward to its full extent. Now, what's happened to your defence? You are now wide open. Bring your right fist up to your chin and open your glove fully to protect your chin. At the same time, your right forearm and elbow covers your solar plexus. Now coordinate those movements while I do the same facing you." We both played our roles and I began to see the point of it all. "Right," said the good corporal, " let's try a little session for real." I was soon into a rhythm, concentrating solely on defence, keeping my distance, slipping his leads without being aware of it, ducking, weaving and swaying from the waist. "Well done, lad," complimented Jackson "If you learn to punch your weight, you could be a good 'un." For the record, I never took up the sport, but some of my group did. None of Doyle's followed suit. The different outcomes had nothing to do with interest or ability, everything to do with contrasting styles of teaching, example, and motivation. Not for the first time, The RAF had taught me a valuable life skill.

My first Christmas away from home was memorable. I was invited to join a group from the Church Army for morning service in the parish church and thoroughly enjoyed the feeling of being part of a family for the day. The church was full, the weather was fine and dry, the singing of traditional carols lusty and enthusiastic. Among the airmen present was Jock, in the company of Brenda and her widowed mother. Unlike Lulu, whom we have already met, Brenda was quiet, reflective and retiring. Not for her the centre of the stage. She seemed content with her lot, and dealt with life as it unfolded its ups and downs. I'm sure her mother kept a vigilant eye on her voluntary role in the evenings, where she was in the company of an ever-changing succession of servicemen in transit. Our group was unusual in being there for seventeen weeks, and Jock was billeted with mother and daughter throughout that period. It didn't need that long for romance to blossom. Shortly after Christmas, Brenda was sporting an engagement ring. She was eighteen. Jock was thirty six. The two of them had the blessing of the widow. I hope things worked out well for all three.

Christmas dinner was held in the dining room at Lavender Gardens, the officers and NCO's serving the rest of us. There was food aplenty and, as I tucked in, I wondered how things were at home with strict rationing in force. There were further celebrations in the evening in the Church Army hostel with Capt. Goodwill leading the community singing. After this was over, he approached me and said, "You have a very pleasant voice. I wonder if you would like to join us on Sunday evenings. There's just a few of us. We meet in a little room upstairs after dinner and sing a few numbers together. Just an informal affair." I said I would be delighted to join them. The next Sunday I did so and was glad to be there. It reminded me of similar occasions back home when the extended family met in my grandmother's house for a soiree. Ere long, I was invited to arrive early and have dinner with the Captain and his wife and one or two others. The couple always dressed for dinner in immaculate evening attire, and the meal served was in direct contrast to RAF grub slapped on your plate. It was here that I was introduced to fine wines.

There was a worldly wisdom in the captain's approach to his role as guardian of his constantly changing congregation. He had an unerring instinct for spotting what he called 'wrong uns'. Taking me on one side one evening, he invited me to share in a little experiment.

"Of all the people in here tonight." said the captain, "would you care to nominate the one you feel you could least trust." My appraising glance swept across the room. I made my choice. "Very good," beamed the good captain, apparently supporting my selection. "Very shortly I shall go over to his table to tidy up. I'll drop something on the floor, bend to pick it up, and leave a half crown coin where, sooner or later, your man will spot it." Shortly afterwards the deed was done. We both watched from across the room. Our target saw the coin, looked around surreptitiously and, ever so slowly, began to shuffle a foot across the floor until it covered the coin. Unobtrusively, he then pushed back his chair, bent down, and collected the coin, transferring it smoothly to his right hand trouser pocket. I drew in a quick breath. "You've hooked one with your first cast," observed the captain in fishing parlance. "Now let's land him." As our objective made his way nonchalantly towards the exit, he found a large, benevolent looking gentleman barring the way. "I wonder if you would mind turning out the contents of your right hand trouser pocket. My friend and I are playing a little game and would appreciate your kind cooperation," asked the captain cordially. To my surprise the request was acceded to, and a collection of small change and a handkerchief were deposited on an adjacent table. "What little game are you playing?" asked the thief, somewhat uneasily. "Well, actually" explained Captain Goodwill, "we're particularly interested in half crowns and their dates." The man began to show signs of growing unease. "I see two half crowns here," continued the observation, "The one I left on the floor by your table was dated 1921. Shall we see if it's here?" The culprit capitulated. "Alright," he said, "on the spur of the moment I picked it up. What are you going to do about it?" "Well," replied my magisterial friend, all geniality replaced by a tone that was magnificently intimidatory, "my usual practice is to call in the police. However, were you to return my coin, and donate the other half crown to the charity box on the counter, I would consider the matter closed." The thief handed over both coins, put the rest in his pocket, and took his hurried leave. The captain beamed at me. "One sinner stopped in his tracks, one half crown to Church Army funds," he said. "This is a regular ruse of mine. Only one person in ten who picks the bait up returns it to the counter. Either you're a good judge of character, or just plain lucky." "Do you suppose he'll have learned a lesson?" I queried. "Difficult to say," came the reply, "The only thing I can be sure about is that he won't be back here again." Captain Goodwill's brand of Christianity was muscular on the outside, but essentially tender at its heart. It was my privilege to have met him. I hope he has handed in his silver half crown and has received a crown of gold.

The end of our long course was now approaching and I reviewed what progress I had made. A sound theoretical grasp of wireless transmission and reception was backed by basic practical skills in the use of appropriate tools and equipment, a rudimentary knowledge of how to diagnose faults, and the ability to repair them. I felt confident that I would pass my final assessment. The only question was, at which grade. We had been told that the top quartile would go to Yatesbury, the rest to Cranwell. The euphoria when the results were posted was high-octane grade; all had passed. My personal reaction was in the 'cloud nine' category. I was bound for Yatesbury. This time I would pass through those doors, previously so summarily slammed in my face, and gain entry to the ultra secret world of the radar fraternity. The wheel had turned full circle.

My stay in the capital had been a rich and varied experience. Apart from the unique treasure chest of opportunities it had opened up for me, and of which I had taken full advantage, mixing with a broad cross section of people, from many varied countries and cultures had enriched my life. To many I was saying, "Farewell and bon chance." A few, among whom was Greg Smedley, would accompany me to Yatesbury.

Yatesbury Revisited

There is something reassuring in returning to a place previously experienced, a feeling not often enjoyed by servicemen. Postings arise for all sorts of reasons, and often at short notice. All the routine of daily life, work patterns, friendship groups are suddenly shattered. You pack your kitbag, take your travel warrant, and head off into the unknown, to establish new life styles as best you can. The golden rule on joining a new unit is to lie low until you've sussed out who controls what. Let the new society make the first moves. Once they've had the chance to weigh you up, they'll accept you. Try to force the pace and you run the risk of rejection. None of these conditions applied as I approached this posting. I was taking with me a well-integrated group. We'd been welded over seventeen eventful weeks, and knew and trusted each other. They would need to familiarise themselves with the camp in general. I already knew it. What we all shared was curiosity about what lay behind that high security fence that surrounded the Radar School.

At this juncture, a short account of the development of radar will help to explain the impact that entering this world was to have on me. Seven years prior to my entry into the Radar School, on 26 Feb. 1935, four men stood in a field a few miles from Daventry, the site of a BBC radio transmitter. The field was in a hollow, surrounded by hills. The four men were A.P. Rowe, a secretary of a secret government committee, Watson-Watt, technical adviser to the committee, Williams, a government scientist, and Dyer, their driver. Of these, Williams was the key man. A year or two earlier, while measuring the time taken to transmit and receive radio signals to the ionosphere, he had been informed by Post Office engineers that they were noticing reflections whenever an aircraft flew overhead. Wilkins reasoned that, if equipment could be designed capable of bouncing radio signals off planes, the position of those planes could be pinpointed. Such equipment was now to hand. With Dyer outlawed from what was a ground breaking technological breakthrough, Wilkins, Watson-Watt, and Rowe monitored a primitive cathode ray tube as they tracked the progress of a Heyford bomber flying at 100 m.p.h. Over a ten-minute experiment, ranges were recorded of up to eight miles. Direction and altitude of flight were impossible to calculate, but the initial vital step had been taken. Further developments would follow, and the imminent threat of war would expedite them.

Neville Chamberlain has had a bad press and an assessment by historians that overlook many of the difficulties he faced. The return from Munich in 1938, that piece of paper held aloft as he alighted from the plane, that phrase 'peace in our time' are now enshrined in the archives, and are universally denigrated. Yet, what if he had not taken those steps? Britain was woefully unprepared at that time to face a rampant Germany, whose mastery of the blitzkrieg on land, growing prowess in the air, and substantial growth in its fleets of surface and underwater vessels at sea, would almost certainly have overwhelmed us. The extra year that Munich bought was to make a crucial difference to the imbalance, and nowhere more so than in the development of radar.

By 1939 there were twenty stations able to track aircraft more than a hundred miles away. These rapidly expanded to the establishment of sites all round the coastline of Britain, known as Air Ministry Experimental Stations. Initially these were Chain Home (CH) stations and were erected on high ground in remote areas. Their 360 feet masts transmitting radio signals probed the skies and seas for evidence of enemy activity. Efficient though they were, it soon became apparent that aircraft were beating the system. One story relates that a station on the east coast detected what appeared to be a large squadron of aircraft en route towards the coastline, only to disappear from the screen several miles out to sea. A plane was sent out to investigate after a succession of similar incidents. The crew reported flights of geese, just skimming over the surface of the sea preparatory to landing. A weakness in the CH system had been detected. Enemy aircraft could avoid discovery by flying at very low altitudes. Thus were born the hundreds of Chain Home Low (CHL) stations that sprang up around the vulnerable coastlines. They had fifty feet high rotating aerial arrays, mounted on stout timber gantries. By the time of the Battle of Britain, Ground Control Interception stations (GCI) had been established to integrate an effective defence / attack strategy. CH and CHL stations fed information to GCI stations which alerted appropriate Fighter Command squadrons to intercept and engage the enemy bombers.

Of Winston Churchill's many memorable wartime addresses to the nation, perhaps none surpasses that which, in a few simple words, summed up the Battle of Britain, "Never in the field of human conflict has so much been owed by so many to so few."

This accolade to the fighter pilots who fought and overcame tremendous odds will echo down the halls of history. Almost like the 'echo' on their primitive cathode ray tubes, a ghostly, attenuated one should follow the first, commemorating the few, who made victory possible as they invented, expanded, and operated a radar system that was to contribute enormously to the final victory of the war and beyond.

It must not be forgotten that the Germans were not without their own radar pioneers and inventors. They were to reach their peak towards the end of the war with their V1 and V2 missiles, and were later to play a significant major role in the American NASA space programme. But for now they were outwitted, outrun, and outfought. German radar stations, covering our eastern and southern coastlines, cast a grid of radio signals across Britain. Enemy pilots, by tuning in to the right frequencies, could navigate along a beam, and across its intersections, with such precision as to locate and bomb targets at night without the need to visually identify them. In the early days of the blitz they did so regularly. One bomber hitting the target successfully lit up the surrounding area sufficiently to enable other aircraft, not equipped with radar, to bomb on sight. The RAF counter to this was to intercept the German signals early, and to retransmit them on a slightly deviant course, with results such as those remarked on by Churchill, at a dinner function one night, "And do you know, the buggers actually bombed Dublin with a cargo destined for Liverpool."

At another place, in this war of the control of the radio waves, a large sector of our coastal defence radar system was subjected to intermittent interference and jamming, rendering it temporarily inoperable. There was no discernible pattern, which made it difficult to detect and counter. Several possible causes were mooted and investigated, including the theory that a German U-boat was surfacing in the Irish Sea from time to time, transmitting on the same frequency as our radar stations, submerging, and then moving on, to repeat the exercise elsewhere. The explanation was more prosaic. On a remote Welsh hilltop, alongside one of our CHL radar stations, stood a WAAF latrine. Protected by an outer wall as a precaution against bomb blast in the event of enemy attack, this facility was in darkness, except when in use. A single naked electric light bulb came on and off at the touch of a switch. Not every user of the toilet bothered to switch off on leaving the building, and after a while the bulb, which was of an ancient carbon filament construction, began to oscillate at the frequency of the RAF radar network. The person who detected this troublesome fault was an RAF radar mechanic who chanced to be male. Many and varied are the theories bandied about as to the circumstances in which he made his discovery. By the time I was admitted to this exclusive world it was developing fast. I was to be part of it for a further five years of exhilarating progress as the aims and objectives of the war effort constantly spawned experimentation.

Meanwhile, the ex-Battersea Polytechnic cohort took up residence with others in the barrack huts of the domestic site, so familiar to me from former occupation. My new hut was next door to that from which I had made my early morning exit to N. Ireland, and I settled down for what I hoped would be a twelve week period this time round. Sundays in Yatesbury were recognised days off. After a late breakfast, which some chose not to take, it was customary to take the morning easy. About nine o'clock the door would burst open and the local newsagent would invade our privacy with Sunday papers for sale. The 'News of the World' was his biggest seller. I usually took my father's choice 'The Sunday Express'. The week after our arrival, things were pretty quiet in the hut when the doors at both ends were flung open to loud shouts of 'Stand by your beds'. We were momentarily thrown off balance. Weekly kit inspections were normal Friday disruptions. However, one does not question orders, especially when bellowed by a senior NCO with Service Police insignia, accompanied by Army Redcaps. We stood by our beds. Four policemen surrounded a bed to which they had made a beeline. Quiet words were exchanged. The occupant dressed fully and, flanked on either side by Army Redcaps, was escorted out of the building. The two RAF policemen started packing what was left of our erstwhile companion's belongings into his kitbag, completed the task and departed. We learned afterwards that the newly taken prisoner, for such he was, had deserted from the army and had reenlisted in the RAF. We now had an early vacancy for a trainee radar mechanic.

Mention of weekly kit inspections provides an opportunity to expand on the topic. Each Friday the command 'Stand by your beds' heralded the entry of an impressive succession of officers and NCO's in single file, from senior rank, in descending order, to lowest rank.

One by one, beds were inspected, items of kit being displayed in prescribed order on the mattress, blankets neatly folded and squared off at the top end of the bed. Floorspace around each bed was polished to a high sheen, bedside lockers were open and empty to reveal their scrubbed surfaces. There was usually at least one token hostage to the proceedings who was put on a charge sheet and directed to a punishment of an evening spent on meaningless 'bullshit'. We quickly adapted to this routine and dealt with it as expeditiously as possible. As soon as the inspection was over, all beds were moved sideways, so as to cover the highly polished former surround that had just passed muster. The beds were restored to their original positions the evening before the next weekly inspection, and the highly polished floor surface, revealed once again, was given a quick buffing with minimum effort. Lockers were emptied before breakfast on inspection days, lugged into the ablutions block at the end of the hut, put under a running standpipe, left for the excess water to drain off, and repositioned by the beds. It was evident to inspecting eyes that effort had been put into cleaning them since the inner corners were slightly damp. Kit inspection was another matter. It was every man for himself, and there was no way of avoiding the irksome bullshit involved.

Weekly exposure to the vagaries of routine discipline was bad enough. Worse still was the weekday round of pre-breakfast parade ground full inspections, reminiscent of Blackpool promenade. There were anything from eight to ten units on parade each morning, each with its own sergeant, or occasionally flight sergeant. Each inspected his own squad. In overall command was a dapper, diminutive, ginger haired Warrant Officer, who was a legend in his own lifetime. He had clearly clocked up umpteen years of regular service, and it was said that, were he and God to meet, it would be God who saluted. Each day, Smith elected to give one unit the benefit of his practised eye and withering sarcasm. One morning with all, as I thought, ready to face up to any scrutiny, one of my greatcoat buttons came off. Panic stations! No time for a needle and thread job. What to do? Greatcoat buttons have a strong, closed metal loop, around which stout thread is normally sewn to attach button to material. Button in place, one pushes it through the buttonhole on the other side of the coat. "Suppose," I thought, "as a temporary expedient, I simply pushed the button, shank first, through the buttonhole and secured it with a cross bar of some sort." The only thing to hand was a box of matches. Three or four matches did the trick. The button was firm. I donned the greatcoat. The button being attached to only one side of the garment, there was a slight gap. Luckily it was at chest level. Expand the chest and the gap closed. So prepared, I marched out for inspection. Once in position, the senior NCO's began their tours of duty. All that is except ours. "Look smart, you lucky lads," he barked, "God is giving you his very special attention today." "Oh Lord," I thought, "here comes big trouble." The W.O. was on top form. They all came out: "Have you shaved today, airman? You have? Then tomorrow morning stand closer to your razor / put a blade in it / try a sheet of emery paper / get your mate to do it." Then, standing behind someone, the whispered question, full of concern, "Am I 'urting you?" Answer from the corner of a puzzled mouth, "No sir." Question restated with rising intimate solicitude, "Are you sure I'm not 'urting you?" Second answer, "No sir, quite sure sir." Third approach, much louder, more intimidating, "Now that's a funny bloody thing," followed by a roar that reverberated round the parade square, "I'M STANDING ON YOUR BLOODY HAIR." By the time he reached me he'd given his all. I took a deep breath and held it. No gap showed. The rogue button shone brightly in line with the others. The moment passed. I breathed out. That evening I sewed the button back on.

This aspect of service life on the domestic site was in direct contrast with that on the technical site. As I entered once again the compound via the single gate where I had once stood on guard, and cast a glance across to the double gated vehicular entrance, where I had also performed sentry duties, I looked forward to a belated entry into huts from which I had previously been banned. They surpassed all my preconceptions. It was a totally different world. A number of different initial impressions struck immediately. It was warm, bordering on stuffy. It was noisy, but pleasantly so, with constant background hum of things electrical. There was a pervasive smell, a mixture of warm mica, perspex, and an indefinable aroma characteristic of such environments. It was redolent of the ink and chalk smell that lingers around school classrooms. It was clean, almost clinically so. The transmitters were large, covering walls perhaps twelve feet wide and eight feet in height. There were meters and neon warning lights all over the set. The receivers were not quite so big. It was their cathode ray tubes that caught the eye, gleaming fluorescently in the subdued lighting.

Alongside the rooms housing these products of man's inventive genius were lecture rooms, equipped with wall-mounted blackboards, demonstration benches, circuit diagrams and charts. All this we were now to study and to practise. No notes, aide-memoirs etc. were permitted to leave the premises. I thanked God for a retentive memory.

The reason for the size of everything was that we were still in the steam age of wireless transmission, adapted to radio / radar purposes. The day of the transistor was yet to dawn, and the miracle of the microchip, miniaturisation, and the hand held computer was in the future beyond that. I recognised the thermionic valves and associated circuitry of the Battersea Polytechnic set up, though Yatesbury displayed more elegantly intricate combinations. What took me aback were the transmitter valves, though I had seen them in crates on the lorry that had taken me to Calne for that journey to Northern Ireland. Installed in pairs in working conditions, they were towers of light, heat, and power, and very impressive. Frankenstein would have loved them. I left the compound at the end of that first day, ready, willing, and hopefully able to imbibe over the next twelve weeks all this special university had to offer.

The teaching was adequate rather than inspirational, and haphazard in its presentation. I found it helpful to take in what I could of discrete modules and then attempt to create some sort of synthesis as we went along. To present a review of what the course content was, I shall regurgitate it as it comes to mind, which is unlikely to be the order in which it was delivered.

The heart of the CHL system, which was now predominantly in use round the coastline of Britain, was its receiver unit, a package that housed two cathode ray tubes, ancillary circuits, and a console shelf at the front with operator controls. The CRT on the left was circular, that on the right rectangular. When operational, each CRT was manned by one operator. A line on each CRT screen was known as a time base and was of different appearance, one screen from the other. On the left-hand screen, known as the Plan Position Indicator (PPI), the time base was a rotating radius, revolving from a central axis. It was fluorescently white and was easily observed as it swept the circumference. This rotation on the screen matched that of the aerial array, mounted on a fifty-foot gantry outside. This array swept through 360 degrees continuously, detecting any object within range and transmitting the information to the screens below. On the PPI this showed as a fluorescent white arc. As soon as that appeared, the operator flicked a strobe switch in front of him/her. This left a diameter time base afterglow as the time base itself continued rotating. The circumference of this screen was etched with azimuth readings. Noting the reading from the afterglow, the operator would call it out.

The second CRT had a horizontal time base, calibrated in miles with a range of up to 300. Its colour was green. When the fluorescent arc appeared on the PPI, and its operator flicked the strobe switch, a downward blip appeared on this second screen, remaining for a few seconds as an afterglow. The operator was now able to call out the range. In practice, the bearing was called out, and followed immediately by the range.

At a large, perspex covered table with a map of the area under observation spread out upon it, a third operator placed an indicator which coordinated the two pieces of data called out. The map was grid referenced. Successive revolutions of the aerial array produced new data, which was similarly logged on the map. Thus was added to the information the direction in which the detected object was moving. After a few more sweeps of the aerial, speed could be calculated. During the time I was at Yatesbury, height of object from the ground remained a problem. It was solved soon afterwards.

This information was passed over the telephone to Ground Control Interception (GCI) stations, responsible for the defence of the area. Knowing the whereabouts of their own planes, they very quickly identified hostiles. Once spotted by one radar station, a hostile immediately came under scrutiny of others. If necessary, fighter planes were scrambled to intercept and engage. It was this system that silently safeguarded us all, vigilantly, round the clock. The technicalities of how it all worked, and what steps to take when it didn't, were mine to grapple with over the course of the next twelve weeks. Come hell or high water, I was determined not to fail.

The receiver was the visible indication that the system was working. It did not explain how what it displayed so graphically came to be created. Without a transmitter, the receiver was just an inanimate box of metal housing intricate but inert circuitry. It is to the transmitter that I now turn. It was a massive brute, an amalgam of engineering, electric, and radio components. Switched off, its appearance was akin to that of a grey, sleek, sleeping beast in hibernation. As you switched it on, via a grey metal lever, you moved through four successive gates, each controlling different parts of the total function. An introductory surge of power decreased by stages to a steady hum, reassuring when you felt in control, intimidatory when you were uncertain of your ability to handle it. It created a presence of restrained power, an aura of mystery, with just a soupcon of the extra terrestrial. Within its solid metal framework, it supported discrete sections which could be removed separately for inspection and repair. These were quite heavy but slid in and out on channelled runners. Along the length of the front ran a sloping console with an array of meters, neon indicator lights, and various push buttons and safety devices. It was all very different from the two-valve oscillator transmitter we had built at Battersea Polytechnic

The key to unravelling the mysteries that lay within the CHL system was an understanding of the circuitry involved, and on this the bulk of our time was spent. Large and quite complicated circuit diagrams were laid out for us to gather round as our instructors pointed out the various functions and how they interlocked. After a while, I became quite proficient at starting anywhere at all on a diagram, and reasoning out its role and function in the whole process. The course encouraged deductive reasoning, seeking cogent conclusions from observed phenomena. Mere parrot fashion repetition of information given was unacceptable and unhesitatingly rebuffed. We were dealing with a very exact science. There was a logical explanation for every situation. If the situation was inimical to the health of the whole, the cause had to be detected and eradicated. Understanding of the underpinning theories was regarded as a high priority by the high-ranking officers monitoring our progress. The real crunch was whether we could apply that knowledge when actively engaged on some remote radar station, with possibly sole responsibility for keeping the equipment on the air.

From time to time, one of these high echelon officers dropped in for an unannounced inspection. I was summoned into the operations room in due course, and introduced to a Wing Commander. "How are you getting on?" he queried. "I believe I'm coping sir," I replied. He consulted his notes. "The reports on your theory appear to be very good," he remarked "You have a receptive but enquiring mind." I made no comment. There was quite a pause. "I am here," he said, in a neutral tone, "to see how you set about finding a fault. Have you done any fault finding yet?" I said I hadn't. He made another note. "Right well," he continued, "I've created a fault on the gubbins here. I'd like you to switch the apparatus on and think aloud, if you will be so good." I switched on. All seemed well as I proceeded through the stages until we were fully on air. I started a visual check of various indicators, commenting as I went along. "Such and such a meter reading normal" "So and so neon light on" "Safety switch in correct position" until "There's an indication of a fault here." "Good," he said. "Now, the 64000 dollar question is precisely what and where?" I proceeded to think aloud. "It can't be that unit because-------or that because--------or that because-------- I'm left with three possible units-------It can't be that one because----------- It's either A or F." "Very good," he said, "Do you have any preference" "Not particularly sir," I replied, "though A is more prone to faults than F." "Let's have it out then," he suggested. I slid unit A out on its runners, far enough for a visual inspection. "Now what?" my interrogator persisted. "Looking for any unusual sight or smell sir," I volunteered. then "There's a duff valve, no filament light" "So there is," he agreed, "I put it there. Would you care to replace it with this one?", producing the original from his pocket. I completed the exercise, and checked that the fault had disappeared. "Very good," he complimented, making another note. "Keep this up and we'll make a radar mechanic out of you yet." With that I was dismissed.

There are a number of tricks in the repertoire of planting faults. Had the Wing Commander left the original valve in place, removed the anode cap, placed a piece of paper inside the anode cap, and then replaced the valve, a fault would have been created, but one triggering different indications. I would still have been led to unit A, but the valve filament would have been glowing, but the non flow of current through the valve would have led me to suspect a fault in the anode circuitry, a resistor or condenser. Really bizarre CRT displays could be produced by the transposition of leads. The golden rule in fault finding is not to panic.

There is a logical reason. Pursue a solution logically. Pull out the unit Use eyes, ears, nose, whatever. The fault is there. Find it. There was purpose behind these apparently random inspections. Blackwood, a blunt Lancastrian on the same course, was visited by the same Wing Commander. Blackwood was known to be very competent with his hands. Show him a fault and he would fix it. Where fault finding was concerned he was usually all at sea. Given the same introduction as that given to me and others, he stood before the equipment, having succeeded in getting it on air, and remained steadfastly silent. The officer prompted him. "What are you thinking?" Whatever was going through his mind, Blackwood's reply was forthright. "Bugger all, sir." The officer directed him to a possible productive line of thought. "Any conclusions?" he asked, after more than enough time for considered reflection. Blackwood gave a deep sigh, followed by another mournful "Bugger all sir." Six "Bugger alls" later, the Wing Commander asked the hapless Blackwood to retire while the former discussed the situation with course instructors. Having done so, he recalled the examinee and informed him, "Blackwood, having consulted others more familiar with your day to day performance, I have to tell you that the marks awarded to you on this occasion are, so to speak, bugger all." The following day Blackwood was off the course, placed on general duties, and subsequently posted elsewhere. It certainly kept the rest of us on our toes.

I have ambivalent feelings about this decision, but recognise the dilemma facing the Wing Commander. At the conclusion of the course, we would be despatched to active service units on which lives depended. There were by now long waiting lists of men keen to enlist on our kind of course. The training was costly. Better perhaps to cut losses early, weeding out unsuitable material, bringing in new blood with more promising potential. Thus far, the Wing Commander's action was sustainable. What bothered me then, and still does, is what happened to Blackwood subsequently. Neither the brightest, nor the most articulate of men, he was, nevertheless, the sort who could turn his hands, if not his mind, to anything. With my own recent experience of general duties, which took no account of attributes I had to offer, I was sceptical about the RAF's use of its available manpower. This was a fault line discernible on posting after posting, where one continuously observed square pegs in round holes. A competent management troubleshooter would have had a field day sorting out these mismatches.

The weeding out continued and further colleagues left empty beds in our domestic site hut. I remember one in particular. Andrews was a natural wireless man. Since boyhood he had tinkered with sets. He was forever taking them apart, retuning them, changing parts, and reassembling them, only to dismantle them again for further modification. He played with wireless equipment as others read books. He never read books, apart that is from wireless magazines. It was suggested by a wit in our group that if, on his wedding night, Andrews' bride offered him a brand new electric soldering iron, in lieu of the traditional first night pleasures of the nuptial bed, she would be sure of an undisturbed night. The leap from wireless to radar was beyond Andrews' attainment. The academic standard demanded was an insurmountable barrier. He too was assigned to general duties. Had I been stranded in the desert with my life dependent on a working wireless set, I would have felt in good hands with Andrews. I hope adequate use was made of his abilities, but suspect he was restricted to painting coal white, scrubbing floors, or peeling potatoes.

As the course unfolded, the pace increased, and twilight shifts were introduced. Beginning at 17:00 hours these continued till midnight with a half-hour break about 21:30. All the lectures were on theory, with much memorising of circuit diagrams. Any subject or academic discipline depends largely on the lecturer for its appeal. I was lucky in that I fell under the spell of Corporal Clarke. He was a rarity among service instructors in that he was exuberantly enthusiastic, ahead of the rest in his knowledge and mastery of his subject matter, and could transmit both knowledge and enthusiasm articulately. Above all, he encouraged audience participation. To hear him develop a train of thought was to observe a creative thinker in action, never losing sight of the original aim, yet never frightened to explore side issues along the way. Today, the world knows him as Sir Arthur C Clarke, an internationally acknowledged expert on space travel and science fiction. His brief with us was to reveal the intriguing mysteries of radar, which he did most competently up to the break. This was always accompanied by a large Harris pork pie in one hand and a steaming hot mug of tea in the other. I'll swear it was the fear of missing those pork pies that spurred some people on whenever they felt their course attainments were slipping.

After supper, someone would pose the question, "Corporal, do you really think that man will land on the moon one day?" It was like applying a match to the blue touch paper of a bonfire night rocket. All existing blackboard content was erased, and the A.C. Clarke version of the space route to the moon began to evolve. Starting at the left hand side of the blackboard, a series of initial, intermediary, and final planetary orbits was sketched out, our space rocket being passed from one gravitational system to another until, with most of the class adrift in space, it circled the moon, preparatory to landing. All the really intricate stuff he had at his fingertips. On the blackboard was a two dimensional series of journeys. These projections involved heavenly bodies continually on the move, in an ever-evolving universe of infinity and eternity. The major obstacle confronting the lecturer was getting his craft beyond the earth's gravitational pull. He reckoned that supportive structures for propulsive purposes would necessitate sitting his spaceship on top of a rocket, or rockets, the size and weight of two or three London double-decker buses. This was not his forte, but he was convinced it would be done. Some of his Yatesbury audience dismissed him affectionately as 'Crackers Clarke'. How wrong he proved them to be. Not many years later, man walked upon the moon, having arrived there exactly as he had foreseen. At a much lower level, he enthused me and others like me to persevere for the following weeks of what could have been the hum drum accumulation of knowledge, into an exciting, imaginative raising of our sights to higher levels than would otherwise have been the case.

For a camp with so many people on site for several weeks at a time, one lot arriving as others left, there was surprisingly little entertainment laid on. It seems we were there to learn, and distractions were discouraged. Occasional diversions cropped up. In any camp there were the inevitable regular lectures on fire precautions, gas drill, first aid, and venereal diseases, to mention but a few. None of the presenters was in the Arthur C. Clarke league. I remember fondly the general duties corporal, a veteran regular serviceman, glaring at his captive audience and bawling out his opening gambit, "There is two types of fire---hinflammable and non hinflammable." Gas lectures were further opportunities for light relief, when read from the official Air Force script by self-important corporals with an inborn gift for mangling the English language. Venereal disease lectures were different. They did not amuse. The text was explicit, the visual aids were graphic, the objective was to deter. It's a wonder those of us who were young, and genteelly brought up, ever looked at a woman, no matter how attractive, with sexual aspirations.

RAF Padgate was a station known to thousands of airmen who passed through, usually on short stays, and had its own cinema. Every Sunday evening, a huge hangar was filled to capacity by several hundred grown men, all reliving the days of their boyhood at the Saturday matinee. When the lights went down, feet drummed the concrete floor and a great roar went up. They giggled through the cartoons, put up with the newsreels, and roared their approval as the main feature film hit the screen. At this time it was 'Kit Carson'. The prelude, every week, paraded the members of the cast, hero white hatted on a white horse, villain black hatted on a black horse. The villain always wore a black mask. Other members of the cast appeared in turn. Each had its own fan club, greeted by cheers or hisses. The film was screened over ten episodes. Few airmen were ever at Padgate for that length of time. While there, they cheered their heads off as the hero achieved unbelievable feats of marksmanship with a revolver that brought villains down at ranges that would test a rifleman, fired a dozen bullets from a weapon that held only six, and did it all from a horse galloping at full speed. Though the hero was the focus of attention, the main question to which everyone wanted the answer was who was the villain behind that black mask. Wherever you went in the world, as soon as people learned you'd been at Padgate the question was always posed, "Who was the villain in 'Kit Carson?" Several years ago, I met a man who claimed he'd seen episode ten, when the villain got his come uppance and was unmasked. My informant swears that the face revealed bore no resemblance to any of the rest of the cast, all of whom had been suspects. My explanation is that the whole set up was a diabolically clever German plot to keep thousands of airmen distracted from their proper task, i.e. fighting the real villain.

I have mentioned the leisurely Sunday mornings in Yatesbury. They were followed by memorable dinners. The food was consistently good, but surpassed all standards on Sundays. Full traditional English roast, potatoes, vegetables, and gravy to die for, were served in generous portions, but the sweet was the piece de resistance, Lyons fruit pie smothered in custard.

Venturesome folk were known to go round twice, heavily disguised, to get past ever vigilant NCO's on duty at the serving points. If you wore spectacles you took them off second time round, and if you didn't, you borrowed a pair. To balance the books in the kitchen must have called for expert creative accounting.

For some, especially those whose homes were not far away, there was a far more attractive alternative way of spending the weekend. One or two occupied our hut, and a scheme was devised to fulfil their aspirations. Suppose Brown was keen to go home. He made an arrangement with Smith to cover for him. Brown would slip out of camp, some time after dark on the Saturday, earlier if he was prepared to increase the risk of being detected and detained. Every night between ten and half past, the duty corporal did his rounds of the many huts, making a roll call. On each hut sheet were listed the names, usually in alphabetical order, of all the occupants. As he called out names and received a reply, he marked his records accordingly. To cover for Brown, Smith was tucked up in Brown's bed, blankets drawn well up, Brown's kitbag alongside, displaying his name. "Not feeling too good corporal," someone would explain, "decided to turn in early." The corporal reports Brown's presence in camp. When he gets to Smith's bed and calls his name, there is no reply. He tries again. "Can't be far away corporal," says somebody. "May be in the bog, or in the hut next door. He has a mate there." "Tell him to report to the guard room before midnight or he'll be on a charge" warns the corporal and notes the absence. About eleven thirty, Smith gets suitably dressed, reports to the guardroom and is registered as in camp. Hut 55 pulled off this stunt almost every weekend. I have no reason to believe that it was exclusive to us. On any given week end there could have been a sizeable number of AWOL's (away without leave).

There was not much organised physical activity at Yatesbury, apart from the nightly exodus to the darker areas of the campus of airman and WAAF couples, armed with groundsheets and a mutual desire to share each other's company. Occasionally someone would find a football and start an impromptu kick about. Seeing a small group throwing a rugby ball I joined in one day, more for the fresh air and exercise than any interest in the sport. A little Welsh sergeant was seemingly in charge. After a while, he came up to me. "Played before, you have," he observed, "Can tell, you know." I admitted to a nodding acquaintance with the game. "Fancy a run out?" he asked "I'm getting a side together for a friendly against my old club. We're meeting half way at Bristol, Saturday." I wasn't really interested. Had it been soccer, I'd have accepted with alacrity. "Got no boots sergeant," I told him. "I've an old pair I can lend you," he offered, "size 6." Relieved, I said, "I take an 8." "Why man," he said, grinning," I did say they were old boots. They'll have stretched to an 8." I gave in. It would be a break to get out of camp.

We travelled by three-ton truck. Arriving at the ground at Bristol, I was surprised by its size, and the quality of its amenities. As kick off approached, a sizeable crowd had gathered, bigger than anything I had played before. I began to change. "You're in at scrum half," the sergeant informed me, "here are your boots." I struggled to get them on. "No can do," I told him. He took the boots, whipped the laces out, stretched the already overstretched leather, and cut a nick in the toes where the lace holes ended. Together, we managed to pull them on. As we took the field, an ad hoc fifteen playing together for the first time, against an established club side, I feared the worst. The ground was now heaving, and the entry of the opposition was greeted by the massed singing that only the Welsh can produce. It was awesome and intimidating. I got the impression that every Welshman for miles around had cancelled everything to attend this fixture. Of the game itself, or of the result, no memory remains, though we did not disgrace ourselves. I remember the Welsh sergeant's post match comments, "Well played boyo. You were really nippy around the scrum." "Not as nippy as your size 6 boots around my size 8 feet," I thought.

The end of our course was fast approaching and the weeding out process was over. Those of us who were left began to contemplate the future. With about a fortnight to go, we were given a form on which to register our preferences as to area of posting. There were by now CHL stations every few miles right round the national coastline. After some thought, I entered the southeast coast of England as my first choice, and the north east as my second. I reasoned that any posting to the first would be handy for London, of which I had pleasant memories. Posting to my second choice would be conveniently handy to home.

A few days later, word got round that the list of postings was up in the orderly room, and we rushed over to see it. It was lengthy and there was a crowd of us. I got close enough to read it. In keeping with RAF custom, the entries were in alphabetical order. I ran my eye down the list and there I was. I followed the line across to the right hand column and read the destination, printed in upper case letters, RAF CRUSTAN. I noticed that no one else was posted there. "Excuse me, corporal," I said to an NCO behind a desk, "where's RAF Crustan?" "Never heard of it," he replied. "There's a map of radar sites in the next room." He accompanied me, looked up a reference sheet, said, "Follow my finger," and beginning at Yatesbury, went up the centre of England, crossed the border into Scotland, bypassed Edinburgh and Glasgow, touched on Perth and Inverness, hit the northern Scottish coast at Thurso, crossed the Pentland Firth, and ended on the north western tip of the island of Orkney. "RAF Crustan," he said, and added, "You poor bugger."

RAF Crustan, Orkney

Before taking up our new postings, we were granted a week's leave. That would have seen Greg Smedley and me travelling together, but it was not to be. He was held back for six weeks extra practical training, and finished up at Hastings. I felt for him on that final morning as the hut rocked to the sounds of packing, and celebrations of a course successfully completed. Greg stayed in his bed, blankets drawn over his head, feigning sleep. We were not to meet again till after the war.

The rail journey home was uneventful until the final stage. Due to work on the line, we had to overshoot my destination and catch a local train back. In the confusion caused, I found myself on the platform at Ferryhill, full kitbag in tow. The train was pulling away before I realised that my greatcoat was still on the luggage rack above the seat I'd occupied. Once home, I alerted the Left Luggage office at Newcastle, and awaited developments. The seven-day leave passed, not quite to plan. I had looked forward to wearing civilian clothes again for a change but found that nothing fitted me. Twelve months of service life had added weight, so a uniformed leave it had to be. Further enquiries at Newcastle station having drawn a blank, I set out, Orkney bound, minus a greatcoat. It was June. It could have been worse.

The journey's initial destination was Inverness, the HQ of RAF 70 Wing. Newcastle, Berwick, Edinburgh, Perth, all slipped by, and then my first encounter with the splendid scenery of Rannoch Moor, Glencoe, Aviemore, and finally Inverness. The stops at the main Scottish stations were memorable for their displays of traditional Scots hospitality, a voluntary organisation called 'Jock's Box' dispensing free tea and buns from trolleys staffed by ladies with warm Scottish accents.

The building housing 70 Wing HQ was a palatial mansion in its own grounds on the outskirts of Inverness. This was Bunchrew House, my billet overnight. New arrivals were given a chit listing all the checks to be undergone before onward posting was permitted. Only when every section had been signed by an appropriate NCO, would travel warrants be issued. I glanced at the list without trepidation till my eye lighted on 'Kit Inspection'. To lose any item of kit is a chargeable offence in two meanings of the word: charged in a disciplinary way, and charged financially for the cost of replacement. I had a problem. Having collected all other relevant signatures, I reported for a kit inspection. A sergeant for whom this was a regular routine with which he was fed up to the teeth said, "O.K. son, we'll use the wee room off the end of the corridor." We did and I laid my kit out, regulation style, on my groundsheet. Meticulously, he checked everything off. Then, "Greatcoat?" he queried. I took a deep breath. "It's hanging up in the corridor, sergeant. I didn't think to bring it along."

"Right, laddie," he said, "pack your stuff up. I've signed your chit. You can report straight to the orderly room for your travel warrant." You may ask what I would have done had he asked me to retrieve my greatcoat. I can answer that one. I'd noticed a number of such garments hanging along the corridor and would have 'borrowed' one for the minute or so required.

So began another lap of what was proving to be an eventful journey. The railway line from Inverness to Thurso was single line, with spurs should trains need to pass. The terrain was bleak open heathland, with only the seascape to relieve the monotony of a seven or eight hour journey. Looking inland, one could imagine scores of enemy paratroopers exploiting the vast territories of uninhabited land, except, as I now knew, our radar defences would detect them before they could land.

We reached Thurso eventually and were transferred to three ton trucks for transport to Scrabster, the port of embarkation for Orkney The bulk of the travellers were army personnel, there being but a handful of RAF, none as far as I could see wearing radar insignia on their sleeves. At Scrabster, there was a large transit camp for troops moving to and from Orkney. It was mid evening when I arrived and reported in. An army sergeant checked my papers and gave me directions for finding my bed, and a place to put it for the night. I would have expected the bed to be already in place. How wrong can you be? I tracked down the hut indicated, where I was handed three pieces of wood about six feet by one foot, and two more pieces three feet long, three inches wide, and three inches deep. To these was added a straw palliasse with minimum straw content. These I carried to another hut on the brow of a hill. In a concrete floored corner, I fashioned my bed out of the pieces provided, and stretched my palliasse upon it. A further trip to the store, and I was one threadbare blanket better off. I was beginning to miss my greatcoat.

June on the north coast of Scotland is a time of almost twenty four hours of daylight. It was eerie to watch the sun set about midnight and rise again two hours later, a touch further along the horizon. I witnessed both phenomena since sleep in my newly won bed was proving difficult. The phrase 'bed and board' had taken on a whole new meaning. I did sleep----eventually-----you do when you're nineteen, and woke to the anticipatory thrill of a voyage across the Pentland Firth. Breakfast was an eyeopener. In single file, men dipped their mess tins into a cauldron of weak gruel that passed for porridge, got that down, and returned for a refill of greasy bacon and sausage. The washing up container was a breeding ground for all the diseases against which we were regularly inoculated. Such fare was standard for Scrabster. Some months later, at a Garrison Theatre performance in Kirkwall I was to hear a stand up comedian raise the biggest round of applause in the show when he bounced on to the stage, wearing his genuine medals on one breast and a huge saucepan lid on the other. "Do you want to know what I got this lot for?" he bellowed, and proceeded to list them. Then, striking the pan lid with his knuckles, he beamed, "This is my favourite. I got this for shooting the cook at Scrabster transit camp."

Breakfast over, we were marched down to the jetty for embarkation. Fierce gales had prevented any crossings for four days and there was a severe logjam of troops housed in Scrabster. Though at the head of the queue with other RAF contingents, we watched squad after squad of army units taken on board. Shortly afterwards, the vessel was declared fully laden and we were marched back to camp.

The army, like the RAF, abhors a vacuum. Something had to be done with us. We were marched back to the main gate by a sergeant from a Scots regiment who, having dismissed us, announced, "Do you see this bloody big pile of coal on this side of the road? The C.O. don't like it there, and when the C.O. don't like anything he takes the piss out of me. He wants it on the other side of the road. Now I'm not as 'ard as 'e is. Shift this lot for 'im, and I'll see you get the rest of the day to yourselves as soon as you've finished." We set to with a will, and were finished by eleven. True to his word, the sergeant dismissed us and we spent a pleasant afternoon wandering round Scrabster. There wasn't much to see, but it beat shovelling coal.

Day two was a rerun of day one up to and including the same Scots sergeant's address at the main gate, delivered word for word as if addressing a squad that had never heard it before. The rest of the day differed from day one in that we had long spells of leaning on our shovels, and finished the job just in time for tea. The term for this two-day training course could well be Motivational Disincentive.

On day three things picked up. Once again we were in the vanguard at the jetty. A few army units went up the gangway, followed by a voice from on board, "Let's be having the bloody Brylcreem boys" and at long last we were on the 'ss St. Ola'. The crossing was quite short, something under three hours, the seas were calm, the sun shone, and life became worth living once more. In such conditions, even in mid June, it was decidedly parky out in the Pentland Firth. Most of the company went below for at least part of the voyage. Without a greatcoat, I found the perfect spot, back pressed up against the funnel on the leeward side. Thus at ease, I was able to enjoy the passing scenery of which the Old Man of Hoy, soaring out of the water, was the most noteworthy. We entered the harbour of Stromness, a small township of narrow, cobbled streets, quaint cottages of solid stone, dormer windowed larger houses, pubs and small shops. I was directed to an RAF office and told that transport to Crustan was scheduled for later in the day. When it arrived, it was a 15 cwt. commercial vehicle loaded with supplies for the camp. I sat among the assorted packages, the front passenger seat being occupied by a fighter pilot bound for Skarra Brae, a squadron base not far from Crustan. We dropped him off and I claimed his vacant seat. I could not recall having seen a single tree throughout the journey, and the landscape grew bleaker the further we went. Every few miles the monotony was relieved by a little cluster of white washed cottages, a cow or horse grazing in nearby fields. These interludes became less and less frequent, and the road became narrower. Eventually we stopped, the driver alighted, and opened a five-barred gate that gave access to a rough track of grass and shingle. "Welcome to Crustan," said the driver, "You'd best walk from here. You can leave your kit on board. Close the gate after I'm through." I did as he asked and watched his bumpy progress up a steep incline. Leaning on the now closed gate I took stock.

Away to my left, some two to three miles distant, the sun glinted on the Atlantic Ocean, which stretched to the far horizon. Dotted about the land in between were small croft houses, some in groups, others in isolation. The road on which we had arrived ran on towards the sea, bending and twisting out of sight. I was not far it seemed from the end of the earth. I turned now and viewed the back of the receding truck. It was time to follow.

Some hundred yards up the track stood a wooden cabin on the left. This was the guardroom. Its single occupant waved me on. A further fifty yards, and still climbing, I reached a double row of rusty Nissen huts on the left, facing each other to form a community. Four of these were living quarters, one a cookhouse and dining room, another a combined office and medical room, yet another a store room, and finally the ablutions and toilet block. I was assigned a bed in the first Nissen on the left, and noted that it was probably protected by the others from what would be the prevailing wind. It was the hut which housed the technical personnel.

Following the original track to its end was to encounter its steepest incline for another hundred yards or so until it opened out on to a broad plateau. On this stood a CHL gantry and aerial with the receiver hut alongside. A narrow concrete pathway from this cluster ran some sixty yards to the transmitter hut. The connecting copper feeder lines twanged and hummed in the breeze. Fifty yards away from the receiver, in the opposite direction to the transmitter, stood the solid, brick built rectangular diesel house. The view from the plateau opened up a new vista. The headland of Birsay was visible. To the west was the sizeable Loch Boardhouse. The arc of the horizon extended unbroken to about 270 degrees. It was of course mid June and the weather was very fine. First impressions were non-commital. What I did not like was the rusty, neglected maintenance appearance of those Nissen huts. In winter gales off the Atlantic conditions would be very different. Time would tell. I returned to my new home and organised my belongings. Tomorrow I would explore further.

The picture that emerged was revealing. The previous occupants, the Royal Navy, had abandoned the site, declaring it to be unfit for human habitation. The rusted Nissen roofs on view were an outer skin, erected over an inner one that, hopefully, was in better condition. In building to this specification, the intention had been to fill the gap between the two shells with insulation material, but to save money this had not been completed. Rats were nesting under the foundations and could be heard, day and night, but specially at night, scampering from one side of the hut to the other, between the two shells. They had gnawed holes in the floorboards along the length of the hut, and, as soon as it was dark, could be heard scurrying across the floor, and along the shelving that ran but a foot above the bed heads along both sides of the hut. Books, papers, and anything edible were nibbled and eaten during night time forays. Crustan was a major health hazard.

Perhaps in recognition of the spartan conditions, the camp was classified as an overseas posting with special privileges, one of which was a weekly ration of fifty Capstan Navy Cut cigarettes in a sealed circular tin, over and above the normal standard ration of cigarettes and chocolate. Nobody was expected to serve on site for a consecutive period exceeding three months. A Saturday liberty run to either Kirkwall or Stromness was normally available to personnel not on duty. Otherwise, the regime was work and sleep, work and sleep, on a three watch system which operated as follows: Day 1: 8am to 1pm and 11pm to 8am. Day 2: 6pm to 11pm Day3: 1pm to 6pm. i.e. every third night was a working night. The cumulative effect of this three-watch system on disrupted sleep patterns was one factor affecting the quality of life. Another was its effect upon the digestive system.

This life style was rendered more arduous in the climatic conditions that prevailed. The site was on the highest point to provide maximum radar coverage, and was subjected to weather systems that built up across 3,000 miles of Atlantic Ocean to hit the coast of Orkney with varying degrees of ferocity. Gales often exceeded 70 mph and could last for days, with constant rain being driven horizontally. Normal footwear was superfluous. One lived in gum boots and heavy sea stockings almost permanently. Black oilskins and sou'westers completed what, in practical terms, became your uniform.

Sanitary provision was primitive. Six Elsan buckets served the needs of the camp complement of fifty men.

There was a duty roster listing the days when named people had to empty any bucket(s) that was/ were full. This involved a 200 yards trek over open ground to a cesspool dug out of the earth. What defined 'full' was a constant bone of contention. Every effort was made to compress the buckets' contents, in order to leave space for just one more day's contributions, thus passing on the trek to the cesspool to the next day's nominee. There were even allegations that the contents of full buckets were transferred to others not yet full to avoid the dreaded consequences. In the same

Nissen hut as the toilet arrangements were wash hand basins and rudimentary showers. There was little concession to privacy.

For the non-technical people on site there was no relief from this spartan way of life, though they did enjoy a less arduous work schedule than the technical staff. It must have been frustrating for them, watching the rest of us coming and going on duty, involved in work so secret that none of us discussed it with them. This division was reinforced by the allocation of living quarters. I shared my Nissen with the exclusive family of radar mechanics and operators. We were thus able to discuss any technical matters freely. This arrangement was also valuable in ensuring reasonable behaviour during the day, when some of us were trying to sleep after the previous night's long watch.

The radar receiver hut was a welcome haven from life on the domestic site. A testimony to the ingenuity of the early radar pioneers, it was one of the last existing prototype installations. The aerial array was turned manually. By the operator's chair was an old car steering wheel, mounted vertically, with a wooden handle attached at right angles to the rim. This wheel was connected, via a series of chains, wheels, pulleys, and wormed gears to the turning mechanism of the aerial array on a gantry above the hut. Grasping the wooden handle, the operator wound the wheel in one direction to rotate the aerial clockwise, and in the opposite direction to go anticlockwise. Even when maintained in top class lubricated condition, the gear was hard work, requiring a good strong right arm. Turning the overhead array in a rising wind was hazardous. Lose control of the steering wheel and the normal relationship was reversed, the aerial spinning the wheel at high speed. A two-hour stint was as long as anyone did. The Plan Position Indicator CRT showed the orientation of the array, so the operator always knew what segment he was covering. It was considered that a closely scanned full sweep should be completed in two minutes, the return sweep to the starting point being a thirty second exercise. The arm strength needed to keep operating in an increasing wind force was taxing. As the aerial came round, head on to the wind, extra effort was required, and the rotating, synchronised time base on the screen provided corroboratory pictorial evidence. The station was kept operational as long as possible.

The operator was in constant touch with the Filter Room in Kirkwall, which received and logged information from radar stations dotted all round the coastline, protecting the naval anchorage at Scapa Flow and the western approaches. Whenever gales reached limits at which (a) operators were reporting the limits of their ability to drive the aerial and (b) the very real danger of the aerial being sheered off as it met the gale head on, Filter Room was informed and lashing down procedures came into play. The array was arrested end on to the gale to minimise risk. As a general rule of thumb, such action was introduced at gale force speeds of 70mph.plus. The crew on duty, except for one left manning the screen, donned foul weather gear, and mounted the fifty foot gantry, often in pitch blackness. Stout steel hawsers, attached to the ends of the array in pairs were unshackled, and paid out very carefully until they stretched to ground level. Loss of control at this stage was extremely dangerous. A thick steel hawser, whipping about in the dark, could wreak havoc, and serious injuries, and at least one death had been reported under such circumstances. With the free end of the hawser safely at ground level, its appropriate stout iron hoop, embedded in concrete, was located and the hawser firmly anchored to it. When the task was completed, four hawsers held the array firmly secured. The whole exercise took an average half to three-quarters of an hour, depending on the weather. You seldom got a gale without rain, and the rain was usually driven horizontally in gusts. Footholds and handgrips in the worst of these conditions were never easy. The gantry deck we worked on was level and as steady as a rock. I was glad I was not on board ship. There were men out there on these nights, performing far more exacting feats in the middle of the Atlantic. Scalding hot tea, and the warmth of the operations room were always welcome after these episodes.

To achieve and maintain a high level of efficiency good teamwork is essential, and compatible relationships within a watch, and between other watches is paramount. Being based in one Nissen during off duty periods helped to reinforce the corporate bonding. We were a mixed bunch. A Canadian sergeant was in overall command. His technical knowledge was eclectic and his man management superb. He knew how to praise and encourage, when and how to give a rollicking. His welcome to me on my first watch was typical. "Forget what they taught you at training school. Here, we do it my way. Suppose you're on night duty, having a little kip, and the operator rudely awakens you to report a fault. Go outside, come rushing in, and show me what you would do." I went, returned, and began to move up and down along the equipment, affecting to look for indications of malfunction. "Mistake number one," remarked Slim. "The first thing you do is sit down and light a cigarette." So saying, he lit two and passed me one. "More mistakes are made by rushing in than even my granny would manage," the advice continued. "A minute's pause to settle yourself down. Then start thinking. I think you'll cope without a nursemaid, but if you find yourself out of your depth, you get me on the blower. O.K? If owt serious goes pear shaped on this station it will be my head on the block. So think on. Till you've found your feet, fall back on me." Some of that advice I have heeded ever since, under all sorts of circumstances.

Second in line was George, a Cockney corporal. With a wealth of experience in the wireless industry before joining up, he was more of a shop floor steward than a manager. He held strong political views and was always ready for an argument. We had a bank clerk, a solicitor's managing clerk, two schoolteachers, an estate agent, a travelling salesman, a news reporter, a local government officer, and a geographical representation that embraced Canada, Australia, New Zealand, Jamaica, and South

Africa. The fortunes of war had produced, on a tiny remote dot on the map, a truly representative cross section of society.

Each of these made contributions to our communal life and, in some cases, shaped my view of the world. The solicitor's clerk could not shake off years of professional conditioning. When passing information on a new plot to the Filter Room, speed and accuracy were essential. If the location was one in which none of our own aircraft should be, the sighting was treated as hostile, and every radar station in the area would be directed to it. The standard message to the Filter Room would be: "Hallo Kirkwall. Crustan calling. We have a new sighting in London Orange 6845." Stan's message would be: "Hallo Kirkwall. There would appear to be the possibility of a sighting, and as far as can be ascertained, its current position is in the approximate vicinity of London, repeat London, Orange, repeat Orange, 6 er 8 er 4 er 5 er or thereabouts." Stan was never definitive about anything, and it was not unknown for the WAAF on the end of the line to acknowledge his call with, "If this bugger is hostile, and we are going to catch him, for God's sake put someone else on the line."

One of the camp's few recreational facilities was a table tennis table. Stan was the unit champion. He took his stance close up to the table, always played on the backhand, simply putting his bat in the way of everything, the power of his opponent's shot being sufficient to return the ball over the net. Stan never won a shot. His opponents lost them.

The bank clerk also displayed evidence of his former activities. When the rest of us tuned into the radio for news on the progress of the war and other items of national concern, Fred hung on for the financial news. He was very fond of advising against the stupidity of keeping your money under the mattress, when it could be invested and earning interest. I suppose that, subliminally, I must have been influenced by him. It was very seldom that any of us left camp. There was really nowhere to go. However, Bob Squire, a fellow mechanic, suggesting that we could do with a break, persuaded me to accompany him on a walk to Birsay. It was a tiny place, just a few croft houses and a shop. While standing outside the latter. I noticed a sign in the window, 'Birsay Post Office.' I went in and opened my first Investment Account with a deposit of £3. I've been saving ever since.

Bob Squire and I continued with occasional trips out after that. A Newcastle man in his mid thirties, he was a typical Geordie, in accent, honest to goodness what you see is what you get attitude, and pride in his roots. We got on well. One Sunday, we decided to take a look at Kitchener's Monument, high on the cliff top beyond Birsay. It was a pleasant day, breezy but warm, and we found the climb easy enough with pauses every so often.

The monument commemorates the loss of the 'ss Hampshire' in 1916 with all hands. On the way down, Bob said, "I could murder a cup of tea." "Fat chance," I remarked, "It's Sunday remember." As we arrived at Birsay again, the shopkeeper cum postmaster was taking a breath of fresh air at the front door of his house adjoining the shop. "Fine day," he greeted us, "Enjoyed your walk did you? I saw you on the way up. Marvellous view isn't it?" We chatted a while since he seemed glad of the company. Then Bob asked, "Is there anywhere round here we can get a cup of tea?" I'm sure he was hoping the postmaster would oblige. "Hm," said that worthy, thoughtfully, "There are three sisters just round the corner who do a very nice Orkney tea for sixpence, but not to my knowledge on a Sunday." He paused for a few seconds, then said, "There's no harm in asking. They can only say no. If you wait here I'll put in a neighbourly word for you." So saying, he disappeared round the corner. Bob and I exchanged glances. When the postmaster reappeared, he had both thumbs aloft. "The ladies will be pleased to see you," he beamed, "You'll find the front door ajar." We thanked him, shook hands, and parted company.

Knocking on the sisters' door elicited a cheery "Come in, please do." and we found ourselves in a pleasant living room, with a peat fire blazing in a spacious grate, surrounded by a well-equipped cooking range. A huge black kettle was simmering on the hob. The delicious smell of home baking wafted across the room. There were little feminine touches everywhere. RAF Crustan was a man's place. This, most definitely was not. Only one of the sisters was present to greet us, which she did most graciously. "Please do take a seat. As you can see, the table is not quite prepared yet. I shall just lay the tablecloth, and my sisters will bring in a few wee bites to eat." The tablecloth was not the kitchen table oilcloth I had expected, but a beautiful lace one, exquisitely embroidered, Cups, saucers and plates were part of a set of fine china. The cutlery was matching. The other two sisters appeared and proceeded to set out a range of small cakes, scones, drop scones, bannocks, oatcakes, barley bread, and a large dish of farm butter, with a container of cream alongside. Tea was poured and the ladies settled themselves in chairs by the glowing fire while Bob and I tucked in. Everything was delicious. As we ate, the sisters began to ask questions. Where were we from? What was it like there? etc. In the short space of twenty minutes they became very knowledgeable about Tyneside and Teesside and Wearside between. "Do you get many visitors?" I asked, feeling the need to stem the flow of their enthusiastic inquisition. "Och yes," came the reply, " and they all sign our visitors' book. I'll get it for you." As good as their word, the book was presented. Bob and I flipped through the pages. The dates went back several years. I scanned the addresses. "You've entertained people from all over the world," I commented, obviously surprised. " Oh yes," came the response, "and we find out as much as we can about where they come from." "That's remarkable," responded Bob, genuinely impressed, then conceded, "You know more about the world than I do."

In further conversation we elicited an astonishing story. The three sisters, all spinsters, were in their seventies. They had been born in Birsay, and educated in the village school in a neighbouring hamlet. They had never been to Stromness or Kirkwall, let alone left the island. Yet, by applying what gifts they had—homespun domestic expertise, and a well-developed skill at putting guests at ease—they had felt no need to venture far afield. Far from going out into the wider world, they were content that the world should come to them. At one point in our long conversation, one of the three put her finger to her lips, crossed the room to a wall on which hung a map of the world. She then switched on an old battery powered wireless set. It was news time and the sisters never missed a bulletin. As items of news were announced, the finger that had called for silence glided over the map effortlessly, always stopping at the correct location. Her two sisters followed that didactic finger dutifully. Bob and I did so almost incredulously. This elderly woman was a born teacher. All too soon, the visit ended. We paid our dues, expressed our thanks, and took our leave. As we strolled back to camp, too full to walk any faster, I remarked, "I thought Crustan was pretty cosmopolitan, but we're not in the same league as those three." I can picture them now, by Peter's side at the gates of heaven, warmly greeting new arrivals, asking them where they've come from, and sitting them down to an Orkney tea. If they are not there, then Paradise is not all it is reputed to be.

Since my arrival at Crustan, I had had no pressing need for a greatcoat. Working uniform, as explained previously, was black oilskins, sou'wester and gumboots. The occasional visit to Birsay was undertaken using my groundsheet as a cape, a common practice among most of us. I was, nevertheless, much relieved to receive a parcel from home which included my long lost deficient item of clothing.

My father had located it in the Newcastle LOST luggage office—our previous enquiries having been addressed to the LEFT luggage office. I put the garment to immediate use as an extra blanket Bed played a large part in life at Crustan. If you weren't asleep in it, you were lying on it reading. There was little else to do. Beds were of a uniform construction, in wrought iron with folding head and foot attachments so that, when folded, they could be stacked easily. The head was a simple curved bar arching across the width. There were no fancy struts or other embellishments. A simple criss cross wire mesh, stretched and secured by hooks inserted into holes in the side irons, provided stability. On to this were laid three padded squares, known universally as 'biscuits'. The whole made a quite comfortable bed. With biscuits in place, there was room for one's head to slip beneath the arched bar of the head frame. A pillow was a protection against that possibility. Most of us used our folded tunics as a pillow.

Wooing sleep while rats were scurrying along the shelving a few inches above your head was difficult, but you soon acclimatised. After a week or two on a three-watch system, you slept whatever the conditions. You did not, however, sleep soundly. Subconsciously, you were never fully relaxed, and constant tossing and turning could cause an awakening during the night to retrieve blankets from the floor. One morning, after a sound and dreamless sleep, I sat up only to receive a sudden blow to the face. I fell back, momentarily stunned, and waited for the world to stop revolving, and the exploding stars to subside. Gathering my reeling senses, I explored my face with probing fingers. They came away covered in blood. Gingerly, I eased my body down the length of the bed and sat up. I was feeling distinctly queasy. In the bed opposite, its occupant was gazing at me, a look of disbelief on his face. "What's the matter?" I asked him. "What's the matter?" he parroted, and then again, "What's the bloody matter? Unless I'm mistaken, you've broken your bloody nose." He was not mistaken. The evidence remains to this day. My folded tunic having slipped during the night, and my nocturnal movements having placed my head under the curved arc of the bed head, I had knocked myself out in trying to sit up.

Talking of beds reminds me of our New Zealand hut mate Cliff. He was nearer forty than thirty, and had travelled halfway round the world to do his bit. An inveterate builder and dismantler of wireless sets, he was a valuable member of our radar fraternity. Cliff had absolutely no charisma. You would never have picked him out in a crowd. Women's hearts would never beat faster on bumping into him. Yet, if they looked into his eyes, and were not careful, they were his for the taking. Cliff was a hypnotist of spectacularly demonstrative efficiency. He first displayed his powers in our hut where he occupied a bed. Having revealed that he possessed this gift, he was challenged to perform on anyone in the company willing to volunteer. He drew two beds side by side, with a gap between them of five to six feet, and announced that he proposed to ask his subject to bridge the gap with the back of the head on one bed, the back of the heels on the other. One of his listeners accepted the invitation. With two others lending a hand, Cliff placed the volunteer in position and asked him to brace his body to form a bridge. He tried but couldn't, collapsing at his midriff. Cliff asked the two helpers to support the midriff until the bridge position was held. He then passed his hands up and down the length of the volunteer's body, intoning, "You will arch your body upwards, make it absolutely rigid, and become a strong, strong bridge." We looked on amazed as the body arched and stiffened. Cliff motioned to the two supporters to stand aside. The body remained in position. He hadn't finished yet, for Cliff was a class act. Seating himself gently on the middle of the bridge, he slowly took both feet off the ground. He weighed just over ten stones but the bridge supported him without flinching. Stepping slowly down, Cliff again passed his hands along the body length, intoning his final instructions, "Time to relax. Nice deep breath and slowly, ever so slowly, relax." The volunteer's rigidity slowly dissipated and he rejoined us flanked by his two helpers. All this was achieved in a familiar Nissen hut at very close quarters. It was staggeringly impressive.

Even more spectacular was Cliff's public performance a week or two later. In the long, silent watches of the night, when there was little activity to report, the Filter Room / Radar Stations network became a chat room, a range of topics being discussed. On one such occasion, the station Netherbutton, near Kirkwall, announced that it had a WAAF hockey team that was looking for fixtures. Our men on duty seized the initiative and asked them to get in touch. In due course, a party of some eighteen or so arrived at Crustan on a Saturday afternoon. The issue of the invitation had omitted to take account of a rather important factor---nobody on site had played hockey before.

However, a scratch side was turned out, consisting of men familiar with either soccer or rugby. We presumed the rules would be pretty much the same, and it was only a bunch of women we were playing anyway. I was placed at centre forward and had my first twinge of doubt when my eyes alighted on the opposing centre half. They could scarcely miss her. She was massive. Sandy Powell, the comedian, used to tell the tale of his wife who sent her night dress to the laundry, only to have it returned, unwashed, with a note to say they didn't do bell tents. This centre half was in the grand marquee class. "Piece of cake," I thought after the initial frisson of fear, "With my speed I'll leave her for dead." Dream on. This mountain of flesh could move with an agility that was astonishing, and had an anticipatory intuition of the direction I was proposing to take. She would have been difficult to handle on her own. With a stick in her hand she was lethal. Around her were slighter specimens of womanhood, extremely well coached in team tactics. We lost. We were annihilated. We were humiliated. I came off that field battered, bruised, and breathless. I have never played hockey again.

Arrangements had been made for a little socialising after the game. We had no facilities for dancing, so we gathered in the half Nissen hut that served as the dining room for an impromptu singsong. Then we played our trump card: Cliff, the Kiwi hypnotist. He started by seeking a non-piano playing volunteer. An attractive, dark haired girl stepped forward. Cliff checked her complete ignorance of the piano, then announced, "With her kind permission, I am going to ask this young lady to perform for us two pieces of her own choosing, one very, very happy, the second very, very sad." He seated the girl at the piano, passed his hands around her head from behind (no eye contact) and said, "Right, young lady, in your own time." The most appalling discordant noises pounded out of the instrument. It was the player's face, however, that riveted attention. A beaming, open mouthed, exuberant expression was followed by one of dejection, despair, and melancholy, with a little tear in the eye. Cliff intervened, those fluttering hands returning the pianist to reality.

The audience clamouring for more, Cliff proceeded to excel himself. Four WAAF's were invited to hold hands and form a circle. Moving around outside the group, Cliff swiftly 'put them under'. Again, there was no eye contact. "You are in a small basket, suspended from an air balloon," he informed them in a slow, deliberate monotone. "You are about to leave the ground. -----You are now airborne. (a variety of facial expressions and body language from the balloonists), You are slowly gaining height. If you look over the side, you will see the Nissen huts getting smaller and smaller." (All the balloonists looked over the side). Suddenly, one of them wrenched her hands free, stumbled out of the hut, and was sick. Cliff dehypnotised the others. The show was over. For the next few minutes, the place buzzed with animated conversation. My contribution was limited to a short observation to Cliff, "See that huge Amazon of a woman over there, goes by the name of 'Big Bertha'? Why the hell didn't you hypnotise her before the game? I'm sure she's prejudiced my matrimonial chances for life."

We were now moving into November and the days were getting noticeably shorter. The daily filling of the diesel fuel tank, always a chore, was now arduous and dangerous. Diesel oil was stored in fifty-gallon drums, a not inconsiderable weight to trundle up the steep incline from storage compound to diesel shed. A gale force wind more often than not complicated matters. I have seen isolated full drums lifted clear of the ground by gales exceeding 100mph. Once a barrel had been manhandled to the diesel-shed entrance, it was rolled up an improvised ramp and dropped into a timber stand, with the bung at six o'clock. Two-gallon metal buckets were used to transfer fuel to the diesel fuel tanks. Among the many articles of knitwear gratefully received at Crustan, the most prized were mittens, slit across the palms, so that fingers could be exposed or covered as conditions dictated. Bare flesh on those drums in freezing weather was difficult to sustain for long.

The technical site ran very efficiently with the mechanic on watch able to deal with most faults. On one memorable night watch I had cause to raise Slim, the Canadian sergeant. The transmitter had tripped. In pitch darkness, with the aid of a torch, I ran along the concrete pathway that connected the receiver hut to that housing the transmitter. We ran a twin system for such emergencies, and I soon had the standby in action. We were allowed two minutes to effect such a change over, and were timed on how long it took us to restore the original channel. I carried out all the routine checks. The chief clue to the possible cause of the breakdown was a most offensive stench beyond my experience. Bearing in mind Slim's initial welcome to me, I got him out of bed. He joined me in a matter of minutes.

"Good God, lad," was his opening gambit, "What the hell is that stink?" Together we went through all the procedures, finally deciding to open the back panels for visual checks. What we found surprised us both. An outlet pipe normally vented hot air that built up in the apparatus. A large rat, attracted by the warmth, and having gained access to the hut, had entered the pipe. A large flat—topped condenser had been its chosen bed. Unfortunately, its nose had contacted one terminal, its tail the other. It had died instantly, the contents of its body exploding, its carcase being baked to the condenser. Nothing in the training manual covered a situation like this. It took Slim and me a couple of hours to clean up the mess, and report the transmitter back in commission. Neither of us bothered with breakfast that morning.

Those of us engaged on the technical side had no difficulty in filling in our spare time. We didn't have much after we had remedied the sleep deficit. For others with normal daytime working hours, the evenings must have been long and tedious. Inevitably, regular card schools arose in which a high percentage of non-—technical personnel participated. Many played merely to pass the time. A few needed the spice of playing for money, within the limits imposed by an airman's pay packet. A hard core played for high stakes, and they were men experienced in such ventures. At weekend sessions, this group attracted its coterie of spectators, enjoying the risks of heavy gambling without personal jeopardy. One Saturday night, large sums of money were changing hands, until, well into the small hours, an RAF Regiment sergeant, on temporary attachment to Crustan, had cleared the pot of just over £30. He retired to bed, his wallet under his pillow. The following morning he reported his wallet missing.

The C.O., a Canadian, called a general meeting and made the following announcement: "There is a thief among us. I want to know who he is. On the table are fifty envelopes, one for each man on the roll. I want forty nine of you to print your names on a piece of paper, place it in the envelope, and deliver it to the orderly room. The fiftieth man, the thief, will place the stolen money in the envelope and deliver it to the orderly room. By the process of elimination, I will know the thief's identity and will deal with him in strict confidence." This ploy did not work out quite as intended. Fifty envelopes arrived with signatures in them. The fifty first contained a £10 note. The thief was wanting the best of both worlds. The victim of his crime was still out of pocket. The C.O. was no fool, and by means known only to himself worked out the thief's identity, and presented him before another general meeting. Three options were presented for voting on: (1) the matter be reported to the civil police (2) it be handed over to 70 Wing H.Q. for them to investigate and punish under King's Regulations (3) the matter be dealt with internally. By a large majority, the last option was favoured. I remember being utterly taken aback when the thief was exposed. He was in General Duties grade, blond and curly haired, with a face that was angelic, and eyes that were of the clearest blue. Butter would have taken a long time to melt in the mouth behind red, cherubic lips. The C.O. summarised the lad's past, a long period in childcare, mainly in a Dr. Barnado's home. I think it was this that swung the vote. He was posted the next day, presumably without any recorded blemish on his service record. What arrangements were made for repayment of the stolen money, I know not. There is, however, a sequel to narrate. Over two years later, in the context of a huge transit camp, I chanced to observe our villain engaged in a card school. He recognised me immediately, and probably wondered what my next move would be. He forestalled it by approaching me, right hand held out at arm's length, and greeted me loudly with, "How nice to see you again after such a long time. World treating you right, I hope. Must get back to my mates. They're a good, honest set of lads." Cool as a cucumber. Older, not quite so angelic, thicker lipped, and definitely thicker skinned, he had not, I doubt, mended his ways.

With Christmas approaching and the weather worsening, we were now subjected to three and four day periods of continuous gales. Of all the aspects, perhaps the worst was being inside those Nissen huts. The privations of getting to and from the technical site, the daily routine of drying out wet clothing, the irksome duty, every few days of carrying full Elsan buckets to the cesspool, filling the diesel fuel tanks, and other unwelcome activities, made the thought of shelter from the elements extremely attractive. There was the rub. You could not find peace in a Nissen hut with rain belting down on it incessantly in torrents, creating a rhythm that bored into your brain. Andy, a little wisp of a man from one of the Durham pit villages, put it most succinctly, seated on his bed. "You'd think the buggers would issue earplugs" and then, after having pulled off his sea boot stockings, and surveying his feet, lugubriously adding, "That takes the bloody biscuit. I'm developing webbed feet."

Christmas Eve dawned unusually fine and dry. I was on the 8am to 1pm watch, and was due back on at 11pm till 8am on Christmas Day. There was a liberty run to Stromness in the evening, and I decided to join a handful of others in the 15 cwt van. Stromness was a pleasant enough little place, and a change of scenery would be welcome. There was also the possibility of seeing a bit of Christmas cheer in decorated shop window displays, and maybe even a tree, an unusual sight in Orkney. As the evening progressed, the breeze eased off, and a full moon shone in a clearing sky. The journey back to camp, a twenty mile run, was like something out of a fairy tale book. A silence alien to Orkney seemed to be settling over everything. I went on watch strangely bewitched by it all. Our Canadian C.O. dropped in about midnight to wish us a Merry Christmas, and invited us outside. "You must see this," he said, "It's simply breathtaking." We congregated under the aerial gantry and took in the panoramic view. Full moon, no clouds, not a breath of wind, an unnatural silence, and everything sprinkled with silver. The landscape below us was silver, the croft roof tops were silver, the placid surface of Loch Boardhouse was silver, Birsay village was silver, and the Atlantic, spreading away to the far horizon, was silver, placid, motionless and silent. It was as though a huge, sound proofed silver blanket had been cast over it all. It was the Canadian C.O. who broke the silence that had engulfed even us, with an apt comment that spoke for all of us, "Peace on earth," he muttered, almost reverently. "And goodwill toward men." someone added. It was a moment to savour. A group of men, brought together by war, engaged in fighting a war, were suddenly and unexpectedly gripped by an overwhelming sense of man's desperate need for peace. How fitting that this particular night should be that of Christmas Eve. Those of us who shared the experience will, I am sure, have recalled it on every succeeding Christmas Eve.

As I came off watch at 8am on Christmas Day, the magic of the moon had disappeared, a watery sun having taken over. There was a gentle zephyr of a breeze, and the silence of the previous evening was now broken. There were indications that the weather was building up to its customary mixture of wind driven rain. Bed looked inviting, and being due back on watch at 6pm, I could have done with an hour or two of sleep. It being Christmas, I decided to forego that option to share what there was of the seasonal spirit. Strings of cards above bed heads, a stunted fir tree in the middle of the floor, and a sprig of holly here and there was about it. By common consent, a wireless was relaying carols. Truth to tell, we were marking time for the big Christmas dinner. As is custom in the RAF, this was traditional fare, served in generous helpings, with free beer on tap. It was a gastronomic exception to the plain fare on offer daily. After the feast came the highlight. Every few weeks, the tedium of life was relieved by the visit of a mobile cinema. On this occasion, it arrived in time to screen "How Green Was My Valley" immediately after dinner. We were ten minutes into the film, and almost at the stage when reality was suspended in favour of a different world, when the power supply failed. I was despatched to investigate. Anxious to minimise the break, I had intended to sprint up the steep incline to the diesel hut. A full stomach preventing this, I strolled up, restored the power, and sauntered back. The hero of the film had been a boy of ten when I left. By the time I took my seat again, he was a young man. "I've seen a few people age like that in Crustan," I thought, and gave myself up again to the realms of escapism of the silver screen.

The turn of the year from 1942 to 1943 brought in a succession of events, the first of which was a tragedy. On night watch, I stepped out of the receiver hut for a welcome breath of fresh air, much as we had done on that memorable Christmas Eve. It was a quiet night, with but a little wind, and no rain. My gaze swept over the by now familiar panorama. Something registered as being unusual and I focussed on it, an isolated croft house, a few hundred yards up the road to Birsay. It was on fire. I dashed back into the hut, alerted the guardroom, and asked the occupant to alert our own people, and the appropriate authority in Birsay. This second approach was a very long shot indeed since the fire fighting equipment in the village was a primitive hand propelled vehicle. The better hope, and probably the only one, was our own response. In double quick time, a full water bowser was hitched to a truck, with all available hands on board, and despatched to the scene. Meanwhile, watching from our vantage point, we foresaw the consequences. The blaze was spreading rapidly, lighting up the surroundings by the second. The building was almost certainly doomed. Our concern was for the occupants. The rescuers arrived to find a bemused, distressed old man, dressed only in night attire, on the grass verge, a few yards from the house. He lived alone. An ambulance was called, and efforts to save the building began. It was an impossible task, and by daylight only a smoking skeleton remained.

The personal cost to the old man was devastating. Never trustful of banks or post offices, he had kept his life's savings in cardboard boxes in different parts of the house. Growing infirmity had necessitated his sleeping downstairs in recent months, a situation that undoubtedly saved his life. The smell of smoke had alerted and awakened him just in time to make his escape. Subsequent investigations traced the site of the initial outbreak and postulated the cause. As with most dwellers in remote areas, the old man kept plenty of stores of essential commodities during the winter months. In his case, this included food, paraffin oil, and matches. He stored them all together. As we knew at Crustan, rats infested any place offering warmth and food. Evidence was produced of rats having gnawed containers of boxes of matches, in the course of which a match had been ignited. I do not know how or where the old man ended his days. I do hope this is not his only epitaph. Sadly, I never knew his name.

Better news followed this episode. Two RAF sergeants arrived on site with plans for a replacement technical block, and a brief to conduct a preparatory survey. A few weeks later, they returned with contractors and the work began. Foundations were dug, filled, and reinforced, with ducts to carry essential cables. Massive reels of heavy-duty cable littered the ground, and we were involved in unwinding them and bedding lengths in place. The new block had everything under one roof, and a motorised unit for rotating the aerial array. No longer would we have to walk that concrete path between receiver and transmitter huts. Above all, the days of driving that ponderous installation by hand, in a system of wormed gears and pulleys were over. Over nigh on sixty years later, I have biceps on the right arm noticeably better developed than those on the left. I refer to this condition as 'the Crustan factor.' To sit in front of our new receiver, pressing shiny, colour-coded buttons, and watching the image on the screen indicating that the aerial array was responding, was sheer bliss.

These improved working conditions on the technical side were not matched by enhanced general living environment. Short of self-generated improvements, it seemed we could anticipate no remedial intervention from higher up. We conducted a survey to ascertain the order of priority of needs as perceived by the men. The results indicated an overwhelming vote for priority number one: RATS. More in hope than in expectation, we filed a report with the C.O. to use as he saw fit. Meanwhile we had a stroke of luck. There were known to be feral cats abroad in the surrounding countryside, and sightings had been made along the shores of Loch Boardhouse. Some of the men visited the hotel by the loch occasionally and came back one evening with news that the hotelkeeper was having trouble with his water supply. Could anyone on camp help? Bob Squire and I went over the following day and repaired a defective water pump, for which the grateful owner offered drinks on the house. Conversation got round to rats. "Don't bother us," he said, "We've adopted feral cats.

They've cleared the place out and keep it that way." We were interested. "Look lads," he continued, "one good turn deserves another. I'll have a word with our gillie. He'll trap a couple of young 'uns for you, one male, one female, and tell you what to do with them." He was as good as his word. The gillie's advice was to keep the two separately in captivity for several days, feeding and watering them regularly but sparingly, housing the cages under our Nissen hut. "They'll get the scent of the rats all around them," he said, "and the rats will pick up theirs. Once your little beauties have accepted their new surroundings, with a ready made food source to hand, you can release them. With any luck, they'll mate, and you'll have permanent rat catchers for nowt."

Within a few weeks, rat activity around and within our Nissen had decreased percepibly. There is always a price to pay. At the height of nightly invasion, just before Christmas, we had bought a dozen spring traps and some rat poison. The plan was to defer use of the latter in favour of the former to see how things developed. Rats, once dead, decompose, creating further problems. Trapped rats can be disposed of, so as to cause no further inconvenience. Each night, just prior to lights out, we had placed our traps around the floor area, adjacent to known entry points. Bets had been placed on numbered traps, the kitty being divided on agreed tariffs: largest rat, first to be caught etc, Type of bait was optional, with cheese the favourite, particularly when toasted on the stove. Our usual haul was six or seven rats per night. The all time winner for speed was the rat, and a monster he was, who sprang a trap as soon as the lights went out, and before some people had had time to get into bed. He made an appalling racket. Someone switched the lights back on and went to investigate. The rat had been caught by his tail and lower hindquarters. It had bolted through an opening in the floorboards. The trap was across the exit, impeding further progress.

It was obviously a two man job. One collected a heavy iron poker from the stove. When the other gingerly got hold of the trap and slowly pulled the rat backwards into full view, it was despatched with more blows from the poker than were strictly necessary. A lot of pent up anger went into that execution. With the arrival of our feral cats, these nightly diversions eventually ceased. We never did use the rat poison. Some time later, I witnessed one of our cats going about his business. Having scented a rat, he was crouched at the opening of a drain, ready to pounce. The rat appeared, then emerged. The cat struck. First taking the rat by the scruff of its neck, he swiftly turned him over to transfer the grip to the throat. Simultaneously, he drew up his rear legs, extending his claws, and raked the rat from top to bottom, disembowelling it in the process. It was over in a second. The rat was a real whopper. I must confess that I hoped he had crossed my bed head one night, and that his demise was my come-uppance.

In the midst of the upheaval associated with the installation of the new technical block, a new arrival had joined us. Corporal Evans, as may be inferred, was a Welshman.

Naturally, he was instantly dubbed 'Taffy' He was an RAF policeman straight out of training school, and zealous in the plying of his trade. Crustan, it has to be admitted, was lax in its standards of discipline. The weather conditions precluded the maintenance of high standards of dress, and we had undoubtedly let things slide rather badly. Ties were seldom worn, people took breakfast with pullovers over pyjamas, nobody saluted the C.O., or addressed NCO's appropriately. We did, on the other hand, maintain an oft commended, high level of operational efficiency. 'Taffy' took a cursory look at this state of affairs and began to set an example. On duty in the guard hut, he was immaculate. Everything gleamed from cap buttons to boots. Webbing was pure white. The hut was in keeping, scrubbed and polished daily. There was a new logbook for leaving and entering camp, unheard of before. After a few minor altercations, it was apparent that matters would come to a head. Mine became the head in question.

I arrived for breakfast just a couple of minutes before the time limit for serving expired. I had no tie. Taffy, attired in all his pomp, charged me with being improperly dressed, and noted the particulars meticulously in his notebook. I did not demur. The man was doing his duty as he saw it. I made to pass by to gain entry to the dining room. "And where do you think you're going?" he demanded truculently. "For breakfast----corporal," I replied in an even tone of voice. He made a display of looking at his watch, then declared, triumphantly, "You're too late for breakfast. That's another charge." "Are you refusing me my breakfast----corporal?" I asked. "I am," he replied, "It says quite clearly here 7-30 to 8 am." "And I think----corporal," I countered, by now thoroughly irritated, "you'll find that Kings Regulations state that you cannot refuse me my breakfast. You can charge me with being late only if I decide to eat my breakfast. No breakfast, no charge." Obviously unsure of his ground, he blustered "Get back to your hut. I'll overlook it this once." "I think not," I said, "I am taking my breakfast, as is my right. If you wish to proceed with the latecoming that is your prerogative, but I must point out that I was not late when I arrived. It was your issuing a charge relating to incorrect dress that caused the lateness." So saying, I passed him and sat down to my porridge, bacon, sausage and egg. The corporal cook had been an avid eavesdropper on the recent conversation, and the helpings were extremely generous.

I informed Slim, my Canadian sergeant, of the turn of events. He was livid. "Who the hell does he think he is?" he stormed. "Did he tell you what he has in mind as punishment?" I said the matter had not arisen. Slim came back a minute or two later. "You're to report to the guard room at six o'clock to scrub the floor," he advised. "Don't worry. It won't happen. Leave it with me." About five o'clock that afternoon, all the lights went out in the guardroom. Within minutes, Taffy was on the 'phone to Slim reporting the fault. "Can't do anything until tomorrow," Slim told him, "All my men are on duty except one, and you've got him on fatigues." "I can't be without lights all night," moaned Taffy. "You won't be without lights," answered Slim. "Have you never heard of oil lamps?" Then, after a pause, "Look mate, you're new here. Let's not get off on the wrong foot. If I put my man on the job immediately are you prepared to drop charges?" The deal was struck.

Slim got straight back to me. "We've got to take this bugger to the cleaners," he said "I've pocketed the fuse that controls the guard house. Pick up three or four of the lads, make sure they've all got gumboots on, wade through all the shit you can find, and leave your footprints over his floor, walls, desk, and. if you can manage it, his ceiling Then light a few candles and tell him you're looking for a fault in the wiring system."

"There are four bulbs in that room. Find the junction boxes, connect the bulbs in series, and report back to me," he continued. We obeyed orders with commendable enthusiasm, leaving Taffy with the assurance, "Power will be restored in a few minutes." Slim replaced the fuse, and we chuckled as we looked back down the hill to see guard room windows showing lights working on quarter power. Taffy came on the 'phone again. Slim listened and then said, "Must be a loose connection somewhere. The lads will soon have that sorted." We retraced our steps through more mud and gravel, reentered the guardroom, opened up the junction boxes, and reconnected the bulbs in parallel. "That should fix it," we reassured Taffy and withdrew. A minute or two later, Slim replaced the fuse, and Taffy was confronted with a guardroom that had muddy footprints in every nook and cranny.

When his dander was up, Slim could be a right bastard, and Taffy had certainly roused him. "We are not finished yet," he snarled, "Every section on this camp has got to show him the door. Right now, he'll be on his knees with a bucket and scrubbing brush. I want at least ten men lined up outside his hut. When you see him scrubbing, number one goes in, and books out of camp. When he has done so, wait till the bastard's back scrubbing, and send number two in. Repeat the process until all ten have booked out. Then you all book in again, on the same lines. If he gives you any lip, tell him from me where to stick his precious bloody log book." Again, we obeyed orders to the letter. Taffy gave no further trouble, but never felt at home after this episode, and applied for a posting which the C.O. was pleased to expedite.

With the days now lengthening, opportunities to escape the confines of camp increased and one day my watch decided to investigate the possibilities of augmenting the monotonous fare we were given on night watches. This was invariably a wedge of hard cheese, a loaf of bread between four, loose tea for the same number, powdered milk and, if you were lucky, a little sugar. We always toasted the bread to make the butter spread more easily. We had a combined kettle cum teapot, a triumph of necessity being the mother of invention. A seven pound empty jam tin, with the top partly cut off, and a metal spout and handle soldered on, did the trick. We boiled it on an electric fire turned on its back on the floor. The same arrangement toasted the bread. I do not recommend these methods for the faint-hearted, but for the record we suffered no loss of life. We did, however, get through a surprising lot of fuse wire.

Of the four members of the watch on duty on the day under review, one went to the Boardhouse Hotel to investigate the possibility of trout, or preferably salmon. He had no luck, but was referred to nearby crofts where he picked up eggs and fresh butter. The other three, armed with ·22 rifles, went looking for rabbits. We'd seen dozens of them scampering along the cliff tops, and if we could get near enough, we should have a good chance of success. We bagged one each and, satisfied with our marksmanship, decided to stretch out on the grass and relax. It was a pleasant day, and, from a recumbent position, the sky became the focus of my attention. After a few moments, a flock of gulls passed overhead, in an arrowhead formation, heading inland. A couple of minutes later, another flock repeated the manoeuvre. Another two minutes, another flock. It was a while before I realised it was the same flock every time. They must be flying in a circle continuously. What could be bringing them directly overhead? I decided to investigate, leaving my companions dozing.

The next time the flock appeared, I followed it inland until it was out of sight, waited, and then repeated the sequence. After three or four repetitions, they disappeared while still within my range of vision. I noted the spot where they had vanished, and approached it stealthily. It was in the midst of taller grass and reeds. I retired a short distance, lay on my stomach and waited and watched. The flock reappeared. Like an arrow, the lead bird shot down among the reeds, the others following in its wake. In a trice, they were gone. I crept forward and found a small hole in the ground. I peered into it but saw only darkness. My ears picked up something that puzzled me for a while, until I bent my head and put my ear to the hole. A far distant sound kept coming and going. Realisation slowly dawning, I actually spoke aloud. "My God, it's the sea." I rejoined the others and brought them to the spot to watch the gulls' disappearing act, and to listen to the distant sound of the Atlantic Ocean. We walked to the cliff top. We were standing on the inland boundary of a deep bay, with high cliffs running out to sea to left and right. We followed the edge of the cliff till we could look back at our original spot, and get a good look at the whole cliff face. At the bottom of it was a sizeable cave. As we watched, gulls were flying out of it, then vertically up the sides, to head inland. The distance from the cliff edge to the hole in the reed bed was over a hundred yards.

Having experienced the full force of successive gales over the previous seven months, with sea spray being driven over the 400 feet cliffs and far enough inland to coat our transmitter feeder lines with salt, I could very readily envisage a future where constant coastal erosion would claim most of the ground on which we were standing.

During a later stroll along these cliffs, with no specific objective in mind, my progress was arrested by nesting terns. It was an aerial bombardment I should not like to undergo again. They attacked repeatedly in groups, their raucous screams rising to a crescendo as they swooped close enough to dislodge my cap. Only when I had been driven to the edge of their territory did they desist, leaving an outpost of hovering, wheeling sentries on duty. Just round the headland at Costa Head, hundreds of guillemots similarly guarded all approaches to their territory. Whenever I watched them, it was always from a safe distance. Orkney is a bird watcher's paradise. For service visitors there was no time to indulge such pursuits.

Our new modern technical block was a joy to work in, but the cumulative effects of a continuous three-watch system did not change. According to the rules, the four-man watch stayed awake all night. In practice, a more congenial regime was in place. Starting duty at 11pm, we prepared supper and drew lots for duty stretches, which were of one and three quarter hours duration. These split the time from midnight till 7am into four. The best spells were the first and the last, since they provided the longest uninterrupted periods. The second and third were the killers. From 7am to 8am everyone was engaged in tidying up and preparing to hand over. After subjection to this regime every three nights for months, it didn't really matter which watch you drew----you were a zombie anyway.

This was brought home to me most forcibly one night. I always slept on the workbench in the transmitter room, which was separated from the main receiver room by a narrow corridor. With my tunic for a pillow, and the warm hum of the transmitter around me, I could fall asleep instantly. On this occasion, a hand on my shoulder roused me. It was 7am, time to tidy up. "Everything O.K?" I asked of nobody in particular, as I entered the receiver room. "No bother since you put us back on air," said the operator at the receiver. "Come off it," I countered, "I've had a marvellous kip since coming off first watch." "We called you at 3am," insisted the operator, "The transmitter had tripped and you set it up. You must remember that." I made no comment and returned to the transmitter room to make my final entry in the logbook. As I began to write, my eye fell on the entry above. "03-00 Tx tripped. Did all routine checks and made fully operational." The handwriting and the signature were mine. A complicated routine of some length had been successfully accomplished, and I would have sworn under oath that I had had nothing to do with it. That's what Crustan could do to you in the short term. In the longer perspective, it could drive you mad in stages. Stage 1: You talk to yourself. Stage 2: You talk to the sheep. Stage 3: The sheep talk to you.

Despite the proximity of the fighter station at Skara Brae, we saw and heard little activity. With the lengthening daylight, we became aware of planes flying low overhead, accompanied by the occasional burst of gunfire. Curious to find out what it was all about, a group of us sauntered down the road for about a mile. Stretched out on grass, on a rising incline running up to the cliff edge, were two large targets in the form of RAF roundels. There appeared to be little huts a short distance away. As we took all this in, we became aware of an aircraft engine to our rear. He flew directly overhead, obviously in the direction of the targets. A few short bursts of machine gun fire rat-at-at-ed, and clods of earth could be seen flung in the air within the target area. The plane peeled away. Little figures appeared from the huts and began checking the scores. Task completed, they retreated to their refuge to await the next plane. We lingered and watched five or six attacks. The last proved to be the most spectacular. Knowing he was the last, the pilot wheeled away, banked and made another approach, the checkers having meanwhile emerged to perform their duties. Obviously believing he had discharged his magazines, the pilot came screaming in to buzz the ground crew, and pretended to attack. There was a split second of ra—ta, turf leapt into the air, and the tiny figures on the hillside leapt higher. Then they scampered for cover. Fortunately, none had been hit. It was like watching an airborne version of a John Wayne film, where he fires bullets at the feet of the villain, saying, "Dance, brother, dance." Though, as far as we could tell, the only effect on the target markers was the possibility of suddenly filled pants, it would be less than justice were the offending pilot not himself shot down later that evening. Whatever the outcome, it had afforded a contingent of Crustan onlookers an unusual talking point.

Though everyone in the technical hut got on well together, compatible sub groups emerged, often reflecting civilian life styles. One such I nicknamed the Rotary Club. It was a select quartet who enjoyed a game of solo whist whenever they could get together. They were engrossed in a game shortly after dinner when the door burst open and a voice bellowed, "Elsan buckets have not been emptied. I want it done NOW." One of the four, Greg, the estate agent, said, "Blast, I clean forgot I was on the roster today. I'll be back in a jiffy." He got togged up nice and warm. It wasn't raining, but it was bitterly cold and a stiff, gusty wind increased the wind chill factor. The other three broke up and began reading magazines—'Lilliput' and 'Men Only' had short articles. Ten minutes passed, then quarter of an hour. "Where the hell is he?" queried someone, "It doesn't take this long to empty two Elsans." After twenty minutes, they decided to investigate. The Elsans had not been returned to their positions in the wash house. They headed for the cesspool out on open ground. The wind was rising and progress was difficult. There was no sign of Greg. They reached the cesspool. One unemptied Elsan was standing a few feet away from the edge. As they drew nearer, they heard muffled sounds. On reaching the cesspool, they were greeted by the sight of Greg, up to his chest in the contents, the other Elsan bobbing about beside him. While someone went for a stout rope, Greg continued to slop around, pawing frantically at the slimy sides of the cesspool. The rope arrived, a running noose was fashioned at one end and cast as near as possible at Greg's head.

After several attempts, he managed to get through the noose, with his arms outside it. Keeping well away from the edge, the rescuers eventually hauled him out. By this time, he was covered from head to foot. The stench was foul and pervasive. He was helped to the ablutions, and a hose was turned on him as he was, fully dressed. Then he stripped off, to be hosed down again. He finished with a conventional shower. In the event, the C.O. ordered every item of clothing to be incinerated.

Greg's explanation of his predicament was that he had decided to carry the two buckets, one in each hand, because he would be better balanced that way. His intention was to empty one bucket at a time. As he stood by the edge, and went through the throwing movements, two things had brought about his downfall. First, a sudden gust of wind had swept him off balance, and second he had lost his foothold on the slimy edge of the pool. Needless to say, he was the butt of much badinage from the rest of the camp. "I bet that beats any dirty deal you ever did in Civvy Street." "May I introduce you to Greg---he's a shitsophrenic." "Greg never actually does anything---he just goes through the motions." are but three examples.

Taffy, our over zealous service policeman having moved on, his replacement arrived. Gabriel was a Jew, as his name implies. You would not have considered him as such by appearance. Fair skinned, blond haired, and blue eyed, he hailed from a West Yorkshire conurbation, where his family owned a number of businesses. He had not wanted to be a policeman and resented the role. Like many others who joined the services, the role you were given had little to do with talent or inclination. Whatever was in short supply was what you were given. Gabriel integrated very quickly. He was fond of walking, especially on his own. At first the walks were short. After a while, they took up to three hours. On occasions, he was away all day. The time came when he was out all night and his little secret was blown. He had a lady friend in one of the crofts in a little settlement just off the road to Birsay. Having seen Gabriel on one of his walks, she had invited him in for a cup of tea, and had set her cap at him. What Gabriel had not grasped, until it was too late, was that her husband worked in Kirkwall through the week, and came home at the weekend. He found this out, as was predictable, when one of the neighbours enlightened him. He confronted his paramour and said, "You never told me you had a husband." "You never asked me," she replied. "What are you going to do?" asked Gabriel "We do whatever you want to do," came the reply, "But you can't do it Saturday or Sunday." Gabriel continued to live dangerously for weeks and, so far as I am aware, never came to grief. I think it's fair to say that, notwithstanding his name, he was no angel.

An affair of the heart of an entirely different dimension was that concerning 'Pin up' Power, a general duties serviceman. Another Welshman, his bed head was adorned with posters and pictures of the glamour girls of the day, hence his nickname. Pin Up's mother, on a good day, might have described him as plain, rugged, or manly. The general consensus on the camp was that he was in the plain and ugly categories, thereby qualifying for the description of plain ugly. A few, less charitably disposed, leaned towards the more definitive ugly bordering on repulsive. These assessments were all by men. How women might view him was unknown. All we knew was that no girl friend wrote to him. His love life embraced his pin ups, and all his fantasies revolved about them. This was to change.

Boredom and monotony drive people to create their own diversions and one of the company embarked on a course of action in which Pin Up was the gullible target. The hut door opened late one morning and a cheery voice yelled, "Letter for Pin Up in the orderly room. Local postmark." Pin Up shot down the slope to the office, collected his letter and read it on the spot. It had been written by the instigator of the practical joke and read as follows: "I have seen you in Birsay once or twice and would like to get to know you. I will be by the telephone box at 7-30 Tuesday evening." (signed) An admirer.

Pin Up's step was lighter going back to the hut. It had been planned to ask him who his letter was from, but he needed no prompting. "It's from a girl in Birsay," he enthused, waving a sheet of coloured, deckle-edged paper in token of proof, "Wants to meet me tonight." A few people whistled excitedly, and someone asked him if he was going. "Too bloody right I'm going," he replied. Now his standards of personal hygiene had never been much to write home about. A whiff of perfumed notepaper and an active imagination worked wonders. We were confronted that evening by a freshly showered, recently shaved, sweet smelling Pin Up, whose cheeks were glowing, and whose eyes were sparkling. He was seen off to a chorus of good wishes, mostly of the lewd variety. We waited for his return, knowing that there was no girl waiting by the telephone kiosk in Birsay.

It was well past 11pm when he came back. In anticipation of the girl's non-arrival, a second letter had been prepared, explaining the circumstances that had prevented her keeping the date, and making another assignment. To our amazement, in answer to our greeting, "Welcome back. How did it go?" we were regaled with a blow by blow account of a fantastic evening of sexual athleticism, in which no details were spared. Someone recovered sufficiently from this unforeseen turn of events to remark, "No need to ask if you're going to see her again then." How he had filled in four and a half hours that evening, in Birsay of all places, is a matter for conjecture, but he had committed himself to a succession of equally unproductive sessions. For the next week he continued the charade, and each night his accounts of his girl friend's apparently inexhaustible passion were further embellished. On the eighth night, he returned earlier than usual, less hyped up. "You're back early," somebody remarked. "Wrong time of the month is it?" "She's gone," answered Pin Up. "Gone? How do you mean, gone?" someone else chipped in. "She's gone back home to

Kirkwall," explained Pin Up. "She's been staying with her aunt in Birsay, on holiday to help with the lambing." We had to hand it to him. He'd dug himself a hole, had fallen in, and had successfully climbed out again. His week of unbridled passion was over. He had passed a week of utterly fruitless lonely inactivity to create the reputation of being a man who could make it with women. It would have been better left there.

Human nature being what it is, someone told Pin Up the truth—there never was a girl: he knew that, and now he knew that we knew that. He went berserk, and the ablutions block was the stage on which he gave vent to his rage, picking up three large cylinders of water and hurling them across the room into the shower cubicles. The following day, when he was asked to lift a similar cylinder, he could not get it off the ground. In his frenzy he had become a man possessed. What one can draw from this account is open to inference. It shows nobody in a particularly good light. The psychological factors involved are intricately intertwined, and can be unravelled only by an expert in these matters. Whatever the rights and wrongs of it, for a whole week it enlivened all concerned, when they might otherwise have been submerged by the unremitting routine of Crustan's relentless pressures.

My time at Crustan was drawing to a close. Having seen and endured the worst it had confronted us with throughout the months from June to early March, I was ready to move on. Not even the recent acquisition of a purpose built technical block was sufficient to hold me. I figured I would get that wherever I was posted. Crustan had been one of the last survivors of the early installations and I had been part of a radar culture never destined to return. The original postings of myself and others had been for three months. We had done nine. On this basis, six of us applied for a move. There were others, who had endured the primitive conditions for as long as we had, who took a different view. In the main they were married men with families. With the worst days behind them, they preferred to stay on to enjoy the improved facilities. As one of them put it to me, "You are single and fancy free. It's all an adventure for men of your age. We have wives and families to consider. While we're here we have relative security. If we press for a posting, we could end up in a far more dangerous situation. The aims of the war are swinging from defence to attack, and overseas postings will increase. I'd rather be left here." We agreed to differ. My request was submitted. His wasn't.

In a matter of days the news came through. Along with Peter Harrow, a schoolteacher in Civvy Street, and inseparable from his violin, I was posted to Rodel Park. I liked the word 'park'. It conjured up visions of open green, well kept lawns and, above all, trees. Orkney was almost devoid of trees. Probably a southern location, I mused. Hampshire, Dorset, or even a return to Wiltshire would be pleasant. We would know when we got to Bunchrew House in Inverness.

It was with mixed feelings that I clambered into the back of the truck that was to take us to Stromness. I was parting from good friends, probably never to meet again, but once the camp was out of sight all my thoughts were on the future. The crossing of the Pentland Firth was scheduled for early morning and we had arrived in good time. The seas were rough and doubts were raised as to whether the captain would sail. A two-hour delay was announced, and we were sent for our second breakfast of the day. Meanwhile, the wind was rising to gale force and the seas were heaving. To our sheer disbelief, we began to embark, with strict orders to go below decks, kit and all. By the time the full complement was on board we were packed like sardines. I secured a stance with a handrail in front of me, and the ship's engines alongside. It would be warm. Slowly, the vessel edged away from its moorings. I glanced through an adjacent porthole and caught a view of the seaweed covered jetty wall as we slid past. It disappeared and I was gazing at stormy skies. A sudden lurch and I was observing the wall once more. It slowly dawned on me. We had not yet left harbour, and already we had climbed one forty-foot wave, and were about to ascend another. I had enjoyed two breakfasts that day. The first was by now well through my digestive system. The second never made it. In a few rapid retches, porridge, bacon, egg, and sausage were swilling around on the floor. I was grateful for the handrail. We emerged into the open sea. Over the next few hours, every man on board, save two, was sick. Actually, only one man escaped, a burly, peak capped deck hand, smoking a foul black pipe with undisguised relish. The other hardy sailor was a woman, a slim, attractive ATS girl in her early twenties. She was genuinely solicitous for the burly men spewing their guts up around her, and helped where she could. There was one well-built army senior NCO whom she approached with the question. "Anything I can do to help?" He shot her a glance of anguish and despair before moaning, "Find the bloody captain, give him my bloody compliments, and ask him to sink the bloody ship."

As we reached mid channel, conditions became alarming. Three tide races, running at nine knots, kept slamming into the vessel's bows, causing her plates to shudder right back to the stern. She dropped vertiginously into each trough, stood still momentarily, then slowly clawed her way up to the summit, engines screaming as the propellers came briefly out of the water, then, contact re-established, swooped down the far side to take on the next monster wave. We were told later that the captain kept his vessel out in this maelstrom while he decided whether to continue to make for Scrabster, or to head back to Stromness. We limped into Scrabster three hours late. The young ATS girl, who had stood up to the worst the Pentland Firth could throw at her, was comprehensively sick as soon as she set foot on dry land As for the pipe smoking A.B., I suppose he celebrated with another pipeful of Black Twist. Orkney had given me some bad times, lashing down aerials in foul weather, but nothing matched the scale and ferocity of her farewell.

The retracing of the railway journey to Inverness was a doddle after this, and Bunchrew House had not changed. Expectantly, I made my first call that to the orderly room "Yes?" said the duty corporal "Passing through on posting to Rodel Park," I said "Rodel Park," he mused, "Here we are---just-----here." I followed his index finger in disbelief. It was resting on the southernmost tip of the Isle of Harris in the Outer Hebrides. "Where've you come from?" asked the corporal "Crustan, north west tip of Orkney." I spat out. "Christ mate," he said, "They certainly know how to give you a good time."

While going through the usual formalities of collecting signatures from various sections before collecting my travel documents, I chanced upon a Leading Aircraftman engaged on a similar mission, only he'd been doing it for three weeks. It appeared he had a girl friend in Inverness and was in no hurry to leave her, so he was wandering around Bunchrew House with just enough signatures to allay suspicion if apprehended. "Where do you sleep at night?" I asked him. "Bed and breakfast in the YMCA," he grinned, "and the girl friend foots the bill." Bearing in mind the recent revelations as to the location of Rodel Park, I was tempted to join him but didn't. For all I know, he is still wandering around Bunchrew House, waving a half-signed piece of paper.

—— RAF Rodel Park, Outer Hebrides ——

The following morning saw Peter Harrow and me, laden with all our worldly possessions, en route for Inverness railway station, a new adventure opening up before us. "Who wants to go to Hampshire anyway?" I thought, "I can go there anytime. Not many people ever get to see the Outer Hebrides. Come to think of it, why would they want to? Still, in my case it's free. Make the most of it. You never know, you may learn to like it."

The journey by rail from Inverness to Kyle of Lochalsh is one to savour and I remained alert throughout, revelling in views, spectacular views that unfolded mile after mile after scenic mile. Leaving Inverness, the broad expanse of Beauly Firth lay on the right, and was behind us as we pulled into Beauly itself. Then north, via Muir of Ord and Conan Bridge to Dingwall, with the long arm of Cromarty Firth stretching away north of Black Isle to the sea. From here we turned west, the countryside becoming bleaker as we passed through Auchterneed, Garve, and Gorstan. At Lochluichart views of the loch of that name were extensive on our left before, in a setting that was both desolate and beautiful, we reached Achenhalt, Strath Barn, and Achnasheen. On both sides of the line, views appeared constantly of rugged peaks up to 3000 feet high, on a day of clear visibility.

Via Glen Carron we steamed into Achnashellach station, then on to Strathcarron. The inland arm of Lochcarron accompanied us on the right to Stromeferry where it widened to meet the sea, of which excellent views were on display as we passed through Plockton, to end our journey at Kyle of Lochalsh. Throughout this magic journey of ever changing countryside, studded with lochs and lochans, and flanked by majestic hillside slopes and mountain peaks, the highlight memories are of station porters calling out a succession of place names bordering on the exotic, with their combinations of resonant vowel sounds and guttural stress patterns. I had embraced a new experience and I liked it.

Kyle of Lochalsh was a tiny village with access to the sea, and was at that time the port of embarkation for Stornoway in the Isle of Lewis. The 'ss Shiela' serviced the voyage. Quite small, but allegedly seaworthy, she was flat bottomed and was expected to ride over, rather than cut through the waves. All of this would have been academic to me had not my recent experience of the Pentland Firth tested my endurance to seasickness beyond breaking point. I was not yet ready to face another ordeal. As things turned out I was needlessly apprehensive. The sun was shining, the sea was calm, passengers were allowed on deck, and the views continued to entrance till darkness fell.

Leaning on the rail, I saw the Isle of Skye on my left and the mainland on my right unfold a succession of lovely seascapes and landscapes. Travel by sea allows time for views to develop. It can seem an age from picking up a specific landmark, reaching it, passing it, and watching it slowly disappear. After an hour and a half, we were out of the shelter of Skye and into the Minch. Though the vessel now rose and fell to a deeper rhythm the motion was not uncomfortable, and, with fewer landmarks now visible, thoughts turned to food. The choice was very straightforward. You either had kipper and fried potato or you went without. The kippers were tasty and the potatoes were fresh. Cynics were to tell me later that it was not always so. After a few successive rough crossings, with little take up of food, it was kept in store until normal service resumed. By that time, the kippers were less tasty, the potatoes less fresh. The tariff remained unaltered. As the Shiant Islands became discernible in the distance, the daylight began to wane, the temperature to drop, and I adjourned to the warmth of the saloon and nodded off.

I was awakened by a change in the noise of the ship's engines, and the bustle associated with journeys' ends everywhere. We were entering Stornoway harbour. I hoisted my backpack and kitbag and lined the deck rail. The water was black and the night equally so. As we hove to and gangways were lowered, a tiny circle of dim light was discernible at the foot of each exit. It was now past midnight and blackout regulations were in force. As I stood at the top of the gangway ramp, from the impenetrable darkness beyond the lit circle sounds of a strange language drifted up.

For a fleeting moment, I had an uneasy feeling that we had made landfall in Russia. I had made my first contact with the Gaelic language, the mother tongue of the native born Outer Hebridean. Another unfamiliar experience assailed my nostrils, the aromatic reek of peat smoke wafting on the breeze. My welcome was epitomised by these two distinctive marks of the culture of the Western Isles. Though I was unaware of it at the time, I had just taken a step that was to shape my future and put me in touch with my past.

The arrival of the mail boat in Stornoway was an occasion which always drew a crowd, and the area beyond the circle of light was thronging with people, some to meet disembarking passengers, many just to feel part of the social occasion. Among many military vehicles we identified a group with RAF markings, and found one the driver of which was there to meet us. He explained that we would be accommodated overnight at RAF Bayble on the outskirts of Stornoway, fifteen or twenty minutes drive away. Sitting at the rear end of a 15cwt truck, I was aware shortly after departure of a strong smell of the ocean. A few seconds later we were in it. Before I had time to panic we were out of it again. We had now entered the Broad Bay area, which was separated from the rest of Lewis at high tide, but never actually cut off. To read about it is one thing. To be introduced to it at dead of night, without due warning is another. Minutes later, we were in yet another orderly room.

Nigh on two o'clock in the morning is not the best time to arrive. We were given directions to our quarters, inevitably a Nissen hut, and were soon asleep. The following morning we were told that a twice-weekly ration run visited Rodel Park, which was approximately seventy miles away. It would be four days before we could be transferred. Meanwhile, we would be taking part in an assault course exercise and mock invasion of the camp. The former I was familiar with. The latter was a first, given added spice in that I was one of a six-man team selected as the invading raiding party. This proved to be exciting, exhilarating, and educative.

Given a plan of the camp, which was guarded principally by a high barbed wire perimeter fence, we identified possible entry points for visual inspection. The defence committee having been allocated an empty Nissen hut as a temporary H.Q., pending its occupation by WAAF's, we saw an opportunity for subtle infiltration, and rigged up a microphone in an overhead lampshade, suitably camouflaged. It worked a treat and we were soon privy to defence deployment of manpower, from which we could extrapolate weaknesses in the timing of manning of vulnerable locations.

Came the night of the exercise. It was very dark, but we had blacked up anyway. We had armed ourselves with long planks of wood, placed outside the perimeter fence the previous day, in locations unlikely to be discovered, and easily retrievable. Strong wire cutters and stout gloves were carried in case of need. Pocket torches were available for minimum use if suitable cover was to hand. At about 2am, we approached our chosen section of fencing and threw our planks across it. One by one we ran up and across them, other members holding them steady. By the time the last man was due, the fence was flattened. We dragged the planks inside the perimeter, and hid them where a patrolling sentry would be least likely to find them, and pushed and pulled the barbed wire back into shape. We'd had no need to use wire cutters, so there was no obvious gap to arouse suspicion. The negative aspect to this was that we were now trapped inside the camp with no easily accessible escape route. We could not afford to be apprehended.

With expert knowledge of the radar set up, we realised that the big prize would be the taking of the technical block. Was it feasible? We decided it was and began to edge in that direction. As we crept closer, we were surprised not to see sentries posted. We knew from our eavesdropping microphone that the security of the perimeter fence was top priority. Surely some provision had been made to protect the technical block. Maybe the sentry or sentries were elsewhere round the block, or had temporarily left to answer a call of nature. We deployed a man to circumnavigate the building and report back. He did so. We could proceed since we were unlikely to be detected. How to gain entry to the building? If we rang the bell, whoever came to the door would follow routine procedures—password etc., which we didn't possess, slam and bolt the door, raise the alarm, and we would be taken prisoner. We needed to get somebody to open that door and step outside.

Any disturbance of the external feeder lines causes interference on the CRT's. The duty radar mechanic would deduce in no time that the cause of the interference was outside and would investigate. We created the external conditions. As expected, the main door opened, the mechanic and a companion operator ran past us in search of clues to the trouble, we stepped out of the dark, held them at bayonet point, escorted them back inside, and captured the station. From our point of view, a most satisfactory conclusion.

The educational aspect of this exercise merits a paragraph of its own. Before we had an opportunity to dismantle and retrieve our microphone from the defence H.Q., the Waaf's moved in. I had been brought up in the genteel belief that, whereas men could, and often did, use foul and abusive language, ladies were ---well, ladylike when venting their spleen. Almost two years' service had certainly confirmed the first assumption. An evening of eavesdropping on the conversations in that Waaf hut turned the second erstwhile belief into profound disillusion. My fellow listeners in, all more experienced in the ways of women than I, were all visibly shaken to the core. In terms of general profanity, blasphemy, and sexual innuendo, what we heard that evening relegated Max Miller to a minor league. We disconnected the speaker, dismantled the wiring, and packed it away. Somebody, sometime, presumably found the microphone.

On the appointed day, the 15 cwt. truck arrived to take Peter Harrow and me to Rodel Park. The four-day break had been irksome, but the rest after the long journey from Orkney had been recuperative. The main benefit had been the break from that incessant three-watch system. Doubtless arrival at Rodel would see a resumption of that regime.

Sitting in the back of a covered vehicle affords a restricted view of the outside world. You have no awareness of what lies ahead, just an appreciation of what stretches out behind. Yet what you have seen, and are currently taking in, prepares you for what is to come. It has to be said at the outset that the road surface was rough, and that the driver favoured accelerator and brake to the almost complete exclusion of clutch. At first this did not matter overmuch, since the roads for the first few miles were reasonably level, with few serious bends. I was looking out on a landscape of rough grass, peat bogs, and small lochs, with groups of crofts appearing every couple of miles or so. Then the journey began to present a slightly less comfortable face. The road began to twist and turn quite sharply, and rise and fall with a rhythm that was irregular. The driver, who was presumably familiar with the conditions, gave scant attention to them, and was intent on reaching his destination as speedily as possible. Passenger comfort was not on his agenda. We bucked and swayed, and bobbed and bounced, as the unfolding backward scene cavorted across our field of vision. We were eventually careering up a series of hairpin bends with what appeared to be precipitous drops perilously close to wheels that were spinning hard to get purchase. Just as we thought we could stand no more, or worse still wouldn't need to, having plunged over the edge, the vehicle came to a sudden, shuddering halt, to the accompaniment of screeching rubber on gravel. Our driver got out of his cab, came round to the rear, dropped the tailboard, and announced triumphantly, "Gentlemen, behold the Clisham."

We scrambled out and took in our first panoramic view. It was breathtaking. We were at the summit of the Clisham, the highest ridge en route at 2622 feet above sea level. Behind us, all the way down to level ground, was a series of sharp bends that snaked this way and that up to where we were standing. The road had been cut into the side of the mount, a rough gravel and shingle mixture being applied as a surface. Once I'd dragged my gaze away from that segment of the view, the rest was stunningly attractive. You couldn't call it beautiful or majestic, but it was mind bogglingly mesmeric in its subtle display of various shades of colour, which underwent continuous change, influenced by a strong sunlight being filtered through different strata of clouds driven by a stiffish breeze, operating at fluctuating speeds at assorted altitudes. "I always stop here," the driver murmured, "and it's different every time.

Even when it's pouring down it takes your breath away." We all clambered back into the truck. The last few minutes had worked wonders on the driver's mind set. The rest of the trip was almost sedate.

RAF Rodel Park, Outer Hebrides – Border between Lewis & Harris.

We stopped at Tarbert for a half-hour break and drank coffee in the hotel. A terminus for the ferry service from Uig on the Isle of Skye, Tarbert was a mixture of croft houses, a shop or two, and the hotel. The croft houses did not, it seemed, have crofts attached. Oats and barley were cultivated in depressions in the ground, where strong winds had deposited soil. The root systems of the crops anchored the grain for a season. After the harvest, winter gales dispersed the soil again, and the crofter had to find new soil filled depressions in which to grow next year's crop. This truly is eking a living out of the soil. Tarbert marks the boundary between Lewis, which we were about to leave, and Harris, which lay ahead. A further twenty four miles lay between us and our new home. Both Peter and I were by now keen to see what awaited us. Crustan was already becoming a distant, fading memory.

We took the west coast route which followed the Atlantic coastline most of the way with increasingly spectacular silver white beaches of shell sand, firm enough to land a light aircraft on. Clean looking croft houses punctuated the coastal fringe, creating a welcome sight after the bleaker Orkney habitation around Birsay. We passed

Leverburgh, the site of an abortive attempt by Lord Leverhulme to seduce Hebridean crofters from the traditions and working practices of generations. We were now within striking distance of our objective. A long narrow valley approach with fenced, well kept grassland on either side, flanked by two commanding heights, Mts. Roneval and Stroneval, led us to the southernmost tip of Harris. We scrambled out of the vehicle and took stock. In a little hollow, at the very edge of a cliff overlooking the Atlantic, lay Rodel Park.

RAF Rodel Park, Outer Hebrides – Harris: Road from Rodel to Leverburgh.

First impressions were favourable. It was a small, compact site of seven or eight Nissens, painted an attractive green, interconnected by walkways of neatly laid flagstones. The surrounding turf was well maintained. Entrance was over a cattle grid, and through a five-barred, sturdy wooden gate, locked in the open position. Peter and I entered the first Nissen on the right to find a corporal seated at a desk. He rose, came round the desk, and proffered an outstretched hand. "Welcome to Rodel," he greeted us "I'll just check your papers and then show you to your living quarters. You'll be assigned to technical duties tomorrow." Our Nissen was at the far end of one of the well-defined pathways, and a matter of a few feet from the cliff edge. The drop to the beach below was about fifty feet. The view from the front entrance was pleasant, a stretch of sea in a sheltered inlet, with a clear view past a headland of the broader reaches of the Atlantic sweeping away to the horizon. There were small vessels dotted here and there. An artist would have thought it a scene worth sketching. It was time to look inside.

Once you enter a Nissen hut, all sight of the outside world disappears. The entrances at both ends house the only windows, the main purpose of which is to let light in, not to provide a view out. The daylight in this Nissen was surprisingly good, and it was a while before I realised why---the interior was painted a light pastel shade. "We have moved up market," I ruminated. There was good, stout floor covering, adequate electric lighting, and the beds, twelve in all, appeared to be in good condition. Adequate locker space and overhead shelving was provided. Two beds being obviously unoccupied, Peter took one and I appropriated the other. Each was midway between the entrance and the first of two stoves that occupied the centre of the floor about a third of the distance from each end. "You'll find the mealtime information on the notice board by the door," advised the corporal. "I'll see you around." "What's the grub like, corporal?" queried Peter, very much in character. He liked his food. "Wouldn't know," came the reply, followed by a pause, then, "I usually eat out." Peter's face fell. "That bad is it?" he groaned. "No, actually it's quite good," grinned the corporal. " I sleep out as well, but that's no reflection on the beds. You see, I'm married to a local girl. We live in Strond, a little village on the hillside yonder," pointing in a direction beyond the confines of the hut. With that he left. "Blimey," said Peter, "He'll be as sick as a pig if they post him."

RAF Rodel Park, Outer Hebrides – Rodel: Foundations of RAF Domestic Site.

Three other Nissens housed the rest of the camp's complement, the others being the cookhouse and dining room, an ablutions block, a combined storeroom and medical centre, a joint guardroom and orderly room and a recreation room. In a brick building near the camp entrance, sheltered under an overhanging cliff, were housed two diesel engines for power supply. If you came out of our Nissen, and walked its length to the other end, and continued a further twenty yards, you reached a grassy knoll, from which an excellent view of the surrounding area opened up. Immediately in front lay a sheltered hollow in which stood a long well—windowed building, with a smaller one alongside. This was erected for use as a NAAFI (Navy, Army, and Air Force Institute) canteen and staff living quarters. As yet, it was not operational. To the left of this compound, nestling in an adjacent hollow, one could see the roof tops of the Rodel Hotel. Even further to the left, looking back to the camp entrance, there was an excellent view of St. Clement's Church, situated on high ground beyond. This was the domestic site. Tomorrow I would be introduced to the technical quarters. All in all, there was every reason to anticipate good times ahead. Compared to Crustan, this place was a palace. No sign of rust on any of the Nissen huts, no sign of rats, and the cliffs adjacent to my hut were but fifty feet high, as opposed to the four hundred feet monsters that had faced the full rigours of the Atlantic fury back in Orkney, with the loss of Lord Kitchener and the 'Hampshire as a reminder of their ferocity. All I now needed were the three sisters of Birsay with their Orkney teas and life would be as it should be.

At nine o'clock the following day a 15cwt. truck took Peter and me for our introduction to our new work stations. The vehicle rattled over the cattle grid, turned right, almost immediately affording us a close up view of St. Clement's Church as we bumped past its front entrance, then abruptly left. Ahead of us stretched a narrow unsurfaced track, ascending steeply to the distant skyline, the Atlantic on our right. Lurching and swaying, and hanging on to the struts that supported the flapping canvas awning, we had covered a mile, possibly a shade more, when we turned at right angles to the left. The steep ascent continued with an occasional twist and turn. A few minutes more and the truck lurched to a halt. "Terminus," yelled the driver cheerfully. "All passengers disembark." We were outside a ramshackle wooden cabin which was the guardhouse. Inside was a Service Policeman, pistol in holster. We were officially introduced, "No need to register from now on," he advised, after checking our credentials "You'll be part of a watch and I know your faces now." The truck turned and headed back to the domestic site, with the driver's final comment shouted as he passed, "I'll pick you up at the end of the watch with the others."

The technical block stood even further up the continuing steep climb, and we made our way up there A hundred yards or so en route we reached the diesel house and glanced inside: Listers, one working, one on standby. A further hundred yards and we were standing outside the technical block entrance. Before seeking ingress, we took stock of the view. It was impressive. We were at a commanding height (radar stations always were) and had views up both the east and west coasts of Harris which demonstrated graphically their distinctive differences. Had we, instead of turning off to visit the site, continued along the road up the east side, we would have encountered a landscape of bare gneiss, indented by a succession of bays that plunge vertically to deep-water anchorages that provide good shelter for fishing boats. It is a moonscape type of scenery, black, desolate, and foreboding.

RAF Rodel Park, Outer Hebrides – Technical Site, Rodel.

By contrast, the west side slips smoothly into shallow water along an unbroken coastline. Plentiful soil, deep enough in most places to grow crops, and with vast expanses of machair, resplendent in Spring with a carpet of wild flowers, and glorious pure white beaches, encourage a broad range of activities. We have noted previously the rough condition of the west coast route linking Rodel with Tarbert. Compared to that on the east side, this is motorway standard. To be avoided, unless your aim is to savour the experience for the first time, this eastern approach is narrow, badly maintained, and accident prone. If your vehicle leaves the road on the seaward side, the drop is sheer, and your watery grave is deep. Should you avoid that and experience a lesser hazard, the chances of passing help are minimal.

Our radar station kept a continuous watch on the approaches round all points of the compass, but most of the traffic monitored was on the Atlantic side. Any attempt to land along that shore would be detected very early, with adequate interventional back up. While even a small vessel would be picked up by radar sweeping the Minch on the eastern approach, it would be lost as it moved inshore, on account of the intervening land mass, and a landing could be effected unobserved by anyone, so sparsely populated was the shoreline. Once ashore, a raiding party, or for that matter smugglers, could trek the few miles across the island, choosing to emerge at any place along the west coast.

Having taken in these shortened views of the panorama, I raised my sights for the longer perspective. To the north lay Harris, with Lewis beyond. To the east, on a good day, mountains on the Scottish mainland were visible. South west was the Isle of Skye. South westwards stretched North Uist, Benbecula, and South Uist with Barra beyond. Away to the far western horizon glistened the heaving Atlantic Ocean. Standing there on a clear day, a stiff breeze fanning my cheeks, and with a whiff of ozone in the air, I felt in tune with the rhythm of Rodel, and completely at ease.

The lay out of the technical block was instantly familiar, being a replica of that at Crustan. I would have no difficulties here. On introduction to the watch on duty, I was given news I had not anticipated. At Rodel, a four-watch system operated. I.e. a three watch system with a complete day off between each cycle. The Outer Hebrides were beginning to strengthen their appeal, and I decided, there and then, to put my unexpected days off to best advantage by learning as much as I could about the area and its people.

I returned to the domestic site, at sea level, when the duty watch signed off at 13-00 hrs. Rodel used the 24 hour clock. I was allocated to the watch team due on at 13-00 the following day, with the sequence of duties to follow. The pattern was: Day 1: 13-00 to 18-00 Day 2: 08-00 to 13-00 and then 23-00 to 08-00 Day 3: 18-00 to 23-00 Day 4: Free As it turned out, this four watch system operated throughout my period of service at Rodel, and established a gentle rhythm of life in keeping with the life style of the local crofters. As one of them, a venerable gentleman in his eighties was to observe, "When God made time he made plenty of it."

It is always advisable, when joining a new unit, to wait for those with established places in the pecking order to approach you, which they will once they've summed you up. I needed to establish myself in two social groups, the specialised technical cabal, and the broader whole camp family. The first would evolve out of shared watches and common living experiences. Radar mechanics occupied one hut, radar operators the one adjoining. Since a number of radar mechanics were Canadian, one of them had decided that our hut should acknowledge the fact and had chiselled 'Canada House' into the stone threshold. This had prompted a wag next door to exhibit a placard in the entrance with the legend 'Operating Theatre' and a sub text that read 'Canadians to supply own anaesthetics'. With such bonhomie and repartee, it was easy to integrate.

RAF Rodel Park, Outer Hebrides – Rodel: Technical Site, Operations Block & Aerial Mooring Ring.

My introduction to a four-watch system had perked me up considerably. The Crustan rats were by now a distant memory. There would doubtless still be the occasional gale and the chores associated with lashing the aerial array, though with summer stretching ahead that threat was minimal. I no longer needed to live permanently in oilskins and gumboots. The only remaining blot on the horizon was one night watch in four. Here again, fortune had marked my card favourably. My watch mates were Paul Berry, a fiery little Glaswegian, Ken Duncan, a native of the Isle of Skye and dubbed 'The Duke', Chris Brown, a Londoner and proud of it, and Burberry, a Russian Jew, who preferred to answer to 'Berry' for reasons known only to himself.

On my first night watch I waited to see how the long hours would be allocated. We finished supper and folk began to organise their sleeping arrangements. "Which stint am I on?" I enquired. The answer was unexpected. "On this watch Berry does the lot." I was told. "Is he mad?" was my supplementary. "The jury's out on that one," someone chuckled. "Sit up with him till you're ready to kip and decide for yourself."

Normally, the night watch is uneventful, with the operator watching one rotating time base and one horizontal. After a while, the rotating one becomes mesmerising, the operator's head begins to roll and droop, and the next thing he knows is a rude awakening as his head slumps painfully onto the console. Occasionally, the tedium is relieved by a little banter with the operator in the filter room. Most nights it's just a long, weary vigil. Not however if your name is Berry to whom idleness was anathema. For him time was money, and money was his god. He had arrived at Rodel a few weeks before me, to find himself in a non-profit making environment. His previous location had been London, where he had honed his entrepreneurial skills to perfection. As soon as war broke out, he rang the Russian Embassy advising them they were in immediate need of blacking out their whole building. He could save them both time and money. He gave a fixed price over the phone, saying, "I can start first thing tomorrow morning." He got the job. He had no materials and no labour force, small obstacles easily overcome by a few more telephone calls. His profit margin was substantial.

With a record like this, he finds himself at Rodel on the southernmost tip of the Isle of Harris. A previous entrepreneur, Lord Leverhulme, having bought Lewis and Harris in 1918, had tried to establish big business in Leverburgh with piers, kippering sheds, new housing, and access roads to cater for the catches of a huge trawler fleet. By 1924, the business was thriving, and at its height. A year later, Leverhulme died, and his executors pulled out. In all his excellent business planning, he had miscalculated perhaps the most important factor of all, the nature of the work force. The Gaelic crofter is a proud, independent man, the progeny of generations who have worked the land. Not for him the cash nexus of an employer-employee relationship. Whether Berry knew all of this I know not. What he did come to recognise very quickly was that there was money to be made out of tweed, and on a big scale at that, if the link between producer and consumer could be expertly developed and co-ordinated. Furthermore, it could be achieved by reinforcing the independence of the crofter weaver.

Wherever one travelled in the small villages and isolated croft houses around Rodel, one could hear, from early morning to late evening, the clickety clack of the loom. The mills in Stornoway distributed yarn to crofts weekly, with pattern instructions enclosed, and the skilled domestic weavers converted it on their handlooms into rolls of tweed 80 yards long by 28 and a half inches wide. There was an allowance for wastage. It was this allowance that set Berry's fertile mind afire. He began by cycling round the district on his days off, using a 'sit up and beg' ancient solid Raleigh he found on site. Visiting croft after croft, he worked his not inconsiderable charm, quoting prices he was prepared to offer for what he termed 'off cuts'. No money passed hands. Berry didn't have any. He needed to find customers willing to pay on delivery. They were all around him. Almost every week, someone was leaving Rodel, either on leave, or on a posting elsewhere. Berry sold them a length of tweed, pocketed the proceeds, and paid his crofters on his next visit. It operated at the outset on a 'small profit, quick return' basis. Weavers' output was soon outstripping customer demand. It was at this stage that I arrived on the scene, to see how Berry occupied a full night shift on the CRT's.

Stornoway was the hub of a communications network linking radar stations throughout the Hebrides, Outer and Inner, and the northern areas of the Scottish mainland. As Berry sat at his console, a stream of orders flowed in and was meticulously noted down The destinations of these orders were many, varied, and far flung. To most people, this would have posed insuperable difficulties. Berry was not in the 'most people' category. He was in a class of his own. Rodel was a tiny port, receiving twice-weekly visits from the mail boat. It was but a short time before a regular consignment of Berry's tweeds was in the cargo hold. At the other end of the voyage, they were routed onwards to a large multiple store with H.Q. in London. The Berry market was becoming national.

A pilot, flying out of Stornoway with a personal purchase of tweed from Berry, soon found himself cajoled into carrying larger bulk orders. High ranking officers, preferably with Canadian connections, were given gifts of tweed to take home on leave, and then persuaded to use their influence and contacts to boost orders. The aspect was becoming international. As I watched the financial empire grow, and the extent to which its tentacles spread, I noted that, at every stage, Berry was implicating people who would otherwise be in a position to bring about his downfall. He was controlling, and very effectively manipulating, a one man Mafia type organisation. It would almost certainly come to a spectacular end, but not before Berry had made a packet.

We all thought that Nemesis had struck some three months after my arrival. There had been rumours of Board of Trade interest, emanating mainly from the source of all gossip, the village post office in Leverburgh. Nothing happened in Harris that escaped the sharp ears of Mrs. Mack. In this tweed conspiracy she was in effect 'piggy in the middle'. Her regular clientele, the local crofter weaver community was quite happy with arrangements that supplemented basic incomes. Accordingly, when Mrs. Mack got wind that something was afoot, she telephoned the camp orderly room. "P.C. Plod is on his way on his bicycle looking for tweed," she said, and hung up.

It so happened that Berry's business was booming by now, to such an extent that half a Nissen hut was packed to the roof with orders awaiting delivery. The corporal on duty alerted the Canadian C.O., who had only recently despatched a consignment home, and was therefore heavily compromised. All available manpower was summoned, a human chain was formed, stretching to the cliff top alongside 'Canada House', and bale after bale was hurled unceremoniously down to the beach fifty feet below. Fortunately, the tide was well out. The constable arrived minutes later, breathing heavily after the long pull uphill, to be greeted by a hospitable C.O., a fine malt whisky in his hand. A pleasant welcoming ceremony over, the refreshed arm of the law was conducted round the camp to find nothing untoward. I can only think that the aroma of the whisky (he'd had a few) prevented him from detecting the lingering distinctive smell of tweed in a now half empty Nissen hut. It took a couple of hours to retrieve the jettisoned bales from the beach, but it was safely garnered before nightfall.

Not everyone helped in the recovery. Some thought it was Berry's look out and he could get on with it. Four of us were otherwise occupied. Directly across the sound from Canada House was a tiny island about a quarter of a mile away. In the midst of all the frenzy over tweed, we observed half a dozen cattle swimming in the sea, obviously intent on reaching the island. We learned subsequently that the grass over there was particularly sweet. What amazed me was the sight of cows swimming, apparently quite effortlessly.

What happened next was a shout from one of the others, "What's that. In the water, beyond the cows?" We all looked. The low sun on the water made the surface shimmer, and it was difficult to focus. "My God," was the next remark, "It's a shark's fin." By now my eyes had become accustomed to the conditions. "Two sharks, possibly three," I said. To see cows swimming was a sight to start with. To have sharks as well was over egging the pudding. We had a problem. Were the sharks harmless basking species or were the cows in danger? Not knowing, we decided to play safe and went for rifles and clips of five rounds of ammunition. Stretched alongside each other on our bellies, we estimated the range, set our sights, and aimed beyond the cows, to as near the sharks as possible. The thinking was twofold in its strategy. First, we wanted to deter the sharks, either by driving them out to sea, or possibly killing them. Second, by creating a disturbance beyond the cows, we might turn them around to head for home. In the event, we succeeded in driving the sharks off, and watched the cows reach the island and land in search of forbidden fodder. Altogether, a diverting little interlude.

Running the village postmistress very close for pride of place as the person whose ears were closest to the ground were the family doctor and district nurse in partnership, and the Church of Scotland minister. Let me, perversely, deal with them in reverse order. At that time, attendance for worship on the Sabbath, though not obligatory, was habitual. Non-attendance attracted the opprobrium not so much of the minister but of members of his flock. The prevailing influence was Old Testamental rather than New. Hell fire and brimstone, eternal damnation, and retribution were preached vehemently. The camel and the eye of the needle were oft referred to. Quite what the local incumbent thought of his parishioners' involvement in the tweed scam is not easy to divine. I met the man weekly in the early stages, not as an earnest seeker after truth, but as a grateful recipient of the bounty he distributed from his Church of Scotland van. Once a week, he appeared without fail at the entrance to the camp, where we all accepted free cigarettes and chocolate, courtesy of his congregation.

The doctor's practice covered the southern area of Harris, with many patients living in isolated crofts, inaccessible in really bad weather. The camp was one of his favourite calls for two reasons. First, he had access to over forty patients en bloc, and second, he was always assured of a warm Scotch. whisky flavoured welcome. Dr. Biggart was an unrepentant alcoholic with a preference for a wee dram. When his visits were to administer regular injections, a regime to which servicemen everywhere are exposed, those on the receiving end hoped he was not sober. This condition, relatively rare it has to be said, was immediately detectable, since the hypodermic syringe was held loosely in a hand that shook uncontrollably. Occasionally, the contents were liberally dispersed before the needle got anywhere near the patient's skin. The thrust of the actual injection was not unlike that of a bayonet charge, and the wound caused was painful in the extreme. This was followed by attempts to disengage, the doctor tugging and retreating wildly in one direction, the patient receding with matching fervour in the other. Fortunately, the doctor was usually drunk, and the operation was conducted with firmness, accuracy, and finesse.

Dr. Biggart and his district nurse Maggie were made for each other. A stout, reassuring woman, she stood resolutely between him and the authorities who handled complaints against him, probably not without reason. The birth mortality rate in Harris was unusually high, and focussed attention on the doctor's arguable incompetence in this particular aspect. It being very difficult to recruit anyone to this isolated district, Maggie's robust defence of her errant colleague was, "Och, he's a good wee man, and a good wee doctor. Where would we find another like him?" Though a staunch Presbyterian, there was something of the Jesuit in Maggie, who was adept at coming out with comments open to a number of interpretations.

Late one evening, after the conclusion of a round of routine injections, I sat in with a small group, as more convivial rounds were experienced in a relaxed mood. After a few generous glasses of malt, the doctor was encouraged to tell us how he came to end up in Harris, Reluctant at first, he was soon in full flow. I doubt if we could have stopped him. I record the gist of his narrative but cannot replicate the accent in which he delivered it. It went as follows: "I was brought up in a strict Scots Presbyterian family, in which my father was an elder of the kirk. He was the unchallenged head of the family. My mother, God bless her, was undoubtedly the heart. I had two older brothers. We were all provided with a good education. Very early on, I decided on medicine as a career, which surprised my parents, since there was no history of such in the family. Notwithstanding this, they supported me, at some financial sacrifice to themselves I suspect, and I embarked on my career."

"It was a good choice and I seemed to have the natural talent for it. I became a junior house doctor in Greenock Royal Infirmary, and was tipped for rapid promotion. Then World War One broke out and I was conscripted. I probably learned more in a year than I would have done in five at Greenock. Then I was gassed. In a field hospital situation they had to remove a lung. I was shipped back home, discharged, and told I had eighteen months to live at the outside." Biggart paused at this point, misty eyed. His narrative had been delivered thus far in a monotone that was devoid of emotion. When he resumed, the tempo, tone, and timbre of his voice were richly animated, as though he was fighting his way out of the trough in which he had left us.

"Well lads. What to do? All the conditioning of my upbringing pointed towards the 'It's God's will' acceptance of personal destiny. I went the other way. If I had but eighteen months left, they would be filled with wine, women, and song. Since I had no voice to speak of, I crossed that off the list. I was left with wine and women There are always women, as you know, who are attracted to a uniform, and when that uniform is reinforced by any form of incapacity, maternal instincts are aroused. I have to admit to a number of liaisons among the nursing staff at that time. What they got out of it God alone knows, but it took too much out of me. The physical effort involved far outweighed the transient joys of sexual relief. I was left with wine. Now I have known many wine lovers in my time, and do not decry the undoubted. solace they derived from their affairs. But I was a Scot. Though never previously a drinker, I embraced whisky, and, in no time at all, whisky embraced me. We have been staunch, dependable, inseparable companions ever since. Forty years on, we continue to mutually sustain each other. What, you may ask, of your doctors' prognosis of eighteen months at the outside? Well lads, I cannot back my theory by any reasoned medical argument, but I have worked on the premise for the past forty years, that as long as I keep the hole where my lung was topped up with the best malt whisky, I'll be alright. Time, I think, for a refill. Mustn't take chances."

Very shortly after my arrival, an event occurred that was to have a profound influence on the rest of my life. A large pantechnicon vehicle drew up outside the NAAFI buildings, and furniture and equipment began to be unloaded. Accompanying the van was a saloon car out of which stepped a middle-aged man and three women in uniform. Something had obviously gone badly wrong with Mrs. Mack's intelligence network, centred on the Leverburgh Post Office, since no forewarning of this development had been issued. Word got around camp very quickly, and a posse of willing helpers was soon manhandling items into the large canteen area in the main building, and on to the hard standing between that and the staff living quarters.

The man in the newly arrived group was a senior area manager sent to set up the new branch. The women (labelled immediately as 'white women') were the manageress, assistant, and cook. They were the main focus of attention. The first was young, slim, and attractive, the second perhaps younger and very pretty, the third much older and worldly worn. She was immediately written off by men whose long separation from the company of nubile young women did not attract them to those old enough to be their mother. Given that the prime purpose of the NAAFI was to provide an attractive, additional menu to that dished up by camp cooks, this evaluation was hardly based on sound reasoning. If the cook did not deliver, the undoubted physical attractions of manageress and assistant would count for little.

RAF Rodel Park, Outer Hebrides – Rodel: Remains of NAAFI Site.

The delivery vehicle departed, followed an hour later by the saloon car, manager at the wheel. A notice appeared advising that the canteen would open for business at 18-00 hours the following day. The staff, now comfortably ensconced in their new quarters, doubtless faced a busy day tomorrow. It is fair to say that everyone was agog as the official opening approached, and a queue began forming at 17-30 hours. On the dot of 18-00, the doors opened and we poured in. The interior was spacious, with perhaps three quarters of the length occupied by tables and chairs of the stacking sort, four chairs to a table. At the far end was a quite sizeable stage, made up of separate blocks. Curtains could be drawn across the front, and there were banks of lighting, including footlights. This was very promising. On the right hand side were serving hatches, three in all, and a door giving access to the kitchen, office, and storerooms beyond. A side entrance, adjacent to the office, opened on to the compound flanked on its other side by the living quarters. On this first evening, the serving hatches opened to a concerted roar of applause and the Rodel NAAFI commenced business.

The menu was the typical fare offered across the Institute's vast trading empire. Quantities were standardised. Quality varies from from canteen to canteen. At Rodel it was first class. The cooking was very good, the baking in the 'Orkney tea' class. We had struck gold. Cynics have said, in discussing the merits of NAAFI tea and coffee, "What is the difference between them?", the standard answer being, "A ha'penny a cup." At Rodel the differential was indeed a ha'penny, but the tea was unmistakably tea, and the coffee was indisputably coffee.

The possibilities conjured up by a stage equipped with lighting aroused expectations none of us expected to be realised, but within a week a mobile cinema, working out of Stornoway, began a programme of fortnightly screenings. My mind boggled at the thought of such a weighty vehicle completing the round trip from Stornoway over roads still fresh in the memory. Alan, the driver/ projectionist, and a canny Geordie, put me right on that one. "You'd need a medal to do that run," he said "I'm all for an easy life. You can stick your medals." He had worked out a splendid itinerary involving a round trip, taking in several outposts like Rodel, with an overnight stop at each. Stations including Brenish, Islivig, and Mangesta in Harris, and Eurodale, Habost, and Broad Bay in Lewis. Alec reported that, on all these other sites, locals were invited to join the audience. This prompted us to follow suit. Cinema nights became so popular that we were despatching transport to outlying villages to ferry people in. The clientele was predominantly elderly, most of the young folk being in the forces. There was a nucleus of still active people, who raised the possibility of a weekly dance, and thus was born the Rodel Saturday Night Dance Society with an eclectic programme. The hall was always packed. The arrival of the NAAFI had instigated a social revolution.

These developments were grist to Berry's tweed business. Instead of having to pedal around the district, custom was now coming to his door. He never missed an opportunity to promote new business. Getting wind of a football match that had been arranged in Tarbert, he joined the truck, assuring everyone of his prowess as a goalkeeper. We played on a quagmire. Most of us were pretty filthy by the end of the game. Berry was covered all over in peaty mud. His goalkeeping, somewhat deficient in technical skills, lacked nothing in exuberance. Hot baths were laid on for us, which we appreciated and enjoyed. All that is except Berry. Scorning such effete ablutions, he trotted across the road with a borrowed towel, stripped at the side of a small loch, leapt in, swam around, emerged, towelled down, and strolled back to the croft house in which he had changed for the game, and donned his uniform. The temperature of the loch would have killed anyone else.

Berry was not the only 'character' in the camp, though beyond doubt the star turn. Jock Fraser, a native of Tighnabruaich on the Isle of Bute, was a highly skilled mechanic, never seen without his toolbox. It was said of him that he not only took it on leave, but took it to bed with him when he got there. Stout, stocky, florid faced, Jock had an engaging frankness, and a most wonderful accent. When confronted by a problem not immediately capable of solution he would frown, put his head on one side, and pronounce his mournful assessment of the situation, "Aye, mon, I'm telling ye, it's a shaky do." The final vowel sound was prolonged and reverberated round wherever he happened to be. He practised a useful sideline, first acquired in the shipyards on the Clyde. He was a competent barber, nothing stylish, just a good neat scissors and comb job. Anyone going on leave from Rodel sat in Jock's chair, and left it looking smarter.

Jim Whittaker, a Lancastrian, was a talented water colourist. I produced six issues of a topical magazine under the title 'Fred's Mag' and Jim illustrated each with meticulous attention to relevance to the text. I recall one article on Rodel sausages, which could be placed in three categories. There was the india rubber version which leapt off your plate if you attempted to spear it with your fork, and bounced along the dining room floor, through the open door, killing a sheep in a nearby field. Then there was the armour piercing sort which skidded off your plate if attacked off centre, blasted its way through the Nissen roof, and brought down a passing seagull. The third type was a hybrid of the other two, and was the deadliest of the breed. It was designed for easy eating, but bounced and pierced after you had swallowed it. Jim's illustrations of these were hilarious. He was a master of caricature as well. A Welsh radar operator, Taffy to all of course, had a set of false teeth of which he was very proud. Taffy had the hottest tongue in Rodel. When he swore, the air positively sizzled. After one particularly corrosive outburst, someone warned him to be careful in case he melted his teeth. That induced a Jim Whittaker classic, a toothless Taffy staring in anguish at his falsies in a glass of water from which clouds of steam were rising.

The pinnacle of Jim's contribution to our quality of life occurred following the posting of Warrant Officer Colman to Rodel. He had been grounded from aircrew duties, and had undergone training as a sort of super disciplinarian. On his arrival, he announced that weekly hut and kit inspections would be held from now on, and that sentries would be posted at the camp entrance, where he could observe their performance from his hut, which conveniently overlooked the spot. Had these innovations had any bearing on the camp's main role, which was surveillance round the clock of air and sea traffic, the men might have gone along with them. It was patently obvious, however, that they were an attempt, on the part of the Warrant Officer, to justify his own existence. We put these points to the C.O. who vetoed the proposals.

Undeterred, Colman tried a new ploy. The camp five-barred gate had stood, locked wide open, for as long as anyone could remember. The W.O. removed the lock and chain and left the gate in the closed position, which meant that pedestrians and vehicles alike would now have to waste time opening and shutting the gate when entering or leaving camp. To reinforce his edict, Colman had painted a notice along the top bar of the gate, reading: 'This Gate Will Close. Try It.' During the following hours of darkness, Jim and an accomplice added, in excellent signwritten characters, prominently displayed on the centre bar, the observation: 'We did. It didn't'. On the bottom bar was a banner headline final judgement on the affair: COLMAN'S MUSTARD. A matching cartoon appeared in the next issue of 'Fred's Mag', too late, as it happened, for W.O. Colman to read. He had disappeared a day or two earlier, posted at the C.O.'s request.

During this episode. The C.O. and I had arrived at an amicable agreement that work was work and bullshit was bullshit, and he fell into the habit of dropping in on the technical site while I was on duty. On one occasion he remarked, "Have you ever thought of taking a trade test?" Not knowing what it was I told him so. "I can give you an assessment test for suitability for promotion to Leading Aircraftman," he explained. "I think you're ready for it." He set the test. I took it. He passed me. Requisite documents were despatched. A fortnight later, I was sewing a propeller badge on my sleeve and was a few shillings a day better off.

The NAAFI staff had settled in to their routine. As a result of company policy, and personal inclination, they kept themselves to themselves, eschewing the delights of both cinema and dance nights. The shutters on their serving hatches were their windows on the world. Off duty, they withdrew into their own domain. Camp rules forbade any airmen to cross the demarcation line, except when official duties necessitated. Such an instance arose when the manageress reported an electrical fault in the kitchen. Since I was available at the time, the duty was allocated to me. It was a simple fault, quickly rectified, during which I fell into desultory conversation with the manageress, who offered coffee and biscuits on the house when the job was completed I asked her how she was settling in, and she replied that things were pretty comfortable on the whole, though the lighting in her office was barely adequate. I offered to fit her up with a table lamp. She said that would be helpful.

Two days later, in response to a telephone call, a contact in Stornoway had one delivered on the twice-weekly bus, operated by Mitchell's Garage. It was duly installed. She was delighted. Thereafter, I was a regular daily visitor. To avoid detection, my route was over the grassy mound between Canada House and the NAAFI, to the rear entrance adjacent to her office. As time went on, more and more of my free time was spent there as our relationship developed.

There was a quiet reserve and sadness in her public demeanour that shielded her from too close a contact with people. Meeting her across the NAAFI counter, customers were kept at a professional arm's distance. All the customary chat up lines fell on deaf ears. She did her job efficiently, closed the shutters, and retreated to her private world. I slowly began to establish in her a confidence that encouraged her to talk about herself. Her name was Annabella, which, by mutual consent we shortened to Ann. She was born in South Dell, a tiny village in the adjoining Isle of Lewis, the third of five children, born into a crofting family. Alastair and Donald were her older brothers, Ishbel her younger sister, and Callum her younger brother. Her father was a self-employed stonemason, who had built the family's traditional two up, two down croft house, with storm porches and dormer windows. Her mother, having been orphaned in her teens, had brought up her parents' family before getting married herself, and was an excellent wife and mother.

RAF Rodel Park, Outer Hebrides – An armful of charm!

Ann's childhood had been typical of that of any youngster born into the island culture, with space in which to roam and explore, with none of the restrictions and drawbacks of growing up in an urban environment. The nearby village school had provided the traditional solid grounding in the three R's, while life on the croft had involved her in a range of domestic, animal husbandry, and agricultural skills. Approaching womanhood, she was very content at home, as an extra pair of hands to lighten her mother's load. Perhaps, one day, she would marry within the community, and continue the traditions of generations.

Abruptly, war broke out. The eldest brother, Alastair, was a highly skilled carpenter, accurate to the point of being fastidious His working standards stemmed from his personal habits, in that he was always clean, neat, well laundered, and clothed, with boots that gleamed, and, most noticeably, the hands of a surgeon rather than those of a carpenter. As Ann related this very detailed description, I realised it was all in the past tense. "You've lost him?" I asked, very softly, Eyes brimming, she just nodded, not trusting herself to speak. "In the war?" I queried, very gently. She shook her head. There was a long silence which I judged it better not to break. Then, taking a deep breath, she sighed, "He died of pneumonia----in Stornoway, in his digs." I left a number of questions unposed. If she wished to tell me more she would. If she did not, I'd need to open up another subject. "He'd caught a chill working outside," she continued. "He told his landlady he was shivering and felt very cold inside, but was feverish outside. He thought he would be better in bed, and went to his room early. When she called him in the morning, she couldn't wake him. The doctor was called. It was too late." "That is tragic," I said. "My mother says it would never have happened had he been at home. She'd have summoned the doctor much earlier," remarked Ann. "I'm sure you must all be beside yourselves with grief," I commented, "but you mustn't blame yourselves. There's nothing you could have done to have changed things. You've still got each other." At this point, she just looked at me in utter despair, and sobbed. I waited, not knowing what to say, in case I said the wrong thing. The seconds passed, she wiped her tears, and continued with further confidences.

"My youngest brother Callum was my father's favourite (again I noticed the use of the past tense), the son born out of his old age. With Alastair and Donald, my father was very strict, whereas Callum he doted on. He was a handsome lad, tall, fair-haired, blue eyed, with a lovely nature. Everyone in the village and beyond knew and liked him. He was conscripted at eighteen into the Royal Navy. We all waved him off as he stood on deck waving back. We never saw him again. His ship was lost with all hands in the Indian Ocean. It's made my father old before his time." "How recently was this?" I queried. "Not quite two years ago," Ann whispered. "And Donald?" I asked. "What about Donald?" conscious that he was now the only brother. "In the Royal Navy," came the reply. I decided not to pursue this. Instead I said, "And now here you are, a NAAFI manageress in a very becoming uniform. Tell me about yourself."

"When the time came for me to be called up, my parents didn't want me to join the Wrens, which most island girls did," said Ann. "There was an advert seeking management trainees in NAAFI so I applied." Again she paused. Again I resisted the temptation to intervene. More confidently, she continued. "They sent me to Maryhill Barracks for training. It was unlike anything I'd ever experienced, and I was terribly homesick." This time, I thought intervention was justified. "Maryhill Barracks," I ejaculated. "That's a rough dump. How on earth did you cope?" "I don't think I would have", came the answer, " if they hadn't allowed me to move into civilian billets where I stayed with cousins." She then smiled for the first time, and I knew the therapy was working. "I was so green," she giggled. "An English officer came up to the counter one night and said, "I'd like some pepper," "Yes sir," I replied, "Black, white, or red?" He gave me a startled look and then barked, "I'd like some pepper, young woman---- writing pepper and some envelopes." We both went into fits of laughter at this point, at which, looking back, a meaningful meeting of minds took place. The ice had been broken, and she felt able to discuss things frankly with me.

The NAAFI system of accounting worried her. Meticulously honest, she was desperately anxious to avoid mistakes. I offered to help out if required. The books were closed every six weeks and a new set opened. This struck me as very farsighted. On a very large camp, the scope for fraud was extensive. Checks at six weekly intervals would provide opportunity for early detection. There were other built in devices to reduce the risks of malpractice, and I was introduced to these in order to help Ann's book keeping.

All raw ingredients were entered in a kitchen book, exact quantities and prices being recorded. Food was produced from a list of standard menus, with ingredients precisely stated. From each menu a specified number of units for sale was laid down at fixed prices. Thus the cost of raw materials could be compared with cash receipts, the expected profit being calculated. Wastage for whatever reason had to be logged. There were ways in which this system could be manipulated. If the recipe for scones produced fifty at a penny each, by baking sixty a profit of ten pence could be made over that built in to the system and, if not shown in the accounts, could be misappropriated. A similar follow through method was used for tea and coffee. A stated number of tea bags was estimated to earn a specific amount of money when sold over the counter. Tea bags could be used more than once, or extra quantities of water could produce tea weaker than that legislated for. It was possible to recoup money lost on account of genuine accidents, such as spillage, burning a batch of baking, and the like. As with all carefully planned record keeping, there were two sides to the coin. The end of an accounting period was always apparent at Rodel. Ann would turn to a cigarette or two, and had a habit of pulling down a strand of thick, black hair and winding it round the tip of her nose to aid concentration.

Cathy, her assistant, also hailed from Lewis, specifically from North Tolsta, in a district called Point. Two or three years younger than Ann, she had a very carefree outlook, with a cheery smile for everyone, but no particular object of her undoubtedly warm affections. Of her family background I had no knowledge, and, as far as I could ascertain, she displayed no inclination to discuss such topics. For Cathy, the past and the future were of little concern. She simply took each day as it came.

Jemima, the cook, was from Renfrew on the west coast of Scotland. She reminded me of my paternal grandmother, who was raised in Fraserburgh on the east coast. In the process of birth, each had been hewn out of the solid granite that lies between both sites of origin. There the similarities end. My grandmother had married, crossed the border into England, and had raised five sons and a daughter. Jemima was a spinster, with the spirited independence characteristic of her kind. A Scot to the very heart of her being, she said it as she saw it, and she saw it very clearly. She could read a person's character as easily as though it were an open book. I would come to value her friendship.

For several weeks now, I had passed St. Clement's Church, on the way to and from the technical site. Realising that it was of quite significant historical importance, and that pilgrims travelled huge distances to visit it, I decided that it would be regrettable were I not to learn something about it. It was, after all, on my doorstep. At that time, the key was in the custody of the crofter living in an adjacent cottage, and, in the company of Ann and Cathy, I collected it one sunny afternoon.

RAF Rodel Park, Outer Hebrides – St. Clement's Church, Rodel.

I had been vaguely aware of the exterior with its tower, square and crenellated, at its western end, and its cross at the east, etched against the sky. The outer walls, constructed out of local gneiss and sandstone dressings, stood solidly against the elements. This was not the original building, which it is thought to have been an outpost of Iona. Since it was the long established burial ground of the chieftains of the clan MacLeod, it is conjectured that it was an early chief, Alexander, who began building around 1500, employing stone masons from Iona. Quite who St. Clement was is unknown.

The most striking features of the interior are three tombs, each of which supports a warrior chief at rest, the figures being carved out of jet black schist, aglitter with granules of quartz. Pride of place is reserved for Alexander MacLeod himself. On the keystone of the arched recess housing the tomb is carved the Holy Trinity and the four

RAF Rodel Park, Outer Hebrides – Rodel: St. Clement's Church interior.

evangelists. Eight archstones on either side depict apostles and angels. Twelve panels are displayed in horizontal fashion. In the centre of the top row is the Sun in Glory, with angels bearing trumpets. On each side is an angel carrying a lighted candle. In the centre panel of the second row sits the Virgin, wearing a crown, a lily in her right hand, the child in her left. On either side are a bishop on the one hand and St. Clement on the other, the latter holding a skull. Beyond these, in discrete panels, are displayed a galley and castle towers. Along the bottom row runs a series of carvings. One scene exhibits an armed chief, two gillies, and four hounds on leashes, embarking on a hunt. A second portrays three stags. A third is of St. Michael and Satan, weighing souls. The final panel declares the provenance of the tomb to be that of Alexander MacLeod of Dunvegan, and is dated 1528. An effigy of the chief, in full battle armour, his claymore between his legs, lies at rest. At his head is a pillow, at his feet a fabled monster.

We emerged into the daylight after perhaps an hour in an altogether different world, having condensed the encapsulation of the history of four hundred years into a brief sixty minutes. I reflected on the mysterious forces that had brought Alexander MacLeod to this, his final resting-place, and on the purpose for which I was but a passing voyeur. He had his claymore. I was a small cog in a technological weapon that could seek out and destroy, at considerable distances, anything that moved on land, sea, or in the air. Yet, the land and seascapes around St. Clement's Church were fundamentally those that Alexander MacLeod had known, and that, increasingly, I was coming to know.

The Australian Aborigines, the New Zealand Maoris, the American Native Indians all knew the mystic powers of land and ancestry, intricately intertwined down the generations. For all these ancient people there was, and is, a spiritual dimension within the land itself. The same deep ethos pervades the culture of the Hebridean crofter, and, that day, a spirit within me seemed to beat in harmony with it. It was like a homecoming.

Not everyone in the camp felt this affinity. A service policeman, one of a team which occupied the guard hut on the technical site round the clock, was on watch at the same time as I one night. It must have been a lonely vigil, with nine hours in a rudely equipped wooden shack, with but a wireless set for company. He was connected to our block by manually operated field telephone, and the drill was to keep in touch every hour on the hour. By mutual agreement, contact between midnight and 4am was discretionary—he deserved some sleep if he could get it. Not having heard from him by 4-30 we rang him. No reply. We rang him three times over the next quarter of an hour. Still no response. His phone was connected, so I was despatched to investigate. It had been a windy night, and the rough path down to the guard hut was littered with debris. A light was gleaming in the window, breaking the blackout regulations. I would need to mention this. I opened the door and stepped inside. He was slumped in his chair, his upper body sprawled across the desktop, his head in a pool of blood. In his right hand was his service revolver. I could see at a glance that he was beyond help.

Various reasons were adduced as to what had driven him to this low pitch. It was rumoured that his wife had been less than scrupulous in her obedience to her wedding vows, that he was experiencing financial difficulties etc. I believe it to have been more basic. What have been postulated were symptoms. The root cause was an alienation from his normal way of life, with which he could not come to terms. It drove some of our men to drink. It had drawn him to suicide.

Another colleague, a radar operator, had been presenting signs of increasing melancholia. Spurning the company of others, he retreated further and further into his shell. At first, people were sympathetic, and offered to keep him company, only to be rebuffed. He went out one day, on his day off, without a word to anyone. When he had not returned, approaching dusk, alarm bells began to ring. He was found the following morning on the beach. He had set off, up the road to the technical site, and for some reason had left the track, and headed off over rough ground to the cliff top, some quarter of a mile away. He may have been attracted by bird activity, or a desire to see the view, or whatever. Had he slipped and fallen to his death? Or had he jumped? We'll never know. Whatever caused his depression, he might have coped with it in a city, for he was a Birmingham man. There is an inherent tendency in the Hebridean psyche towards bouts of depression, with which those so afflicted learn to cope, since it is accepted as part of their make up. It would be as devastating for them to place them in an alien industrial background, as it had proved to be for our late colleague from the Midlands. Island bred folk, transferred to work in the Clyde shipyards, have suffered in similar ways.

A third colleague dwelt in a psychological half way house. Glaswegian by birth and upbringing, he was adjusting well to life in the Outer Isles. He had, in his own words, 'got his feet under the table' in a croft on the seashore, less than a mile from camp. Gregarious by nature, and not afraid to get his hands dirty, he had helped with the peat, cleaned out the cow byre, and lent a hand around the croft. Almost every crofter kept a long, bamboo fishing rod in the barn, and regularly fished for his breakfast off nearby rocks, accessible from the bottom of the croft. Ten minutes was often all it took to catch enough for the family. Having been introduced to this recreation, Jock slipped out on his own one evening, to bring back a surprise catch for the family. He never returned. While his back was turned, a freak wave swept him off the rock on which he was standing. His body was recovered from the sea. His mentors had taught him how to fish. They had failed to demonstrate how to fish safely.

Jock's tragedy was that he was a city bred man, showing growing signs of adapting to entirely new rhythms and ideas, and thoroughly enjoying the experience, only to be cut off before he had savoured them to the full. 'Cash' Clark was a different proposition. He too originated from a big city, Newcastle upon Tyne. Far from integrating with the background into which he had been posted, from the start he hated, resented, and rejected it. A super salesman in pre-service life, he had lived at a hectic pace, governed by sales targets, intense competition, and financial returns. He was essentially a loner. He had no friends in camp, and seemed to hold everyone else in aloof disregard, and, in some cases, disrespect. 'Cash' was always immaculately turned out, the ingrained habit of his training and experience. All these traits came together one stormy night on watch.

Strong gales in Rodel were unusual at this time of year, but they did occur. When they did, the site was exposed on all sides, and the initial lashing down of the aerial sometimes needed subsequent repetition as the wind veered. On the night in question, such was the case. We climbed the gantry at about 01-00 hours, did what needed to be done, and returned to the usual scalding hot tea and a seat in the warmest spot. It was customary for all operators but one to assist the duty mechanic in these emergencies. 'Cash' never contributed, being conscious of the effect it would have on his uniform. Everyone else on watch stretched out fully dressed during their spells off. 'Cash' took off both tunic and trousers, placed them on a coat hanger, and wrapped himself in a blanket. A significant change in wind direction drove us on to the gantry again at 03-30 hours. This time the job took longer and we were shattered, freezing, and frustrated on return. The sight of 'Cash' sleeping soundly in his woollen cocoon instigated ill feeling that demanded retaliation. A number of alternatives were suggested. The one adopted was highly relevant. His trousers were taken, and a willing volunteer climbed the gantry for the third time and tied them to the end of the array.

Came the end of the watch. 'Cash' was frantic. "I can't go back to camp like this," he remonstrated, trouserless. "Don't have to," someone suggested, "The relieving watch can bring your spare pair up." 'Cash' settled for this, apparently having no choice. Having searched high and low, he had found no trace of his missing article. We were seated in the back of the 15 cwt. truck, with a view back to the technical site, when the aerial array swung into full display, trousers flying full length as the installation revolved. "Your trousers have turned up," a cheerful voice informed a despondent 'Cash' "And very nicely aired," added another. As I have said, 'Cash' was a loner. I can add now, that he had no sense of humour.

In due course I was granted a fortnight's leave. Truth to tell, I didn't want it. I had everything I needed at Rodel. Home, they say, is where the heart is. Mine was in Rodel, focussing ever more, I was becoming increasingly aware, on one person. Nevertheless, I took the leave, and spent the morning on a mammoth laundry exercise. Practically everything I had in the way of clothing went into buckets, heated on the stoves in 'Canada House', and were soon displayed on two long washing lines, stretched between hut and cliff edge, securely pegged in a good stiff drying breeze. Feeling quite smug, I went for my dinner. Returning about half an hour later----panic. Every stitch of clothing had vanished, presumably over the cliff. Gingerly, I peered over the edge. No sign. Devastated, I crept over the grassy knoll, and into the NAAFI rear entrance. Ann, Cathy, and Jemima listened sympathetically to my tale of woe, upbraiding me for my carelessness. Utterly fed up I went on watch at 13-00 hours. Signing off at 18-00 hours, I returned to the NAAFI. On a table, in a storeroom, were all my clothes, beautifully ironed, and arranged in neat piles. They'd stolen the lot off the lines during my dinner break. "If you bring your case over, we'll pack it for you," offered Ann. It would have been churlish to refuse. When I unpacked at home three days later, I found my pyjama trouser legs had been stitched closed at the bottom, that the sleeves of the jacket were similarly treated, and that a digestive biscuit had been stitched to the jacket pocket as a medallion. Underneath was a handsome plaque, bearing the following inscription " Awarded for Meritorious Service to the Three White Women of Rodel. Haste Ye Back." I needed no bidding. With added travelling time, I had been away nearly three weeks. During that period, the ties already established had strengthened.

In my absence, our Canadian C.O. had departed. No longer would we enjoy little chats during his visits to the technical block, when he had regaled me with tales of his upbringing in the Rocky Mountains, and of the magic moments he had experienced there. I sensed that we were kindred spirits, each with a developing awareness of the aura unique to the Outer Hebrides. I am sure he was sad to depart. I would miss him.

His replacement was a different proposition. Not for him the mysticism of the wide, wild open spaces. Toronto was his birthplace, and city slicker was his disposition. His private quarters were a Nissen hut on the edge of the camp, isolated from the others. He had lost no time in propositioning both Ann and Cathy with blatant invitations to spend a night (or two) with him. Both had given the kind of point blank refusals that brooked no further approach. Jemima was more direct, committing him to his face with dire threats of ' black, burning, hellfire and shame'. I don't suppose he'd ever run up against her like before. It didn't deter him from looking elsewhere, and every weekend saw a different Waaf from Stornoway alight from the service bus to bestow her favours on the Toronto adventurer.

Meanwhile, an incident occurred that scared me witless at the time. The relief transport having failed to arrive at the end of an 08-00 to 13-00 watch, an operator located an old bike round the back of the diesel hut, and proposed riding it to the domestic site. "Room for one on the crossbar," he announced, not really expecting any takers. "You're on, Bert," I said, anxious as ever to resume life in the NAAFI. Bert straddled the machine, and I took up position, sidesaddle on the crossbar, hands resting lightly on the handlebars. We cruised gently down the road, passed the guard hut, and on to the road home. You don't really notice slopes or bends when you are in the back of a motor vehicle. You do when you're on a bike. This road was steep, the surface was loose, and some of the bends were challenging. We were doing quite nicely until we were approaching the last lap, where I knew a pronounced right angled bend awaited. To go straight on was to head for the sea. "Take it easy, Bert," I yelled, over the noise of flying stones, and the wind in our ears, "There's a nasty bend ahead." "O.K.," shouted Bert, and applied the brakes. There was a snapping sound, and a sort of ping—ing. "Christ," screamed Bert, "the bloody brakes have gone." The next few seconds live with me yet. I knew everything depended on Bert. I was locked in. I took both hands off the handlebar and shouted, "Peat, look for a peat exit." We were almost at the bend when I shouted again. "Peat bank. Just ahead. Go for it." Mercifully, he did. The softness of the ground slowed progress almost abruptly, and we toppled rather than fell, landing in part peat, part heather. As we surveyed the drop from the bend twenty yards down the road, Bert turned pale and spewed up. It could so easily have been curtains for both of us.

The one member of the NAAFI staff unaccustomed to the Hebridean way of life was the redoubtable Jemima. None of us probably realised that she was more singularly isolated than anyone on the site. She was excluded from the services members, since her role as cook was largely behind the scenes. She was never asked to serve at the counter. Though she was observably on excellent terms with Ann and Cathy, she was old enough to be their mother, which created a generation gap not easy to bridge, since her life's experience in Renfrew had little in common with their shared upbringing in Lewis. Jemima received little in the way of post, which served to increase her isolation. For a period she became increasingly withdrawn, until she had to take to her bed. The doctor was called. She had shingles, a painful condition. Hospital was advised but the idea terrified her. Ann asked if she could be nursed at home, with support from the district nurse, and after a little liquid persuasion, Dr. Biggart agreed. For some three weeks, Jemima was on the sick list, the other two taking over the cooking. There were no complaints from the customers.

In the final stage of her convalescence, she asked if I could be allowed in to see her. "I think she's fed up with our company," said Ann, "She needs cheering up." So saying, she led me across the courtyard and into the staff private quarters. Jemima was propped up in bed in a tiny room of her own, looking frail and flushed. "I'll leave you two to it," said Ann, "I know you'll have plenty to talk about." "Now lady," I greeted Jemima," "Are you feeling better?" "I'm well on the mend," came the reply, "Yon wee lassie's a lovely woman." She paused before adding, "But I don't have to tell you that." "No, indeed you don't." I concurred. There was a longer pause as though she was wondering how to proceed. "You've made a wonderful difference to her since we all met." she said. "She never smiled all the time we were together before we came here. These days, she's like a wee flower that's opened to the sunlight." A further pause, then, "It's you who've driven the clouds away." I looked her straight in those candid clear blue eyes and said, "Jemima Renton, are you match making?" Her gaze did not waver. "That is God's work," she replied, and then, placing her frail hand over mine, "but I am one of his workers." Squeezing my hand, she continued "Lying in this bed these past days, I've had plenty of time to reflect. Ann reminds me of myself at her age, when life was full of promise. It was wartime then, and I had a boy around whom all my hopes were built. He was killed. I was not alone. Thousands of women lost their men in that war. Today, I have no family to speak of. This, here in Rodel, is my little family."

"It is indeed," I enthused, in an effort to lighten the mood. "You're as good as a mother to Ann and Cathy, a very good and valued friend to me, and a grandmother to all the lads out there, who enjoy your cooking and baking." She withdrew her hand. "Och, away with you," she mock scolded, "You haven't lost that smooth tongue," then "but it goes with a warm heart. Listen to your heart. What does it tell you?" "You know the answer to that," I said seriously. "The question is, what does my head say?" She inclined hers and requested, very softly, "What does it say?"

"In war time," I said, "we are all ships that pass in the night. Nothing is as it appears to be. Ann and I know nothing about each other's real backgrounds. We come from different cultures. I have no idea yet how I'll earn a living once the war's over. I'm twenty. I've never felt for any other girl what I feel for Ann. How do I know it's not just infatuation, arising out of the circumstances in which we find ourselves. Then there's the age difference. She is twenty seven. She probably looks on me as a younger brother, filling the gap left by the one she lost." At this point, the flow ceased. She took my hand again. "In her eyes, you may be a substitute for Callum, but you're not a boy. You're a man and, unless I'm mistaken, for her you are THE man. But you are wise to hearken to your head. Give it time. You'll both be parted ere long, and a period of separation will determine whether it's love, or temporary infatuation. Keep in touch. Don't lose her. She's a girl with a heart of gold. She deserves the best, and you are the one for her." I was much moved by not only the warmth with which these kindly words of advice were spoken, but by the fact that they were offered at all. Behind the physical frailty of this tiny Scotswoman was a lifetime's hard won experience. Of her own volition, she had created the opportunity for this little tete-a-tete. Just one thing puzzled me. Had she, I wondered, had a similar session with Ann?

Jemima's return to work was timely. Normally, rations were varied, and the camp cooks produced adequate meals. For a period of some ten days however, rations hit the buffers, and the only item coming through from Stornoway was kippers. Now this dish is considered a delicacy by many people, and Stornoway kippers are among the most sought after. Not even putting them on the menu under various headings, of which 'Stornoway turkey' was the most pretentious, refreshed the palate after ten days of the dish for breakfast, dinner, and tea. Indeed, it was years afterwards before I felt able to face kippers again.

It being an ill wind etc., Jemima came into her own, and the NAAFI profits soared. Even her much derided 'Nelson cake' was ordered with gusto, and eaten with enthusiasm. The take up of this particular recipe had previously declined, when it became public knowledge that its ingredients were the left overs from all other dishes. As long as it didn't include kippers, it now went down a treat.

Berry, never one for shunning the limelight, produced a characteristic display of showmanship during this period of culinary desolation, by consuming his kippers raw, proceeding to gnaw his way down one side of the backbone, back up the other, flip the fish over, repeat the process, and finish with a perfectly filleted skeleton between very greasy fingers. Though he smacked his lips, and declared his meal to have been both nutritious and delicious, nobody followed suit.

Though I could forgive Berry his eye-catching display of frankly disgusting table manners, his final contribution to life at Rodel earned neither applause nor approbation. It had far reaching impact on almost everybody's lives. The Harris Tweed industry was fast approaching its zenith, and vast profits were accruing, with government revenues benefiting significantly. Berry's activities had attracted the attention of officials in the Board of Trade, who had decided to investigate. We have discussed the network of people embroiled in Berry's machinations, from crofter weavers, individual airmen, high ranking officers, RAF pilots, ship's captains, through to large multiple companies. The heart of all this activity was a tiny radar station on the southernmost tip of Harris in the Outer Hebrides. The investigation would doubtless start there.

It was Mrs. Mack who broke the news from her spider's web in the Leverburgh Post Office. I was down there with a stack of outgoing mail. As we conducted our business, she looked at me over her glasses and remarked, "I hear you're leaving us." "First I've heard of it," I said sharply, genuinely taken aback. This obviously pleased her. She loved being first with hot news. "Oh yes," she expanded, "about thirty of you are being moved out." I concluded the transaction and raced back to camp "Idle gossip," was the comment of the orderly room clerk.

I went to bed that night reassured. I had no wish to leave Rodel. As far as I was concerned, they could leave me there for ever. The following morning, a signal arrived over the secret official line of communication. Thirty plus postings were listed. I was one of them. They were to take effect immediately. My first reaction was to curse Berry. My second was to hope that Mrs. Mack was working for us and not the enemy. She had been spot on, black spot on.

Some of the postings were to individual radar stations within 70 Wing, and destinations could be identified. Peter Harrow's news was dire: he was returning to Crustan. I was obviously destined to leave the geographical area of 70 Wing for pastures further afield. The precise location would be revealed when I reached Bunchrew House. The speed of this mass exodus threw the whole camp into turmoil, and questions were asked as to the reasons. We all knew the real reason but were interested to hear the official ones. The one given in my case was plausible. The war was beginning to swing from defensive to offensive. Revolutionary new radar systems were coming on stream, and radar mechanics of proven ability were being hand picked for intensive training. I was, allegedly one of these. Nobody could tell me where the training would take place. For a fleeting moment I thought about giving Mrs. Mack a call, on the basis that she was bound to know. Deciding against it, I conjectured that a third visit to Yatesbury was on the cards.

There was no time for protracted farewells. The NAAFI girls gave me an emotional send off, placing my kit in one peat wheelbarrow, and me in another, wheeling both ceremoniously to the waiting three ton truck. Under the laughter and bonhomie there were genuine tears. The previous evening, I had promised Ann that I would keep in touch, and she had reciprocated. As I sat in the back of the truck, along with others, the three waving 'white women of Rodel' receded rapidly into the distance, and then were gone.

As we negotiated the testing hairpin bends of the Clisham, clouds that had been gathering all day unleashed unbridled tears in torrents that were a fitting accompaniment to the break up of associations built up over the past gloriously happy months. What lay ahead none of us knew. What was written in the stars would be revealed. Meanwhile, it was a case of accepting what is to hand, adapting to it, reshaping your life, and who knows, God willing, you'd retrace your steps to where you'd left your heart, and hear it beat again in harmony with another.

Sennen Cove, Land's End

I have little conscious memory of that trip back to Bunchrew House in Inverness. Truth to tell, I was on auto pilot, dwelling in a sort of limbo land. It was a reasonably pleasant crossing of the Minch, and the autumn colours in the Highlands, for it was early October, were glorious. Bunchrew House hadn't changed. The familiar routine of booking in, chit signatures etc. completed, I reported for travel instructions and documentation. I had to smile. My destination was Land's End, specifically Sennen Cove, which was adjacent. There was a special training unit to which I was being posted. Someone, somewhere, seemed determined to ensure for me a comprehensive acquaintance with the remotest outposts of the British Isles.

It was a long and tedious journey, culminating in arrival on a Sunday. En route, I developed a heavy cold, a high temperature, and a raging fever. By rights I should have sought medical attention. Between Inverness and London I dozed, sweating like a pig, and feeling awful. In London, I visited a Salvation Army canteen, behind Kings Cross Station, where a member of staff gave me aspirin or its equivalent. I took refuge in a newsreel cinema between trains, sleeping through most of the programme.

It was an overnight journey to Truro, the H.Q. of my new Wing. By the time I'd arrived I was on the mend, fairly weak, and a pound or two lighter. Another bureaucratic routine of acceptance and clearance completed, I was entrained for Plymouth. From here, no RAF transport being visible or available, I took a taxi to

Sennen Cove. Never the busiest of resorts, it was somnolent on Sundays, and it was some time before I located my home for the next fortnight.

The course was demanding. A new radar system, code named 'Oboe', was coming on line with miniaturised components. I had to soak up the principles involved, and commit to memory an array of circuit diagrams. There were no practical sessions since the equipment was not yet available. It was a case of sleep in one hut, and work in the one adjoining ad infinitum. There was no respite. I saw nothing of Land's End though it was on the doorstep. A very real sense that I was taking part in something highly significant was inescapable. At the end of the fortnight, I reported back to Truro. I'd have welcomed the opportunity to have remained in 78 Wing to explore the beautiful scenery over which it presided. It was not to be. My next posting was to RAF Trimingham. It would not have surprised me had it been in the Shetland Isles. It was in fact in Norfolk…

—— RAF Trimingham, Norfolk ——

Having taken a crash course on 'Oboe', I was expecting initiation into the system's practical application, while all the new technology was still in my head. No such site was yet available it seemed, so back I went to familiar ground, The station at Trimingham was a replica of the old CHL at Crustan and Rodel. I was shown my quarters in the now familiar Nissen hut, the standard being well above Crustan's, well below Rodel's. It slept about eight men, pending the allocation of a civilian billet. These arrangements, unlike the bed and breakfast I'd known at Battersea, were for full board. The orderly room corporal informed me that there were no vacancies, and that there was a waiting list. If I could find a landlady willing to take me in, I could jump the queue.

It took a couple of days to assess my companions in waiting, by which time Alec MacIver, a Scottish graduate Grammar School teacher, agreed to team up in the search for more desirable accommodation. It helped that we were on the same watch. There was a cosy little teashop in the village, appropriately named 'The Singing Kettle'. There we repaired to draw up a plan of action. A direct approach seemed the best. We would walk down the streets, select a house that looked promising, ring the doorbell, and politely state our case. It would be possibly some time before we struck lucky, but it was preferable to doing nothing. We left the warmth of the tea shop and began our quest. A newsagent's shop window caught our eye. Prominently on display was a large notice advertising a Garden Party in the local Parish Church with stalls, games, tombola etc. All were welcome. The date was for Saturday. It was now Friday.

We reorganised our schedule. Why visit prospective landladies when they were inviting us to visit them?

It was a fine day, but on the cool side, when we arrived to join the festivities. "There's bound to be a Queen bee around somewhere," said Alec. "Why not approach the vicar?" I suggested. "Well," observed Alec, "first, he might offer us a bed in the vicarage. I don't know about you but I'd almost rather stay in the Nissen. Second, he's not the boss around here." His eyes roamed around the groups manning the various stalls. "She is," he said, positively. "Come on son. Just leave it to me." He homed in on a small group of ladies, engaged in animated conversation, in a space between stalls. One of them appeared to be conducting proceedings. Excusing himself, Alec joined the group, and, a second or two later, emerged with the lady in tow. Addressing me, she said, "Your friend tells me you are offering your services for the afternoon. It is so good of you to give so much of your free time. What exactly did you have in mind?" Alec shot me a warning look, afraid that my reply might be along the lines of "We thought someone might have a couple of beds available." He needn't have worried. "Back home I'm an active church member," I said, "and always help on occasions such as this, wherever the organiser detects a need." Alec positively beamed. "I've just the thing for both of you," the lady boomed, "Our ladies are always chary about running the raffle. They always fall short of the target I set." Alec and I exchanged glances. "It will be our pleasure, madam," he said. "And hopefully to your profit," I added.

We set to with a will and attracted continuous business throughout the afternoon, exchanging snippets of conversation with customers in the process. In announcing the takings at the end of the proceedings, The Queen Bee said, "I'm sure you would want me to propose a special vote of thanks to our two fine RAF boys, who have helped to raise what is a record sum for the raffle. Thank you, boys." As the applause rippled round the gathering, I saw Alec whisper into the lady's ear. The applause ended. "Our two airmen arrived in Trimingham only two days ago, and already they are almost one of us. At present they are accommodated in camp. I'm sure that some of you ladies will have spare rooms and feel able to express our appreciation for the help we have received today in a really practical way. Thank you once again boys." Within minutes we were approached with offers, none of them direct, but addresses where vacancies might be found, and with notes of introduction. On Monday, we took up residence.

Our new home was a mile or so up the road in Cromer. Its geographical situation faced the North Pole, and the winds battering the coast were bitterly cold. The street in which we lived was a long row of substantially built stone properties, used mostly to cater for the large peacetime holiday trade. Our billet was at the seaward end of the street, the gable end being exposed to the full blast of the elements. There were about eight of us in residence, along with the proprietrix, her mother, and a daughter of

Junior School age. There was some doubling up in that single beds were squeezed into every available space, sometimes three to a room. I had a separate room in theory, but it was an access to a three-bedded room beyond. Privacy was at a premium.

The food was good, hearty cooked breakfasts, a cooked dinner at midday, and a plain tea. The landlady was married to a regular RAF serviceman who was serving abroad, and the lady was keen to make it known that, understanding an airman's needs, she would pull out all the stops to meet them. A few days after our installation, Alec quizzed me, "Has Brenda propositioned you yet?" Seeing my puzzled look, he said, "She ran into me in the corridor at the weekend and said she was going for a walk along the cliff top, and would I like to go with her?" I thought, "Why not? What better way to see the sights than in the company of a local?" Alec went on to describe the walk in some detail. Brenda had enthusiastically drawn his attention to various landmarks and then, the wind getting up, had snuggled up close, and drawn his arm around her waist. They had walked thus for a while when they came to a sheltered spot, where she suggested they might rest awhile. "The blatant bitch had obviously been there before," snorted Alec. "Anyway, she came straight to the point. Would I like to make love to her?" "You're having me on," I protested. "I am not," Alec replied. "What's more to the point is she was trying to have it off." "O.K., I'll not ask whether she got her wicked way with you or not," I commented, with a grimace. "She bloody didn't," was the rejoinder. "I told her I didn't share with anybody where women were concerned." "I'll bet that pleased her," I remarked. "She didn't turn a hair. Just smiled and put my arm around her waist again, and brought me back home," answered Alec. "No hard feelings. What an incredible woman."

It turned out that Alec was right about the sharing. One of the lodgers, a well built, taciturn service policeman, enjoyed the pleasures of her bed three nights out of four, being on duty on the fourth occasion. Another resident took his place then, not always the same one every time apparently. Brenda erected no barriers in pursuit of her declared aims of meeting her airmen's needs. Alec and I contributed two observations in summing up the unusual situation in which we found ourselves. His was, "When her old man comes home on leave, do you suppose he has to take his turn with the rest?" Mine was, "I find it ironic, to say the least, that in our search for accommodation, we should be directed by pillars of the established church to the amenities of what is tantamount to a house of ill repute." For the record, the protection of my virginity was never put to the test. Brenda was drawn to men of experience, and there was a wide choice available, not all of whom rejected her advances.

As I had learned, on previous occasions, the RAF did not like to see any opportunity slip by to expose its personnel to wider experience. It was obvious that I was marking time at Trimingham. It therefore came as no surprise to be seconded for a fortnight's assault course training at RAF Staxton. Out came the map, with a touch of trepidation. You never knew with this lot. It could have been worse. Staxton was a few miles inland from Filey on the North Yorkshire coast, on the edge of the Yorkshire Wolds. We were now into January, 1944, with heavy snowdrifts, biting winds, and short days. The course was tough, the Army NCO's running it tougher still, and uncompromising. It is only when you have been without regular physical exercise that you realise how far down you've allowed yourself to slide. The first two or three days were gruelling, with long marches through testing conditions, to gradually build up general fitness levels and stamina.. Most of us did not join in the evening relaxation sessions in the nearby pub—a facility embraced with gusto in the latter stages—preferring instead to crawl wearily into our twin bedded bunks as early as possible.

Reveille techniques were simple. No rousing bugle calls for us, or a shake on the shoulder by an impatient NCO. Oh no. A batten of wood, dragged along the side of a Nissen hut, by a lusty voiced sergeant bellowing, "Wakey, Wakey" did the trick. You were on your feet in a trice, with the dead that he'd awakened alongside. It would have aroused even Tom Burns, of Crustan memory. I'd forgotten Tom until now. He was the soundest sleeper I've ever met. Rousing him at 4am to take over from you on watch had been a regular problem till we hit on a solution. We lit a cigarette, stuck it between his lips, nipped his nostrils together, and waited. He coughed himself awake in seconds..

In retrospect, I enjoyed the Staxton experience, and returned to Trimingham in peak physical condition. Fortunately, before Brenda became aware of the fact, I was on my travels again. This time the destination was quite palatable. I was bound for a radar station based at RAF Cleadon near Sunderland.

—— RAF Cleadon ——

Having left the north east in June 1941, and having seen a fair selection of the British Isles since, I disembarked from the train at Sunderland station in February 1944, a much wiser and more experienced person. I'd left as a callow youth. I was back, not yet twenty one, fully aware of what life was all about. What new experiences would I encounter on this latest posting? The beginning augured well. I stepped on to the station forecourt, to be confronted by a line of waiting taxis. Before any of the drivers could begin touting for a fare, a stocky little man, with a shock of tousled ginger hair, came up to me. "Howay, bonny lad. You have the look of a stranger in want of directions. Can I help?" "I'm a stranger to Sunderland," I said, "but not to these parts. I was born and bred hereabouts." "Why man, you're as good as one of us," he grinned, "Where are you bound for?" "RAF Cleadon," I informed him. "No sweat," he chuckled, "There's a bus stand just round the corner." So saying, he hefted my kitbag on to his shoulder, and I followed. He perused the timetable on the notice board. "D'ya take a drink?" he asked. I said I'd never been known to refuse one. We crossed the road to a nearby pub, where two pints of Samson's best were soon on the bar. "We've got half an hour to wait," he said "Let's sit down and enjoy the beer."

An ex pitman, one of a wonderful breed of men, he was good company, and the talking never faltered. He looked at his watch. "Right son," he said smartly, "time to catch your bus." He again hoisted my kitbag. Seeing me on to the bus, he called to the conductress, "RAF Cleadon for me mate here. Look after him and see he gets off at the right stop." "Will do," she shouted back, " and you make sure you find your way home sober, you old bugger." It was good to be back among my own again. You can't beat the north east for genuine neighbourliness.

Cleadon turned out to be an unusual posting. It began by my being despatched, armed with a billeting order for bed and breakfast accommodation, to a house in Prince Edward Road, on a council estate. I was welcomed by the lady of the house with open arms. "Come in, honey, and make yourself at home," she invited. For the next few weeks, I was one of the family. Nothing was too much trouble. Married to a manual worker, she knew how to feed a man, and good plain food was the order of the day. Rationing did not seem to pose a problem, and there was always plenty on the table. On a Friday evening, a hot bath was always run for me, with a large, thick, hot towel to hand. She treated me like a son.

On the technical site, an unusual situation existed. This was no operational site as such. A huge hangar had been converted to store hundreds of electrical stores, and there must have been a fortune standing there. Most of it had been intended to service defensive radar systems, and recent developments had rendered them redundant. Alongside was the operations room of the now defunct radar station to which I had been posted. On arrival, I was the only one authorised to enter the premises, not even the camp commandant, who was non-technical, being allowed across the threshold. Duty consisted of turning up between eight and nine in the morning, filling in time, and signing off about six in the evening. It was a doddle but rather lonely. Until that is another radar mechanic arrived.

It's hard to say who was the more taken aback, Alec MacIver or I. "How did you pull this one off?" I greeted him, "Welcome to skivers' paradise". "Entirely out of my hands old boy," he beamed, "But I suspect that Brenda was involved somewhere along the line. You, she didn't want. Me, she couldn't have. So she decided to get shot of us both. How do I set about finding a good billet? And don't tell me to try the local church garden party." As it happened, Alec fell on his feet too, and we spent a few happy weeks together.

One evening, I decided to introduce him to the night life of Cleadon, and we visited Marsden Grotto, an underground pub with bars set out in caves, with views of the sea. It was probably unique at the time, offering all the amenities of the traditional hostelry, with built in, salt laden air conditioning. After quitting the premises, and wending our way back home, we caught the smell of fish and chips. Our noses led us unerringly to a long queue outside the shop. We joined it, noting that it wound its way back on itself inside the shop, before reaching the counter. I anticipated a wait of twenty to twenty five minutes. A woman's voice from inside the shop called out, "Haway hinnies. Divn't stand queuing out there. We think mair aboot war serving lads than that. Haway up to the front here." We did as we were told. Everyone made way for us. "What's your order?" asked a lass behind the counter, all smiles. We placed it. Out of the sizzling pan of hot fat came two huge portions of cod, a dash of salt, a sprinkling of vinegar, all wrapped snugly in plain waxed paper, with an outer covering of newspaper.

A handful of loose change at the ready, I proffered the right amount. "Put it back in your pocket. Someone down the queue's paid for it," smiled the server. We publicly thanked our anonymous host, and sat on a bench up the road to eat our supper. "Good hot meal," said Alec enthusiastically. "Good warm hospitality," I countered, with genuine pride.

Being so near home, I took the opportunity at least once a week to board a United bus for the hour's journey involved. I never bothered with a pass. As long as I wasn't stopped en route and asked for my papers, nobody would be concerned. I was just a touch apprehensive, during one return journey, to observe a service policeman come on board a few stops before Cleadon. When he too alighted there, I braced myself for trouble. I needn't have worried. As we both passed the guard room door, the policeman on duty greeted him with, "Can I see your pass, Bill?" to which Bill replied, "Bugger off, you silly sod." Even service policemen play hookey.

The Cleadon way of life was too good to last, though we expected a fair lapse of time before someone in authority cottoned on. Alec and I were, in effect, outside the system, attached to a radar station that was no longer in action, and beyond the reach of even the C.O., who was unauthorised to enter our place of duty. Somebody did eventually assess the situation, and took swift, appropriate action. We were ordered to have everything packed for a posting to RAF Tilly Whim, Swanage, on the night train. It was mid afternoon when the news broke. Our documentation had to be collected before 17-30 hours. We decided to pick up our papers first, and then pack.

On checking our authorisation, all seemed in order until Alec asked a question, "Where do we collect our rations?" The orderly room clerk said he had no instructions to issue rations. "We'll be travelling overnight to London, and then there's the extra journey to Swanage," said Alec, reasonably. "If we're not issued with rations, we'll need subsistence allowance in lieu." The clerk was out of his depth, and rang for a corporal. He sought advice from a sergeant, who arrived within a few minutes. "Can't issue rations," he stated, authoritatively, "Cookhouse is closed." "Subsistence allowance it is then," remarked Alec. "No authority to release subsistence money," barked the sergeant. "Only an officer can do that." "Better get one then," was Alec's immediate response.

By now the temperature was rising, and Alec was in the mood to dig his heels in. An officer arrived eventually, not best pleased. After a briefing from the sergeant, he turned his attention to the resolute Alec. "Well now, airman," was his opening gambit, "I'm sure we can sort this little contretemps out." "I hope so—sir," said Alec, "I very much hope so." The officer was very perceptive. "Unless I'm very much mistaken," he smiled, "I detect a Scots accent. I too am a Scot." Scot he may have been, but his accent was almost pure Received Standard Pronunciation. I could see Alec's hackles rising. "What part of Scotland are you from?" continued the officer. "Glasgow—sir," came the reply in unmistakable Glaswegian. "Well, well," enthused the officer, "I come from Glasgow myself—Kelvinside---west side." Alec's face was a picture. "Is that so? I also come from Kelvinside---east side---sir." he snarled, banging his clenched fist on the table. There had been no meeting of minds here. The officer conferred briefly with the sergeant, took out his wallet, and counted out enough to cover the tariff in accordance with King's Regulations. "Thank you---sir," said Alec, picking the money up. "Is there anything to sign?" The officer nearly choked. "The documentation will be completed in the morning," he said. "Someone will sign on your behalf." So saying, he left the room.

It had been an interesting exchange, in which a clash of service ranks, class status, and personality traits had all influenced the outcome. Alec was an articulate, well educated product of the then wrong side. The officer, equally articulate, was from the right side. Today's meritocracy had not evolved, and the one was the holder of the King's Commission, the other was in the ranks. Sixty years on, Alec would undoubtedly be regarded as officer material. Demarcation lines still exist, but are less blatantly based on class social differences.

Alec and I boarded our overnight train, and enjoyed the meals on offer all the way to Swanage. What new adventures awaited?

RAF Tilly Whim, Swanage

My precipitate departure from Cleadon disrupted plans to celebrate my twenty first birthday at home. Instead of a party among family and friends, I spent the day among strangers. RAF Tilly Whim was a newly emerging radar station on cliff tops high above the Dorset town of Swanage. As I arrived, it was still in pre-operational guise, with equipment in course of installation. A huge under cover area was to house a number of separate units, and floors had only just been constructed, and awaited polishing. It was on this task that I was occupied throughout the whole of my birthday, which appropriately was April the first.

The whole vast organisation was a paradise for those with a penchant for carving out opportunist niches, and such a one was Flight Sergeant Cromwell. He had taken the manpower by the scruff of the neck, and had established a hierarchy over which he exercised unrelenting control. The enterprise was already known as 'Cromwell's Flying Circus'. Such regimes depend on subordinates of a particular subservient disposition, and Cromwell had eyes and ears all over the place. An L.A.C., in charge of the floor area assigned to me reported to Cromwell at the end of the day that my work was not up to the standard required. I knew at once where he was coming from. Anxious to establish himself in the Flight Sergeant's good books, he took an early opportunity to do so at my expense. Anyone else in his charge that day would have suffered the same treatment. I was duly marched into Cromwell's office.

The L.A.C. put his case. The Flight Sergeant asked for my comments. I told him I had been instructed to polish a certain area of floor space and had done so to the best of my ability. Was the L.A.C. complaining about the quality or the quantity of the work done? No quality standards had been specified when the order was issued. I had completed the task in good faith. If the final results did not measure up to unspecified standards, perhaps consideration should be given to a review of the quality of materials supplied. At this point, a Ft. Lt. In the background intervened, "What is your trade designation?" he asked. "Radar mechanic, sir," I replied, "recently trained in 'Oboe' and assigned here on posting to A.M.E.S. 9412 mobile unit." Cromwell looked uncomfortable. The Ft. Lt. had a brief word and Cromwell announced, "No further questions. Just wait outside." I withdrew, to be joined, a couple of minutes later by the officer. "Sorry about that son," he said, "As you can see, things are a bit chaotic here at the moment. I'll have someone take you to your unit." Ten minutes later, I was led along a narrow concrete path, past two mobile units, to the one at the far end. I had arrived at Air Ministry Experimental Station 9412. The floor area was minimal. It hardly ever got polished.

There being no living quarters attached to the unit, I had to be billeted in Swanage. The road down to the main street was very steep, and almost half a mile long. My billet was well over a mile uphill, going west from the town centre. Reporting for duty entailed walking into the centre, there to catch a 15cwt truck up to the unit. One needed to allow three quarters of an hour at each end of a watch period as travelling time. Walking these steep stretches kept me in good trim. I shared the accommodation with two other airmen on different units. The landlady was a homely widow of about sixty with a married son and a daughter, also married. John and his wife Lucy lived in. Rose, the daughter, rented a house round the corner, joining the family at meal times. Her husband was serving in the army abroad. I soon became integrated, and found the experience both enjoyable and entertaining. Rose and Lucy were complete opposites. The daughter was quiet, reflective, and reserved, missed her husband, and constantly worried about his Italian posting. The daughter-in-law was openly dismissive and derisive of her husband, and was out every night with any Yank that was available. Her parting comment to her husband as she departed was always the same, "Don't worry, gormless. I always look before I jeep."

It was the period leading up to D-day, and all along the south coast were vast camps of American G.I.'s. They poured into the nearest town in the evenings, to be welcomed by local businesses, and the female population. They were not too popular with the indigenous servicemen for three reasons: they were overpaid, over sexed, and over here. Another version concerns a Yank who received a letter from his wife, telling him she had heard he was being unfaithful, and asking, "What has she got that I haven't?" to which the reply was, "Nothing, honey, but she's got it over here."

Rose kept out of the way as much as possible, obviously hurt by her sister-in-law's open contempt for her brother, who simply sat smouldering, at a loss to know how to handle his erring spouse. She coped with separation from her own man by taking long walks in the countryside adjacent to the house. One Sunday afternoon, she invited me to accompany her, and we strolled over rolling meadows covered in Spring flowers, primroses in particular growing in profusion. She obviously felt the need to unload a lot of pent up emotion, and talked a lot about brother John "He's a lovely lad, but he's never been what you would call positive," she explained. "He wasn't particularly bright at school, but he's always been good with his hands. He works as a construction foreman for a local firm, and has a good wage. He stints her for nothing. In fact, that's probably part of the trouble. She's got him round her little finger. He's in a reserved occupation, and she throws that in his face. Not man enough to be called up she says. If he were more of a man, she tells him, she wouldn't need to chase after Yanks." I made no comment, but switched the conversation round to her. "Well, you seem to have made a better deal. How long have you been married?" I asked. "Oh, Frank and I were school day sweethearts," she replied, "We'd been engaged for about three years, saving for a house of our own. I always said I didn't want a council house like my Mam—she's paid rent all her life, and look at her today, struggling on without my Dad. Anyway, the war broke out, and we got married. We've the little place around the corner from my Mam. It's a struggle to keep the payments up, but it's ours, and one day we'll be together again."

"It's strange, isn't it how things work out in families?" I said. "There's you and John, brought up together, with totally different marriage situations." "We're very different personalities," said Rose, reflectively. Then, quite vehemently, "He'll probably put up with her till she leaves him for someone else. Me, I'd swing for the bitch." I'd enjoyed the walk and the conversation, and Rose had given vent to emotional pressures probably best dissipated. There might have been further walks but for an unforeseen development. The authorities introduced new billeting arrangements. To avoid the long walk down to the town centre, to catch the official watch transport up the hill to the technical site, those of us billeted on the western outskirts of Swanage had taken to walking across country, in effect using the hypotenuse side of a right angled triangle. This had been quite pleasurable, affording plenty of fresh air, preparatory to being cooped up in our confined trailer for several hours, and giving excellent views of the English Channel, with occasional sightings of wild life, especially birds. In places we were crossing private land, and though we had never been challenged, a couple of farmers had submitted official complaints. The RAF met these in customary fashion. There was an obvious need to shorten the distance between technical site and living accommodation. On the steep slope that connected the High Street and the radar site were a number of small avenues, groves, and crescents. As the names infer, the houses were in the main quite large, and in some cases stately, and often had generous plots surrounding them. A number were requisitioned, including 'Woolloomoolloo' on a corner site, about equidistant from the High Street and the radar site. To this solidly built mansion I was moved, along with about a dozen others.

Everything about the property was solid, including the timber floors. To this I can testify since I slept on one on the first floor, in a bay windowed front room with extensive views. 'Bed and board' took on a new meaning. We ate in premises in the High Street, commandeered by the authorities, so I no longer had the pleasure of Rose's mother's good plain cooking to sustain me. Such was the steepness of the incline to be stumbled down, or toiled slowly up, that most of us gave breakfast a miss, settling for coffee and a scone an hour or so later, in a café adjacent to the mess. Over time, we gathered odds and ends of storage, but in the main we lived out of our kitbags. All in all, we were a good bunch and got on well together.

Having settled domestically, I was by now integrated into A.M.E.S. 9412. The watch system was the familiar four watch one, which is as good as it gets. Regular watch teams were soon established, with two or three operators, and at least one, preferably two mechanics. From the outset, we always had two of the latter, Jack Home and myself. As long as 9412 was in operation, Jack and I were inseparable. He was a Canadian from the Peace River territory of British Columbia, tallish, very slim, laconic in speech, laid back in manner, and a well-trusted friend and companion. A schoolmaster by profession, he had married just prior to being posted overseas. He was a few years my senior.

'Oboe' or '9K' as it was sometimes called, was a sophisticated radar system designed to spearhead specifically targeted bombing raids on enemy installations. Its operation entailed two radar stations working in tandem, many miles apart from each other. From the day after my arrival, I had been involved in operations twinned with another station on the east coast.

This unit was known as the Cat. We were the Mouse. For a specific operation the roles could be interchanged. The Cat worked with the aircraft pilot, the Mouse with the same plane's navigator cum bomb aimer. The aircraft used were Mosquitos, flown by pilots dubbed Pathfinders. Pathfinder piloting was a highly developed skill, on which the success or failure of a bombing expedition was primarily dependent. Simply put, the pilot had to fly unerringly along an invisible beam, identifiable through sounds in his earphones. That beam, transmitted by the Cat station, ran directly through the target area. If the pilot successfully located the beam, and flew unerringly along it, the first stage of guaranteed accuracy could be met. In training, the pilot learned to lock on to the beam, which for explanatory purposes can be likened to the white line in the middle of a road. If he began to deviate to either side, he received appropriate indications in Morse code. a series of dots for one side, a series of dashes for the other. Deviations of over five miles were indicated by repetitive A's in Morse, over ten miles by B's, over fifteen miles by C's.

At Tilly Whim, we built into our equipment a replica of that available to the pilot, so that we could follow his progress, even when we were not working directly with him. It was reassuring to track a crack pilot in action. His system switched on, you would hear him locate the beam, and then the continuous whine would start, and continue as long as he stayed on course. An initial deviation changed the whine to 'dit dit dit dit dit' and he would make the correction and a return to the whine. If he over corrected he heard ' dah dah dah dah dah' and swung back to the continuous whine again, after which he stayed there. After an experienced pilot had switched on to the beam, all we would hear was a couple of minutes of weaving from side to side, and then absolute perfection, as if the beam were visible to him in the sky.

The Mouse station's partnership with the navigator cum bomb aimer was the second essential requisite to guaranteed specific target accuracy. Before any raid, all the relevant data was fed into a computer (a huge mechanically driven monster). Airspeed, ground speed, height at time of bomb release, wind speed and direction, weight of bomb load, parabola of bomb trajectory etc. were all fed in. With the continuous whine in his headphones, the pilot was taking his navigator dead over the target. Twelve minutes from target, the latter received Morse D's, at nine minutes C's, at five minutes B's, at two minutes A's. The computer took over, clanking its way through the data. At precisely the second it cut off, the navigator pressed his bomb release button. Had everybody done his job efficiently, and had all components worked as programmed, fifteen yards accuracy was guaranteed whatever the weather conditions. There was no need for visual sighting of the target. If the pilot ignored anti aircraft fire and enemy fighter planes, and stuck to that beam, and the navigator co-operated, the chosen target would be hit.

The Pathfinder Mosquitos were used primarily to identify the target area for Lancasters following in their wake. Equipped with magnesium flares, which they dropped dead centre of target, they lit up the night sky sufficiently to enable a thousand heavily laden Lancasters to unload their cargoes, peel away, and head for home. The occasional use of a Pathfinder led to successful raids such as that in which a senior officer was air lifted from prison, after the wall had been breached by low flying precision bombing, and co-ordinated seaborne Commandos moved in to escort the escapee to a waiting ship and freedom. A single Pathfinder was also used in diversionary tactics. A major raid having been planned for one area, a Mosquito would be despatched to another, perhaps two hundred miles away, to unload thousands of aluminium strips, which showed up on enemy radar screens as a concentrated marauding attack force. Thus were German fighters diverted from the actual scene of attack.

From the beginning of April, we were engaged with sister stations in softening up German coastal defences and industrial areas vital to their war effort. We realised at the time that we were playing a vital role in the build up to D-day, when Allied forces would attempt to secure a foothold once again on a Europe from which we had been banished at Dunkirk.

Setting up the equipment for a huge bombing raid was time consuming and, in the cramped conditions in the radar trailer, could be claustrophobic. Heat built up. The atmosphere became soporific, and energy levels, over a period of long days, and even longer nights, often fell dramatically. The regime was particularly hard on the WAAF operators, with relentless stints of duty, concentrating on mesmeric cathode ray tubes.

As with CHL, the defensive systems of Crustan and Rodel, the offensive 'Oboe' technology had two screens. On the left was one with a horizontal time base, calibrated in miles up to 250 – 300. On the right was another horizontal time base in light green. In the mid point of this was a bright highlighted section in two parts, with a slight gap between them. The two highlighted parts represented four millionths of a second. The gap between was one millionth.

In the course of a raid, the Mosquitos would be known to be well on their way to the target area. Each had a specific call sign, e.g. KP (King Peter). At the prearranged time, the Cat station would manually transmit in Morse KP—KP---KP on the agreed frequency. The pilot would switch on his radar. A downward blip would appear on our left hand screen timebase, indicating the distance between us and the plane. Simultaneously, the central section on the right hand time base would appear, with a downward blip straddling the one millionth of a second gap, confirming that the aircraft was on the beam. There was always a couple of minutes in which the blip moved either one way or the other, after which it resumed the desired position, and we knew we were watching an expert at work. What we did not know were the conditions in which the pilot was operating. We were snug and safe. His crew would almost certainly be under heavy fire, and possibly fighter plane attack. Yet, the blip never wavered. If it suddenly disappeared, we could infer either that the plane's radar equipment had failed, or that the aircraft had been hit and was in trouble, or both.

It was the tension that built up in the trailer during operations that cumulatively drained the operators. One instance will suffice. We had a tiny girl from Middlesbrough, who turned the scales at barely seven stones, but was possessed of tremendous mental and nervous stamina. After a series of night watches she was like a zombie, and at 2 am we suggested she retired to the rest trailer for a nap. Reluctantly, she acceded, asking to be awakened to resume duties at 3 am. She was still asleep at 8 am when the watch ended. We carried her gently on to the transport taking us all back to our billets. She was still asleep. We arrived at the WAAF hostel, carried her up the path, and stretched her out gently on the front lawn, slumbering on. We rang the door bell. A WAAF came to the door. "Good morning," we greeted her. "We've brought Becky home. Do you mind if we lay her on your front room settee?" Permission granted, we lifted her once again, and ever so gently arranged her on a very comfortable couch. "When she comes to, tell her we all love her to bits," I said, "She's our own Sleeping Beauty. We all kissed her in turn but she wasn't roused by any of us." She was back on duty for the next watch, as fresh as a daisy. "Did you really?" she asked, "Did you really all kiss me?" "Poetic licence, Becky," someone said. "But we will now," chimed in somebody else, "if you feel you've missed out." "Cheeky buggers," said Becky, then "My mum's never going to believe this." In times when the glory tended to go to the more glamorous roles, the contributions of the Becky's of the back room brigade must never be understated or forgotten.

Not all WAAF radar operators had Becky's impeccable attitudes and dedication to duty. At the other end of the league table was Bunty, a sumptuously dark haired, well formed, big busted girl with a cut glass accent. Her vowels were impeccable, her consonants clipped. Her pedigree was apparently beyond doubt. Bunty's interest in and commitment to the integrated team work essential to the efficiency of a mobile radar station was minimal. She was on the make, intent on annexing a meal ticket for life. Her hunting ground was the officers' mess. She was not beyond a spot of blatant flirting on watch, and was in full cry one evening while everyone else was fully engaged preparing to launch yet another important strike on enemy territory. Not as yet having succeeded in catching anybody's eye, she perched herself on the work bench, hitched up her skirt revealing shapely legs, placed both hands flat on the surface beside and behind her curvaceous bottom, and thrust her well formed breasts forward till they were straining her shirt buttons. Straining even further back, the heel of one hand came to rest on an electric soldering iron, only recently in use. Her instant reaction drew immediate attention. "Ow! f-----g hell," she yelled, in an accent far from cut glass, and jack knifed convulsively into an ungainly, spreadeagled heap on the floor. Someone commented in exasperation, "For God's sake make yourself useful. Make us a cuppa tea." Bunty gathered her composure and made for the kettle. Five minutes later a brew was ready. Gratefully, we reached for our mugs, took a swig, and spat it out. "What the hell have you done now?" asked one angry voice. "She's only put a full week's ration into the bloody pot in one go," groaned another. "Quarter pound of bloody tea, four mugs, can you bloody believe it?" Bunty had never made a pot of tea in her life. In the RAF you were guaranteed to meet a cross section of the social strata. Not all of them were what they seemed.

On two other occasions Becky displayed another side of her character that further endeared her to the watch. It was a sunny afternoon and we were making modifications to the radar equipment. Jack and I needed to concentrate and Becky chatted incessantly as was her wont. "Shut up, Becky, there's a good girl," I said. "We've a ticklish job on here." She took not a blind bit of notice. "Can't you do anything with her?" Jack asked, rhetorically. Becky cast me a quizzical look. Then she resumed her idle chatter "One more word out of you," I threatened, " and I lift the lid of the seat you're on and put you in the locker underneath." Game on. Becky started up again. "Right Jack," I said, "that's it. Give me a hand will you." Together, we lifted her off the locker seat, opened the locker, stowed her inside, dropped the lid, and got on with our work. I'll swear we'd almost forgotten her when there was a knocking noise from inside the locker. Hastily I lifted the lid. Becky's impish little face appeared. "Any chance of a cup of tea?" she asked, angelically—"two sugars." She got her tea, and drank it, seated comfortably in one of the operator's chairs. You couldn't be angry with Becky for long.

The other episode was not dissimilar. Again, we were on a tight schedule. Again, she was nattering. After a series of warnings, we threatened to take her outside, wrap her in camouflage netting, and tent peg her to the ground in the long grass. I think the idea appealed to her. She didn't shut up, and we did what we had promised. She'd been there a few minutes when Jack said, "Oh my God, the C.O.'s coming down the path. If Becky makes the slightest sound, we'll have some explaining to do." The old man kept us talking for the best part of five minutes, with a captive Becky but a few feet away. At last he departed, and we pulled out the tent pegs, and disentangled the camouflage netting. Becky gave us a wicked little giggle and said, "I bet you two were close to shitting yourselves just now." "Too right," said Jack, feelingly. "Join the club," observed Becky. "I'm off. I'm bursting for a pee."

As with most radar stations, Tilly Whim had a proportion of overseas people, with Canadians being particularly well represented. One such was Sgt. Jack Munro, our radar mechanic overseer. Big built, bluff in manner, open, honest, and always on the look out for new experiences, Jack was fascinated by the beach and the rolling sea beyond. He'd been raised in Manitoba, where almost everything was different from Swanage. He would stand outside our trailer, taking in great draughts of the air coming in off the sea, and exclaim, "Gee fellas, just get a load of this in your lungs." One afternoon, he went off on his own along the cliff top. Finding a little ravine that led to the beach below, he arrived to see sand dunes dotted along the strand. Keen to explore, he clambered over the roll of barbed wire between him and them. A few yards along the wire was one of a series of notices, 'BEWARE. KEEP OUT. THIS AREA IS MINED.' Jumping off a dune on to the beach, he landed on a mine and was blown apart. Having formally identified the body, an experience embedded in my memory, I still find his loss, and particularly the manner of it, hard to accept.

A less harrowing memory of sand dunes, within the safety zone, is that of another senior NCO, whose name escapes me. He was a member of that group, found on any large site, committed to inflicting regular doses of retraining in their range of subjects. This man's line was automatic weapons, on this occasion the Browning machine rifle. Jack Home, myself and a couple of others were detailed to meet him, on the afternoon of a day off, to be instructed in the use of the weapon in beach landing conditions. Accordingly, we assembled in front of him among the dunes. He stripped the gun into its major components, wrapping each part carefully in protective material before stacking it. "Mustn't get sand in, lads," he cautioned, "Mustn't get sand in." He then got to the release of the buffer spring. "This is the tricky bit. Just watch me carefully. Unless you know what you're about, it's easy to lose the bloody thing." He pressed the block holding the spring hard into his midriff, and exerted pressure with his thumbs. "This is it lads," he puffed, growing redder under the strain. "Right, I've got the bugger." PING---something shot past us with a high pitched whine. "Christ," blasphemed the sergeant, "that's never happened before." "What do we do now if the enemy pops up from behind a sand dune?" asked an earnest seeker to the solution of a possible practical problem. Never short on initiative, Jack suggested, "Point what's left at him and shout 'Bang Bang. You're dead'." The hapless sergeant had a better idea. "Look lads, it can't have gone far. Find it and we'll call it a day." We retrieved it in about five minutes, pocketed it, and let him stew for half an hour before shouting triumphantly, "Found it, sergeant." The rest of the afternoon we spent in a café in the High Street relating the incident to anyone disposed to listen.

As night after night we conducted relentless bombing raids on targets just across the Channel and, on occasions far into the German hinterland, speculation increased as to when and where the Allied landing would occur. Free time was usually spent in a convivial café in the High Street, scanning the morning papers, listening to portable radios, and playing solo whist for modest stakes. We discovered the municipal tennis courts, which charged reduced rates for servicemen and women, and the watch as a whole relaxed with mixed doubles. Nobody was particularly good at the game, but it was healthy, enjoyable recreation.

Inevitably, in the restricted confines of the operations trailer, and in shared leisure activities on the tennis courts liaisons developed. Jack Home and one of the girls on our watch evinced signs of increasing mutual interest. To what extent it developed I know not. I had the impression that she was the front runner, with Jack prepared to go along on his own terms. It was now almost eight months since I had left Rodel, and Ann and I had kept in touch throughout. I was more assiduous than she, her letters being less frequent, but always warm and affectionate. No longer at Rodel, she was managing a large NAAFI in Stornoway, catering for a constantly changing transient clientele. I still knew where my heart lay. My head, as yet, had reached no definite conclusion.

Almost imperceptibly, D-day crept upon us. I had been on watch the previous evening, as raid after raid pounded the defensive shore batteries. D-day itself dawned fine and bright, and Jack Home and I were up and about early. The skies were full of aircraft, passing overhead in a constant stream, engine-powered and gliders, all in a one way system. We breakfasted, joined others in the usual café, and met up with watch members at the tennis courts. Everyone knows where they were on June 6th. 1944. I have to confess to almost non-stop tennis in Swanage, while momentous events were unfolding overhead, and, just across the Channel, thousands were risking their lives to establish a foothold in Europe.

As the day progressed the temperature rose, and it was uncharacteristically humid. Jack and I, both sweating profusely, stripped to the waist, tossing shirts and vests behind the baseline. At the end of the game, an attendant emerged from an adjoining building and requested us to put our shed garments back on. A local bye-law apparently regulated the dress code in force. Thus reprimanded, we donned vests and shirts and carried on playing. One of our WAAF partners mischievously suggested that she cast off her upper vestments to test the system to destruction, to which Jack quipped, "Wait till we get home."

The set over, I noticed a handkerchief waving from the other side of the expanded metal fence surrounding the playing area, and its owner beckoning me over. I went across. "What did you do that for?" I was greeted. "What did I do what for?" I asked. "Put your shirt and vest back on," came the reply. "Oh," I explained, "some bye-law apparently." My new found acquaintance exploded. "Look lad," he snorted, "Up there in those planes men are going perhaps to their deaths, and here in Swanage hundreds like yourself are fighting for freedom. That officious little bugger thinks a peaked cap entitles him to throw his weight about. Never allow yourself to be pushed around by the likes of him." He paused, then asked where I was living. "Woolloomoolloo," I told him. "Thought so," he said, "I've seen you around. I live just up the road. Fancy dropping in about four o'clock. I'll have a bite to eat laid on." After a moment's hesitation, I accepted. I had nothing to lose, and this man's attitude appealed to me.

I arrived in due course at what proved to be an intriguing location. The main, and possibly the only entrance, was via a very solid timber door set into a ten feet high brick wall that seemed to stretch forever. The security on the door itself was impressive, with multi-levered locks, a Yale, and heavy bolts at top, middle, and bottom. I pressed the bell button, but heard no sound, the bell itself probably being some distance away. Almost immediately however, there was the sound of footsteps, the door opened, and I was invited inside. The wall enclosed a large area, some hundred yards by fifty. In the middle was a fairly substantial timber building. Well laid out walkways linked plots of land under cultivation. With the owner, for such my new found acquaintance turned out to be, was a small cross bred terrier We proceeded along a walkway to the cabin and entered. Deceptively spacious, it was divided into three functional areas: living and dining room, kitchen, and bedroom with separate bathroom and toilet beyond.

It was connected to the electric mains, and water was laid on. The immediate impression was of comfort, warmth, and relaxation. At my host's invitation, I took a seat. He sat opposite and lit his pipe. I declined the offer of a cigarette. "You've certainly got a nice place here," I said by way of an opening remark. "I'm glad you like it," he countered. "I've everything I need, and most of it is to hand." He swept an arm around the room. "Good library, eclectic music collection, radio, and Rex here." At mention of his name, the dog barked, head on one side, and wagged his tail. "Rex is my paper boy, and runs other errands as you will see, all in good time. Meanwhile, feel free to look round while I put the kettle on." So saying, he went into the kitchen. His library was extensive and contained nothing lightweight. Shelves from floor to ceiling were crammed with volumes, all neatly sectioned and labelled, according to subject classification. It was as though I had stumbled into a high class second hand bookshop in a university city. The music was equally impressive, mostly classical, but covering a broad spectrum. This was the home of a seemingly well educated man. He returned with a tray, and set out plates of what appeared to be home baking, and a larger than usual pot of tea. "I love my tea," he said, as if in need of explanation. "Now, would you like to hear how I acquired this place?" he asked. I said I most certainly would. "It's a longish story," he warned, "Just stop me when you've had enough. I don't want to bore you." With that he started.

"I've had two major upheavals in my life. The first was being forced out of civilian life into the army, the second being turned out of the army back into Civvy Street. The second was worse than the first. I was born into a pit village in County Durham, and all around me, at eighteen, men were being conscripted into the county's Light Infantry regiment. I didn't fancy that, and started looking for alternatives. Some of the Scottish Highland big names had vacancies, and I managed to persuade one of them to take me on. As you can see, I am not all that tall but, as the recruiting sergeant said, you don't need to be tall to play the bagpipes, as long as you have a good pair of lungs. They kitted me out, and I soon became proficient on the pipes.

We were drafted overseas, and I went into battle at the head of the lads, spurring them on with the skirl of the pipes. I had a charmed life. Men fell all around me. It seemed I was invisible, possibly invincible as well. I felt like the old Roman Legion standard bearer. If he was hit, somebody was always there to take over. With me, if I'd copped it, no other bugger knew how to play, so they did their best to protect me. Anyway, I came through right to the end of the war, and they demobbed me. Times were hard then, with few jobs, and I had no trade to fall back on. Talk about a land fit for heroes. I had a little money put by, and my army bounty, but that wouldn't last long. I'd soon be on the streets. I put my thinking cap on. There was only one thing I could do well, and that was play the bagpipes. Why not take them on the streets?

I bought a second hand set of pipes, and the finest Highland regalia my money would stretch to, and started busking. I used to do the London theatre queues during the winter, and the major seaside holiday resorts during the summer. Because I was impeccably turned out, and could play the pipes really well, people didn't put pennies in my box, but silver—'tiddlers', sixpences, shillings, florins. I even got the odd half crown. I lived in digs all over the place, had only minor expenses, opened a bank account, and over the years had a tidy bit put by. When it looked as though this second war was on the cards, I decided it was time to settle down, so here I am."

"You say you've performed in all the major holiday resorts," I mused "Why did you settle in Swanage, rather than any of the others?" He held a forefinger up the side of his nose, winked conspiratorially, and replied, "I always got bigger takings here than anywhere else. I still do a summer season on the prom, along with Rex here. I think he's a bigger draw than I am. The kids love him. As you can see, I've got this place sorted. Very private. Do my own thing. No sweat." "I notice you grow a lot of your own produce," I remarked. "Ay," he grinned, "and I've got a live-in gardener." So saying, he rose to his feet, as did Rex immediately. Both went outside and I followed. "Here boy," said my host, standing at the end of a row of potatoes, and putting a wicker basket on the ground. "Fetch," he ordered, and Rex began digging furiously, forepaws throwing soil between his back legs. As each potato was unearthed, the dog took it in his mouth and dropped it in the basket. When sufficient had been harvested, Rex took the wicker handle in his mouth and, tail wagging, carried the basket to the kitchen. "He collects the newspaper every morning," said Rex's master, fondling the dog's ear. "You can see him if you're in Churchill's just after 9am. I let him out, he scampers down the hill, round the corner and into the shop. They put a folded 'Telegraph' in his mouth and he brings it home."

"That is a most remarkable story," I said, "Thank you for telling it. I'll remember it as an object lesson for when my time comes to be demobbed." "Always remember son," he advised, "never be pushed around by others. Be your own man. Make your own way." "I take it you never married," I ventured. There were no photographs on display, and the place, though neat and tidy, bore no evidence of a woman's hand. "No, never married," he answered. "There was someone, a long time ago. Couldn't ask her to share my itinerant life style. By the time I'd settled down, it was too late. Mind you, in the winter I do a shift in the Coastguard's Station. There's a nice little widow lives next door. I might think of asking her to move in, but Rex here would probably object. Rather have my dog on the whole." I visited this engaging personality several times over the next few weeks, and recall him with respect and affection. It is a privilege to have known him.

The week or two following D-day were very tense as the Falaise gap continued to be held, but a breakthrough out of it remained unachieved. We read the morning papers assiduously, anxious for any sign of progress. Then the news broke. A three-pronged assault had seen Allied tanks making for the Brittany coast to the west, Paris to the south, and Germany itself to the east. We were a mobile unit in a static situation. We had played our part in the assault so far. When it was apposite, we would move across the Channel, truly mobile, to continue the attack.

Around mid July, three-ton Bedford trucks and a few Matadors appeared on site, and anticipation turned to excitement. Trucks and Matadors were allocated to the four A.M.E.S. units, and drivers were nominated to them. Neither Jack nor I drove, but shared the delight of those who did, and were engaged in painting and camouflaging their vehicles, all of which had to be fully waterproofed, a process in which all lent a hand. The WAAF operators were not expecting to be posted overseas, and one or two sad partings were foreseen. Drivers took to naming their vehicles after girl friends. One that comes to mind was registering the driver's frustration at not having persuaded a WAAF on whom he was sweet to develop the relationship to his full satisfaction. His three-ton Bedford bore the name 'Ice Cold Kate'

For some weeks, there had been no leaves granted, on account of the run up to D-day. Now people were being granted fourteen days in quite large numbers, as if in preparation for a new phase. My turn came at the end of August. I gave a passing thought to taking it in Stornoway, but hadn't time to arrange accommodation. As it turned out, it was just as well. I'd been home three days when a telegram arrived recalling me to Swanage. The A.M.E.S. mobile unit 9412 was going overseas.

On reaching Swanage, I made straight for Woolloomalloo, to find it deserted. Propped up against the wall of my bedroom was my kit bag, thoughtfully packed in readiness. I slung it over my shoulder and, for the last time, descended that steep slope to the High Street. At the orderly room, I was told that the unit had been transferred to a large tented camp site at Worth Matravers, a few miles up the coast. Transport would take me there. En route, large areas were occupied by troops, mostly American, and it was in such an encampment that I rejoined my watch mates. Jack had insisted that a place be reserved in his tent for me. Predictably, his greeting was, "Had a good leave, partner?"

All was hustle and bustle, and the underlying excitement was tangible. The rest had all been re-vaccinated and inoculated over a period of a few days. In company with other late arrivals, I got the lot in one go. The process would have gladdened the heart of even the most zealous of time and motion experts. We formed a line, both hands resting on hips, and walked between two rows of medical orderlies, each armed with a fully charged hypodermic needle. I didn't count the number of injections, but it exceeded four. Reaching the end of the line, the hitherto bright blue sky began to darken, went into a spin, and was rapidly totally eclipsed. I came to on the lush grass on which I'd passed out, confronted by Jack's concerned face. He was holding his upturned forage cap in his right hand. "Excuse me sir," he greeted me, "Care to make a contribution to the Royal Society for Sick Airmen?"

We spent but two nights at Worth Matravers before being sent to RAF Cardington in Bedfordshire. On arrival, the place seemed enormous, with aircraft hangars all over the place. We were there for one night only, to pick up Bedford three tonners, specially prepared for cross Channel transport. Drivers had previously been delegated and notified. Shortly before lights out, a senior NCO entered our hut and asked, "Any mechanics among you lot?" One or two hands were raised. Mine was the nearest. "You'll do," he said, "follow me."

I found myself on hard tarmac in the rapidly waning twilight. "Ever driven before?" asked the sergeant. I told him I hadn't. "Right," he said "Just hop up there, and I'll get in the passenger seat." We were standing alongside a hulking great Bedford truck. Utterly bemused, I clambered up and occupied the driver's seat, which was about half way to heaven. The view was terrific. "Now," came the sergeant's voice, through the haze, which had temporarily taken over my brain, "This here is the gear box, and this here is the gear lever. You move the lever through an aitch like this." He demonstrated a few times. "Got it?" he queried. "Think of the letter H. This is how you select your range of speed. Forward left= first gear; Backward left= second gear. Forward again to halfway, bring her across to the other side of the H then Forward right= third gear, Backward right = fourth gear. Go on, have a go." I played for perhaps half a minute and got the hang of it. What the ranges of speed were he did not say, and I had no wish to complicate matters. "O.K. that's your hand controls taken care of," continued my instructor, "now for your feet."

He switched the interior lights on as if by magic. "Three controls," he explained, "from left to right, clutch, brake, accelerator. You press the clutch pedal down every time you want to change gear, the brake to slow down or stop completely, the accelerator to increase or decrease speed Get the feel of them and we'll do clutch and gear lever together." Quite quickly, I began to cotton on. "Excellent," he enthused. "I'll start her up. It's this button here." The engine roared into life and the structure began to throb. "Now, I'm just going to slip her into first," he said. "I want you to ease the pressure on the clutch gradually, and she'll begin to move forward." Beginner's luck. She began to glide forward. "Good," said the sergeant, "Let's move into second." We moved into second. The sergeant sat back. "Drive her round the hangar," said the sergeant, nonchalantly.

A Bedford is a heavy brute, quite easy to keep in a straight line. Turning her is another matter, and I had to haul the steering wheel pretty hard. I quickly discovered that you've got to start dragging the wheel back again to resume forward progress while turning through ninety degrees. It was a huge hangar. I don't know how long I took to circumnavigate it, but eventually we arrived. I managed not to stall. "O.K." said the sergeant, "let's get down." Back on terra firma, he began scribbling on a small rectangular buff coloured card. "There you are lad," he grinned. "Report 09-00 hrs. tomorrow morning. This little beauty's all yours." In my hand, I held an RAF licence to drive motor vehicles up to and including three tons. I did not sleep too well that night.

Into Europe

The following day I drove that Bedford in convoy, with servicemen in the rear, down to Gosport on the south coast. With one vehicle in front, and one behind, I concentrated on keeping equidistant. In the process I learned a lot about the use of the gear box rather than the brake. The technique of double declutching when changing down was postponed for another day. There was a driver's manual in the compartment and I carried that with me for days. The most important omission in my crash course had been my instructor's failure to point out, let alone practise, reversing procedures. I learned this the next day, when I was required to reverse up a ramp into the bowels of a Landing Tank Craft.

Having observed a few vehicles successfully complete the manoeuvre, I was in position, an officer with a flag in each hand in front of me to indicate appropriate corrections of the steering wheel, when a motor cycle despatch rider sped past on to the ramp. He skidded. His bike went into the water on one side, he on the other. There was a hiatus while they fished him out. The bike they left for later. By now I was not all that keen to continue. However, the ramp having been inspected and declared safe, I riveted my gaze on those two flags, heard the clank as the Bedford mounted the ramp, saw the flags urging me to go for it, put my foot down, and closed my eyes. There was a loud thump. I opened my eyes in the semi-darkness and braked. I'd made it. I was directed to a marked area where my vehicle was shackled at all four corners to iron hoops, in case the sea got rough. All around were similarly secured vehicles.

I sought the clean fresh air on the open deck, prepared to enjoy my first crossing of the English Channel. A corporal in charge of the ship's galley grabbed me, along with others, and we were soon peeling potatoes as the English coast receded and we were in the middle of an amazingly busy sea lane. For the record, that Cardington driving test is the only one I've ever taken. Since its issue, I've driven thousands of miles in a variety of vehicles without causing an accident.

It was mid afternoon as we entered the D-day landing area with its Mulberry harbour and floating roadways still visible and in use. Three months earlier, bitter fighting had secured the unopposed landing we now accomplished. By early evening, we were settling for the night on the outskirts of Caen, once but a name on the map, now a reality. Three events of note come to mind. Among the cocktail of inoculations recently injected was the first stage of a triple dosage. If I missed the second and third, it would be back to square one. I took the second at the back of the truck, the hypodermic being sterilised in a candle flame. The third I received a week later. The second event involved a change of uniform. RAF blue having been mistaken for German field grey, there had been a number of incidents of French freedom fighters firing at allied airmen, with several woundings and one or two deaths resulting. Accordingly, we handed in our uniforms in exchange for Army khaki battle dress. I was quite pleased with the fit and general condition of mine, except for one particular. On the tunic were three neatly stitched bullet holes. Somewhat poignantly, they were in the back, just above waist level. I found out that the former wearer had been a Canadian infantryman. Not a happy note on which to go to bed, which brings me to event number three. We slept on the ground under our trucks. I slept on my back.

Only our C.O., F.O. Armitage, was aware of our destination as we set off next day, our trailer hitched to a Matador, with Bedford three tonners and Fordson 15 cwt. vehicles completing the convoy. Since we were now truly mobile, we relied on iron rations for subsistence. These came in packs, one between several men. The food was adequate, bland, and monotonous. Until we arrived at wherever we were heading for, any opportunity to live off the land would be taken. The first place of note we reached was Rouen, birthplace of Gustave Flaubert, site of the burning of Jeanne d'Arc, and famous for the paintings of Claude Monet. Of greater significance to us, as we passed through, were market stalls selling fruit. Bunches of grapes were plentiful and cheap. Almost to a man we indulged. Here we discovered, for the first time, the purchasing power of cigarettes. I bought a half kilo of luscious green grapes. Most opted for the full kilo. We resumed our journey, popping grapes into our mouths like kids at a Christmas party. By the time we reached Amiens, bladders were bursting in every case, bowels in some. We stopped at a pissoir and became acquainted with French public sanitary provision. I needed a leak, and the relief afforded was worth the conditions the exercise imposed. Jack Home had to go the whole hog, and emerged in shocked disbelief. "Go inside and get a load of that," he groaned, "but don't bother feeling for the seat. There ain't one."

I investigated. One hole in the floor, a studded metal plate on either side for your feet, and two straining bars set into the walls. I decided there and then that a roadside halt, when next I felt the call of nature, would suffice for me.

At Arras, the birthplace of Robespierrre, the C.O. called a halt and we drew our vehicles into the kind of stockade formation used by the early American settlers opening up the west, as protection against marauding Indians. We attracted a lot of attention, children being especially curious. My Grammar School French had included an oral module, and I would have been prepared to practise it, had it not been for the presence in our group of David Stanley, a Scots graduate whose French was polished. I tagged along with him and learned a lot. A group of girls, aged about nine or ten, caught his eye and he beckoned them over.

"Comment vous appelez vous?" he asked each in turn. They gave their names. David was obviously drawn to a lovely, fair-haired youngster and squatted beside her. "Alors Helene," he said, "Est-ce que vous avez des freres?" Yes, she had three brothers. "Et quels ages ont-ils?" She gave their ages. He repeated the catechism for her sisters. There were two sisters. Dave produced a small diary and asked the names of all the siblings. He then sat on a nearby bench and invited Helene to sit beside him, which she did quite naturally, apparently completely at ease. Dave drew a little sketch of a flight of stairs. "Eh bien, ici l'escalier de votre famille," he smiled, printing the names and ages of all the children on the appropriate step. Taking the slip of paper, the entranced Helene thanked him, ran to the door of a nearby house, and disappeared. A few seconds later, she emerged with a stout lady, who watched as the child returned to David, and said that, if we had any soap, her mother would like to do our laundry. It would be ready very early in the morning. Four of us accepted the offer and, true to her word, beautifully laundered items were delivered on time. We rewarded the mother with toilet soap and Helene with bars of chocolate. Vive L'entente cordiale.

Into Europe – Travelling through the countryside.

Still unaware of our ultimate destination, we assembled the convoy and proceeded further east, passing through Douai and Valenciennes, the centre of exquisite French lace production. Travelling through this countryside, I was aware that, over the centuries, many invaders had traversed our route in both directions, leaving a legacy of racial, religious, and cultural tensions in their wake. What was to us a great adventure was but a blip on recorded history. By mid afternoon we had arrived at Mons, and again the C.O. called a halt. Wagons once more drawn up into a defensive formation, and sentries posted, those of us with free time wandered round the main square. The townsfolk were wary. Not so very long ago, German troops had swaggered about these streets, and had done so for a number of years, rendering their presence familiar. Our uniforms were strange, and possibly threatening. We were the first RAF unit they had encountered.

Around the square was a scattering of estaminets, each emitting its own musical invitation to step inside A group of about six of us approached one such and entered.

It was attractively set out with small tables and matching chairs, subdued lighting to create a relaxed ambience, a small bar with a good selection of drinks, and an angular, sharp eyed custodian behind it. Those eyes swept across our group, with the appraising assessment of years of experience. She selected Johnny White, the only senior NCO, and trilled, "Bon soir, mon sergeant. Qu'est ce que je vous faire?" Johnny looked blank. I translated. "She wants to know what she can do for you." "Not a lot," was Johnny's reaction "Tell her I'll have a beer instead." "Bier pour tous madame, s'il vous plait." I requested. We drank them standing at the bar. Accustomed as we were to our national brew, the local tipple did not go down too well. The old girl kept the conversation going as landladies do when trade is slack, asking questions I noticed rather than making comments. She had a surprisingly good command of English, though the accent was mangled. From time to time, locals came in and sat at the tables, from which snatches of animated French drifted across to us. Occasionally, a customer, having finished his drink, would approach the bar, pass through the gap created when the barmaid raised a hinged flap, pull aside some curtains beyond and disappear. I suppose we spent an hour and a half there, before deciding it was time for bed. Returning to the convoy, we all agreed it had been a pleasant break from routine. The following morning, notices were posted, listing amenities declared off limits, on account of the risk of contracting venereal diseases. Ours was on the list. We'd enjoyed an evening in a brothel. Sgt. Johnny took the news philosophically. "What can I do for you, indeed? She never told me what was behind that curtain."

Venereal disease was a constant threat to military efficiency, and every effort was made by the authorities to control it. Before embarking, we had attended lectures, depicting in the most graphic detail the ravages of syphilis, gonorrhoea, and associate forms. Free advice was available on how not to contract it, what to do if you'd put yourself at risk, and where to go when you realised you had it. In some continental towns, public charts recorded the daily statistics of the numbers being treated. It was reckoned that one brothel could have a greater sustained impact on troops' fitness for action than a unit of enemy soldiers.

We stayed another night in Mons. Jack and I had no need to seek alternative drinking quarters, since we were on guard duty from dusk till dawn. This entailed patrolling the perimeter of the convoy formation, ever alert for anything suspicious. To make matters a little more irksome, a light drizzle, interspersed with short, heavy downpours, constantly reminded us that not everyone hated the Germans. Sabotage was ever a possibility. Such ideas, always in the back of the mind, concentrate when you are patrolling valuable equipment and your comrades in arms, at 2am.in conditions ideal for a surprise attack. Jack and I had reached a corner of the convoy for the umpteenth time when he pulled me to a halt. "What's up?" I whispered. "Ssh," he hissed, "Listen." I listened but detected nothing. "Listen," he hissed again. "Can't you hear it? Like an alarm clock." We both concentrated. Then I heard it, faint but discernible-tick, tock, tick, tock. We followed the sound till it became quite loud-TICK, TOCK, TICK, TOCK. We were standing by an inn on the corner. The sound seemed to be coming from part of the building in deep shadow. "What do you think?" asked Jack. "Time bomb?" I ventured. "Could be," agreed Jack. "Better notify the old man." I said. We got the C.O. out of bed, he woke a few others, and the proprietor of the inn was roused, and his premises searched. The 'time bomb' was eventually found. A leaking gutter under the roof was dripping rainwater into a puddle on the pavement, shrouded in darkness-tick, tock, tick, tock. "Thank you lads," said the C.O. "Better safe than sorry." We did not seek the innkeeper's opinion.

Pushing further east, we passed through Charleroi, a centre of coal, iron, and glass industries. Among previous visitors had been Napoleon, who had spent two days here before the Battle of Waterloo. We didn't linger, and were still unaware of our destination. On we drove to Namur in the valley of the Meuse, the site of numerous invasions and much destruction. I noticed that the countryside was beginning to change. As we approached La Roche, the scenery became more open and appealing. We were in terrain I associated with our operational conditions, and I sensed my new home was not far away. Truth to tell, we were all ready to settle down. Several days without properly cooked food was beginning to pall, though latterly our compact watch group had fared better than the others.

Jack Home, having been raised in British Columbia, in an area close to the source of the Peace River, had learned a thing or two about living on the move, Appropriating bits and pieces of discarded angle iron, old tin containers and the like, he had rigged up a portable stove. The technique was primitive but effective. Two metal containers were supported about two feet above ground level, one containing diesel oil, the other water. Very little of each was needed. The two liquids were fed down V shaped angle iron conduits to combine, above a source of heat. The combustible mixture was directed, by more lengths of angle iron, into an oven of mud and twigs that conserved the heat. Easy to erect and dismantle, and eminently portable, this primitive stove delivered hot iron rations every evening for over a week. It moved one of the party, a good trencher man who had missed his grub, to declare, "By God, Jack, if you weren't so damned ugly, I might even consider marrying you." Never lost for words, Jack riposted, "And if you were the last man on earth, apart from me, I'd let you starve to death."

Shortly after leaving La Roche my inclinations were confirmed. We had arrived at Baraque de Fraiture, the second highest point in Belgium, and on the crossroads between Liege to the north, Bastogne to the south, La Roche to the west, Vielsam to the east. It was the ideal site for us to resume our attacks on enemy targets. Welcome to the Ardennes.

The Ardennes

The C.O. gathered the technical staff around and opened the last of his sealed orders. "Within spitting distance is a high plateau with pine forest on three sides. I've the appropriate grid references here. I'll need half a dozen of you to accompany me. I know how diffident you are about volunteering, so I'll take (he read out a list including Jack and me). You'll all go in one of the Bedfords. I'll take a Fordson. We keep the Matador and trailer between us. Can't be too careful. I'll brief the others on the domestic arrangements. You'll join them later."

The entry to the site was over a log bridge, spanning a deceptively deep ditch, then up a gradual grass sloped incline that levelled out into a large plateau about half a mile from the road. The pine forest was about thirty yards distant. "We're looking for a wooden stake," said F.O. Armitage on dismounting, adding "over here if I'm not mistaken." Within a couple of minutes, the marker was found. "Splendid," said the old man. "Our transmitter goes smack on the nose where that stake is. Everything's been calibrated from that point. Tonight or tomorrow, we'll be in business again." It was an exciting moment. We had spent weeks directing raids calculated to prepare for the invasion of Europe, were now in Europe, and the German hinterland lay exposed before us. In Churchill's language, we had passed from 'the end of the beginning' to 'the beginning of the end'.

We set our equipment up to be available whenever instructions were received. With the arrival of the relief watch, we were driven, that late September evening, through a glorious section of the Ardennes, travelling south to the tiny village of Manhay, two or three miles up the road to Liege. The forest came almost to the roadside on both sides, and was resplendent in the autumnal glow. We turned off the road at the head of the village, through open gates, on to a gravelled approach. Ahead of us stood our domestic quarters.

It was a purpose built small to medium sized hotel, constructed in local stone. Attractive on the outside, it lived up to its promise inside. Spacious rooms, decently furnished, lounge and dining rooms at the front, kitchen and ground floor bedrooms at the back, created an initial impression of quiet satisfaction. We'd be alright here. The main sleeping arrangements were upstairs. Two major drawbacks emerged. One, there were no beds. Two, Jack and I had drawn the short straw. The lack of beds posed no problems: we'd been sleeping on bare boards for weeks. The short straw was the result of being the last to arrive. While we had been engaged on the technical site, the others had exercised first choice of accommodation. We had been left with a little room directly over the entrance porch. It would be colder and noisier than the others. It proved to be very comfortable, nevertheless.

The Ardennes – AMES 9412 Mobile Radar Unit.

The building as a whole was extremely warm, with central heating throughout, a luxury unknown to most of us. The cellar housed a wood burning stove, of capacity to serve the whole building. A powerful electric circular saw was provided to cut the adequate store of logs. The requisitioning of the hotel had included the appropriation of the owner's large stocks of logs piled up in the clearings in the forest just across the road. We were unlikely to want for fuel.

A new benefit was about to be disclosed. We were now in the American sector, with all that that implied. There were basic differences between the British and American systems of logistics. Under our dispensation, you kitted troops, goods, vehicles, and anything else going overseas, spending vast amounts of money and manpower keeping track of them. Hence our regular kit inspections. If you lost anything, you were accountable for it. The Americans sent overseas what was essential plus a great deal more, and simply wrote it off. Neither time nor money was wasted on repetitive checks and needless accounting.

The rationing regimes also differed. Hitherto, we had been used to a daily ration of five cigarettes and a weekly bar of blended chocolate per man. Under the American PX system, Jack Home and I needed an extended army blanket to carry our joint weekly ration of cigarettes and chocolate. One man's allocation was a carton of 200 cigarettes a week, with a wide choice of brands, and any number of extra cartons at half a crown each. The chocolate ration was two dozen assorted bars, again with a wide choice of makes. In addition, all sorts of gadgets were available at discounted prices. It seemed obscene that we should be cocooned in such luxury, while our folks back home were restricted to the barest of rations.

The staple diet of three meals a day was equally lavish. One example will suffice. On my first visit to collect a week's rations from a depot in Bastogne, I presented my credentials to the G.I. sergeant in charge. "How many men ya got?" he demanded "Twenty eight," I replied. "Twenty eight," he muttered, consulting a printed sheet, then "Seven turkeys," he bawled. Everything else was in proportion and I returned to Manhay with a three ton Bedford fully laden. There was just one drawback which seriously diminished our delight amidst such bounty. We had a lousy cook. He could do little to reduce the appeal of canned goods, however, and I became a devotee, indeed almost an addict, of tinned fruit juices, peanut butter, jams, marmalades, and packaged cereals. The C.O. passed acid comment on the cook's uncanny ability to ruin almost anything he committed to the oven. "We get seven turkeys, which is bounty indeed. He abuses six of them beyond man's capacity to digest, and we have to fight for the one that's left. Even the bloody birds turn up their beaks at the six we throw out."

Settled in one place for the foreseeable future, I wrote to Ann, letting her know the sequence of events since last I had written from Swanage. It was by now just over a year since we had been parted, and the absence had only served to confirm my feelings. More than ever, she was the woman with whom I wished to spend my life. I could not, as yet, offer any prospect of the future, but I wanted to tell her that I loved her, and would always do so. Aware that, in the interim, she too had moved on, and may have found someone else, I wanted to keep the friendship we had known at Rodel alive and meaningful. Whether the feeling had ripened into love on her part, she had yet to say. The reply came rather more quickly than usual, and I remember the circumstances of its delivery with vivid clarity.

Normally, the post was laid out on the dining room table. It was always a time of mixed emotions. Men with letters to read would find a quiet place, those without expressing their disappointment in their individual ways. On this occasion, the C.O. was visiting the technical site while my watch was on duty, and brought our mail with him. There was something for all of us, which was good. Had any of us been left out, it would have heightened the sense of disappointment. Mine bore a Stornoway postmark. It was an unusually long letter, the gist of which was that I was in her thoughts and prayers constantly, that she had treasured memories of our time together, that there was nobody else, and that she hoped we could meet on my next leave. For the first time, I dared to hope that my dreams would eventually become reality.

The Scots charmer of young Helene with 'l'escalier de votre famille' had struck up a close friendship with a colleague of a much different approach. Bob Bolsover was a bluff, florid faced hulk of a man, lacking in the social graces, and quick to call a spade a spade. In civilian life, he had been a salesman for a large engineering company. David Stanley was an academic. An unlikely pair at first sight, it was soon apparent that, when fused, their joint attributes could achieve far more than either could alone. This was specially so in mixed company, when the one could open avenues normally barred to the other, allowing entry to both. They were drinking in a hostelry nearby, and David was conversing as eloquently as ever, when he was introduced by the landlord to the local lord of the manor. Talk turned to matters literary, artistic, and musical, and a warm invitation was issued to visit the baronial hall for an evening. David introduced Bob, and the invitation was extended to include him. What ensued was revealing.

Over the next few weeks, the pair were regular dinner guests, and were treated to the delights of a magnificent library, displays of priceless art, particularly the works of Watteau, and pianoforte playing by the lady of the house to almost professional standards. Choice wines flowed freely. All this of course was David's natural habitat. Yet it was Bob who regaled us all with detailed accounts of each evening's entertainment, and did so with enthusiasm and pride. David just sat back beaming.

Observing these two was to see a natural born teacher, and an originally unpromising pupil, prosper to their mutual delight. By natural instinct, Bob Bolsover was a philistine, an enemy of the privileged classes, a beer swiller rather than a connoisseur of fine wines, a dancer to any of the modern big bands as opposed to a devotee of classical music, a man who dressed down for dinner at midday, as against dressing up for dinner in the evening, a revolutionary not an aristocrat. In a short crash course of a few weeks, David Stanley had proselytised him. I shall cherish the memory of this as what the essence of teaching is all about, finding potential, creating a favourable environment, and lighting the spark that sends the pupil into orbit.

Among the Manhay contingent, a number of interesting personalities began to emerge, some of whom would be but temporary acquisitions, a few destined for more extended tenures. Ray Durness had only recently joined our watch, and had been readily assimilated. About five feet eight inches tall, he was broad for his height, sandy haired bordering on ginger, had intense candid blue eyes, and was Gloucestershire born, with a slight burr in the voice to go with it. His most pronounced attribute was his walk. As he moved along, the height of the top of his head maintained an unvarying distance from the ground. From any angle, no rise or fall of the head, or indeed its movement in any direction, was discernible. He was a drill sergeant's dream. Companionable, dependable, utterly trustworthy, Ray was a good man to have alongside. We got on well and we'll meet him again.

A late arrival had been Sgt. Barnes, a hustler with a chequered history. Born in the east end of London, he'd come up the hard way, and had been a press photographer for one of the national dailies before being called up. Shy and reserved he was not. Within hours of arriving, he had taken over the ration run. At a stroke, the seven turkeys for twenty eight men became fourteen turkeys for twenty eight men. He delivered seven as usual. The other seven, along with the rest of the rations provided pro rata, were disposed of on the return journey. Barnes' ration run occupied the whole day, with deals struck in every village and farm en route. His trade in cigarettes was huge. He eventually expanded his activities in collaboration with like minded Americans, organising rackets on a massive scale. There had always been petty pilfering, but Barnes and his accomplices exploited what they perceived to be ideal conditions for organised crime.

As we have seen, once American stores went overseas they were written off. That was the supply side of the opportunity. All around, was civilian population vulnerable to the black market. That was the demand side. The wide boys bridged the gap. At first, the odd truck was emptied. Then the next truck was stolen, both it and its contents being sold on, in whole or in parts. An isolated train wagon would be looted. On one occasion, a whole train was annexed in a Calais siding, driven a few miles into the Normandy countryside, and disposed of under cover of darkness. One thing Barnes was not was discreet. It was not easy to assess where he stood in the Mafia like hierarchy, but I have no reason to doubt the substance of the rumour that, many months after our ways had parted, he bought a large hotel in Mons, paying for it with a huge consignment of cigarettes.

Meanwhile, the assault on German strategic targets continued relentlessly. Nightly, towns, cities, and industrial areas were pounded, in what became routine to us. Four people sitting in a small trailer, co-operating with another quartet, perhaps a hundred miles away in another, were leading a few Pathfinder planes to open up destruction on a hitherto unprecedented scale by hundreds of Lancaster bombers, in which undoubtedly defenceless civilians became casualties. It was a depersonalised process, in which we, the perpetrators, were distanced from the consequences. As soon as the ritual had been completed, we tucked into our American rations, smoked our American cigarettes, and toasted the Pathfinder and Lancaster crews, 'God speed and a safe flight home'. The following night another watch would repeat the process.

What we did not realise at the time was the time scale in which we were operating. Germany, and particularly Hitler, was not finished yet. They still had aspirations for the future, based on technologies fast approaching operational access. We began to become acquainted with one of these. While on watch one night, we heard the sound of an aircraft engine flying very low, and apparently in trouble. The throb of the engine was spasmodic and faltering. We dashed outside. Just passing overhead, about a hundred feet above us, was an apparently wingless device with flames belching from its rear. We watched it out of sight in a direction that took it directly over Manhay. Several minutes later, we heard a loud explosion, and the sky lit up. "That's a bit close for comfort," exclaimed someone. "Better ring the domestic site," suggested somebody else. We did. All was well there. The target had been Liege, and apparently the objective had been hit. The ensuing conversation was both revealing and alarming. What we had witnessed was a German 'doodle bug', a pilotless bomb, calculated to just clear Baraque de Fraiture, the highest point between launching site and target, and timed for the engine to cut out over Liege. Supposing German intelligence was to learn of the precise position of AMES 9412, we could be taken out at a stroke.

Night after night thereafter, 'doodle bugs' enlivened our watches, always passing directly overhead, never mercifully cutting out.

With V2 rocket launching pads being established, preparatory to attacks on Britain, the war was now at a crucial stage. The Fuhrer was meantime mounting his final gamble, that was to find us in the wrong place at the wrong time.

The nightly 'doodle bug' procession did not disrupt equanimity at the domestic refuge at Manhay, which was a few hundred feet below the height of the technical site. It was therefore a surprise, whilst participating in a game of solo whist one evening, to be disturbed by the sound of a low flying aircraft---very low flying. To a man, Jack Home, Ray Durness and I dashed out into the rear garden. What confronted us was both spectacular and hazardous. Flying but feet above the forest was a four engined Lancaster, markings plainly visible in the light of the flames belching from the rear of both wings, and licking their way towards the tail fin. Though on a level course, she was clearly doomed. In the few seconds of sighting, we saw no signs of crew still on board. We waited, convinced she was about to crash. I suppose it was about a couple of minutes later when an almighty explosion created shock waves, and the night sky was lit up by a massive conflagration. We went inside and waited. It was forty five minutes later when the call came through from the police station in Bomal, a tiny village, the best part of twenty miles away. They were entertaining a British airman. Would we care to pick him up?

Jack and I climbed into a Fordson and drove off into the night. Navigating on strange roads in the dark, without benefit of signposting is never easy. We considered our man was in safe custody, and that we could take our time. It was well after midnight when we arrived. The police had transferred their charge to a nearby hostelry, to which they directed us. It was well after closing time, and we had to hammer on the door to gain entry. Seated on a comfortable settee, a delightful pair of nubile young ladies one on either side, a glass of something in one hand, and with an array of opened bottles on the table in front of him, was a tousle haired Warrant Officer navigator in stockinged feet. "Good morning," I greeted him. "We've come to rescue you." "Bugger off," he replied, "Do I look as though I need rescuing?" He had a point, so we lingered and helped him with the drink. He didn't seem to need any help with the women. Eventually, we persuaded him to get into the Fordson, where he told us his story.

"We'd reached our targets and dropped our bombs, and were on our way home when we were picked up by one of their searchlights. It must have been radar controlled because in a matter of seconds we were spotlighted by several more. We knew what to expect, and it came, intense, concentrated very heavy ack ack. We didn't stand a chance. The skipper kept her flying but we all knew we'd never reach the Channel. I calculated that we'd come down in friendly territory, and the orders were given to bale out. I don't know what happened to the others. I came out with the captain still on board. He may have gone down with her. It had been like a furnace in there, even before we were hit, and I'd loosened the straps on my flying boots. My 'chute opened, pulling me back with a jerk, and my boots fell off. I drifted down into the trees, and the 'chute got tangled in the upper branches. I had to cut the strings, and dropped several feet to the ground. Luckily it was soft. I was busy dragging my "chute in when the locals arrived and, well the rest you know."

"Have you done many ops?" asked Jack. "Two more and that's my lot." replied the W.O. "I'm not keen mind you. Bloody war's nearly over. Almost bought it tonight. Don't be in too much of a hurry to get me back. They'll put me straight on the next mission, and I reckon I've done my whack. I've probably lost some good mates tonight." We took him back to Manhay, where the C.O. gave him a couple of days to recuperate before notifying the appropriate authorities. I often wonder what happened to him.

A salutary warning that we were at war came one evening when I was driving F.O. Armitage up to the technical site. The darkness as we left the hotel intensified as we entered the forest flanked main road, and headlights were essential, since the journey, though by now familiar, was a succession of twists and turns. Incidents had occurred of fallen trees creating an unforeseen hazard, and the possibility was ever present of deliberate sabotage. We were about half way there when a sharp burst of small arms fire broke the silence, and Armitage gave a sudden yelp of pain and surprise.

Instinctively, my foot went down hard on the accelerator, and we sped round the next bend. "Good God, I've been shot," exclaimed the C.O. "Only a flesh wound as far as I can tell. We'll get it checked on the site."

It was a minor wound in the upper left arm, and was dressed and bandaged in no time. "What do you suppose that was all about?" Armitage asked me. "Someone on his own," I ventured, "or on her own" I added. You never could tell. "We were travelling fast at the time, it was dark, so it was probably a hasty pot shot, rather than calculated marksmanship." The C.O. pondered for a while. "Why me?" he asked. "Why not you?" "Too dark to pick out a specific target," I replied. "It was an opportunist, spur of the moment attack." "Supposing you wanted to disable a vehicle, or capture it, which side would you attack from? ---the driver's side, surely," said Armitage "You're the lucky sod here. Think about it. Which sector are we in?" "American," I answered. "Exactly," said the C.O., "and that bastard thought he was attacking an American vehicle, and shot to disable the driver---on the left hand side." I whistled. "Thank God for right hand drive Fordsons," I said. "I think I owe you one, sir."

We were now into early December and the days were growing shorter, and noticeably colder. On the 8th. Jack Home, Ray Durness and I had a full day off and, the weather being glorious, decided to pack a few rations and explore the forest. One of the unit vehicles had a call to make on the far side of the section immediately in front of our hotel. We estimated that a walk from there back to base would be about a couple of miles. Accordingly, we were dropped off there.

Ray and I deferred to Jack as leader. After all, his background was far superior to ours where forests were concerned. As we left the road and crossed low scrubland, dotted with saplings, I noticed a woodman's cottage with blue wood smoke curling from its chimney pots, and a winter's supply of logs stacked nearby. We entered the forest proper. But a few strides found us beyond the reach of sunlight, the canopy being very dense. The air temperature dropped considerably. Progress was not straightforward. At every few yards, detours had to be taken, on account of obstacles. The air was pervaded by the musty aroma one finds in these conditions, and the silence was palpable. After a while, there was almost a sense that we were invading, and that watchful eyes were on us. None of us spoke much, each reacting to the situation in his own thoughts. After perhaps an hour, Ray ventured a suggestion, "Can't be far off now." "Yea, shouldn't be long, agreed Jack, laconically. "Never been among trees this dense," he continued. "Back home they're huge and more widely spread. You can usually glimpse the sun from time to time." I said nothing. By now I knew Jack well. I knew he was lost. He knew he was lost. Admitting it was another matter. Doggedly we plodded on in his wake.

Some twenty minutes later, the canopy began to let in a little light. Five minutes later, glimpses of sky broke through, still a bright blue. Quite suddenly, we emerged into scrubland, with saplings dotted about. Of our hotel there was no sign---just a woodcutter's cottage, with blue wood smoke spiralling from its chimney pots. "Oh no," I groaned in disbelief. Jack was more explicit. "Christ," he exclaimed, "we've come full bloody circle." "Put not your trust in Canadian backwoodsmen," was Ray's contribution. The day ended with a long walk round the forest to the hotel. The weather continued to be favourable, and we enjoyed the views. "Soon be Christmas, Jack," said Ray, as we sat down to tea. "I'm going to give you a compass."

Battle of The Bulge

A week to ten days later, on a Sunday, we travelled to a village a few miles up the road to Liege, for an afternoon and evening of mixed social activity. The C.O. had met one of the local dignitaries at some function and had agreed to play the local eleven at football. Tea, social, and dancing were to follow in the village hall. As it happened, we could muster quite a useful eleven. We'd never played together before, had done no training, but fancied our chances.

One of our three ton Bedfords dropped us off, arranging to return at full time with another contingent to swell the numbers for the dance. We saw the truck drive off, took to the field, and set to. By half time, in going that was heavy, we were struggling but holding our own. I remember having a vicious attack of cramp in my right calf. As we took a welcome break for oranges, the Bedford lumbered into sight, and we were hastily ordered to get changed and climb on board. No explanations were given, nor, as far as I could make out, were any apologies extended to our hosts. Three quarters of an hour later, we were back in Manhay.

On the gravelled approach, round the side, and at the rear of the hotel were American vehicles of various types and sizes. Inside the hotel, American voices were ubiquitous. It transpired that, despite increasing inclement weather, German Panzer divisions had launched a concerted and unexpected attack on that sector of the front defended by U.S. forces. In some places, a breakthrough had been achieved. What we now had in residence was the forerunner group that had been repelled, about twenty in all. I recall one particularly loud mouthed sergeant, who could have stepped straight out of the shooting lot of a Hollywood film, assuring everyone, "There ain't nothin' to worry your fat arses over. Our tanks are stuck in the snow, and if we can't move, as sure as hell the goddam Krauts can't."Thus emboldened, I decided on an early night, and was soon sound asleep on my floorboards.

It was still dark when I was aroused by a hand on my shoulder. It was F.O. Armitage. "Things are looking distinctly dicey," he said. "I want you, Home, Durness and a couple of others to get up to the technical site to supervise the watch on duty. Prepare for evacuation of the trailer, and the possible destruction of ancillary equipment. I'll keep in touch by telephone and advise you of developments. On your way and good luck." I dressed hurriedly and joined the others downstairs. We had to step over recumbent American bodies, occupying every available inch of floor space. There must have been in excess of sixty men. Outside, the area was crammed full of vehicles. I glanced at my watch. It was 3 am.

It being December, and approaching the shortest day, it was still dark, and would be for hours yet. To make matters worse, there was a damp, swirling mist at the Baraque de Fraiture crossroads, which thickened as we crossed the log bridge and drove up the slope to A.M.E.S. 9412. We began the task of preparing both Matador and trailer for withdrawal, hampered considerably by the conditions. About 6am we heard on a portable radio that the German advance was rapidly developing, and that American troops were everywhere in retreat. Shortly after dawn, we received positive orders from the C.O. We were to get our unit on to the road as soon as possible, and head west, with Mons as our objective.

The Matador was found to be low on water in the radiator, a problem solved by the use of drinking water we might well need, topped up with the bladder contents of the ten or so of us involved. We destroyed what we couldn't load on to the trailer, dismantled the aerial and smashed it beyond use. As it grew lighter, we could see a few yards ahead, but the mist deadened sounds from the road. We could tell, however, that traffic was continuous. Approaching the log bridge that gave access to the road, we received our last message from F.O. Armitage. German Panzers had overrun a sister A.M.E.S. unit at Vielsam, some ten to fifteen miles to the east. All personnel were presumed to have been cut off. We were to get our trailer on to the road at all costs.

We edged on to the log bridge and saw, for the first time, a long continuous flow heading west. There was no discernible break as we waited and waited. Nobody wanted the delay a Matador and trailer of our length would cause. It was when trucks with unused ammunition, Press jeeps, and vehicles with staff officers began to go by that we decided enough was enough. A Cockney sergeant radar operator and I took the initiative, stepping into the road as the Matador edged forward. Bit by bit, the traffic slowed, Matador and trailer swung into line, and we were on the way to freedom. Again, I consulted my watch. It was noon precisely. The Panzers arrived at 12-15. It was a close run thing.

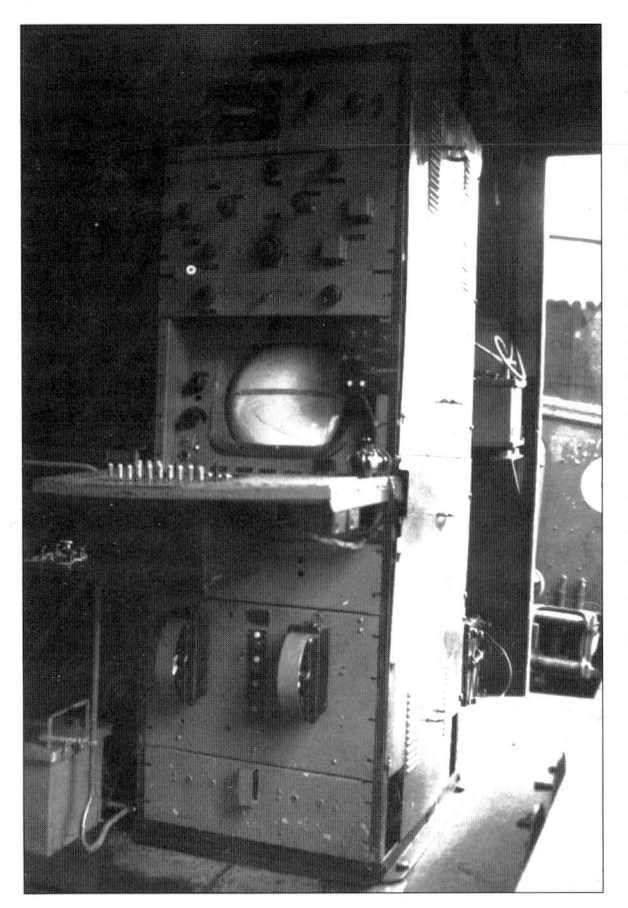

In the scramble to get the unit on to the road, Sgt. Frank Webster and I had had to use the trailer as transport, entering by its hinged rear door. As we increased the distance between ourselves and trouble, we decided to enjoy the scenery by sitting in the open doorway, our legs swinging freely, the door locked back in the open position. It was pleasant enough relaxation after a night of continuous and unlooked for tension. The road had long upward stretches, alternating with downward gradients. On the upward ones, the trailer moved at a walking pace. This encouraged Frank into a little gentle exercise, and he dropped to the road to stretch his legs. "If our lass could see me now, she'd laugh her bleeding head off," he chuckled. "Fancy walking when you can cadge a lift," she'd say. Unnoticed during this brief observation, we passed over the brow of a hill, and Matador and trailer began to pick up speed. Frank gave a yell from about five yards away, and began to run. I'm sure it was the longest five yards of his life. The combined weight of Matador and trailer is about seven tons, and once that starts rolling, the rate of acceleration is impressive. Not as noteworthy as that of Frank on this occasion. It took a supreme effort, and my outstretched arm, but he managed to make it, to collapse in a heap on the floor. If Frank Webster was subsequently subjected to nightmares, I'm certain this was one of them.

Battle of the Bulge – Radar scope in trailer.

We stopped that night, short of Mons, at an isolated farm where we were given a barn with plenty of straw for a bed. Next morning, we shaved in cold water from a stand pipe, and were grateful for the gift of eggs from the farmer's wife. By midday we were in Mons, and joined comrades who had escaped from Manhay. They had brought with them as much of our personal belongings as they could. By my bedspace had been a half-filled kit bag, which they had picked up in good faith. It contained nothing but dirty laundry. Among possessions left behind were several hundred cigarettes, and a large parcel of assorted toilet soaps, sent from home as an early Christmas present. I had what I stood up in, and would need an almost complete kitting out. About a week later, rekitting took place. They were unable to supply a cap badge, and issued a deficiency chit with the legend: Deficient—one cap badge. Reason---enemy action. In telling Jack this I chuckled, "I'll dine out on this for years, explaining that it was shot off by a sniper." Jack showed me his chit, which read: Deficient--- one pair of socks Reason---enemy action. "I'm going to tell the tale of a narrow escape from someone else's marital bed." he said.

At this point, a broader view of what became known as the Battle of the Bulge will place A.M.E.S. 9412's place in it. In September 1944, at the time of the unit's landing on the D-day beaches, Germany was clearly facing defeat. The Russians were advancing from the east, Allied bombing was devastating the interior, and their armies were making rapid inroads from the west. In that same month, Hitler convened a meeting, outlining his plans to initiate a drive on Antwerp, using the Ardennes as the approach. Here, he was probably guided by history, for it was this route that had been so successful for his rapid incursion into France in 1940. Geography was almost certainly another factor. Massive concentrations of tanks, troops, and supplies could be achieved in a highly densely forested location.

Battle of the Bulge – Night stop at isolated farm.

On Dec. 17th the day of our retreat from Baraque de Fraiture and Manhay, American Seventh Armoured Division troops confronted the German Sixth Panzer unit at St. Vith, which was about twenty miles due east of our site. This engagement slowed the German advance, which detoured to the north towards Malmedy, where American prisoners were taken, of whom eighty six were shot. Bastogne, from which we had drawn our rations while at Manhay, became the focus of both American and German aims, its strategic position being crucial. Had the Germans taken it, the progress of the Allies across Germany would have been slowed sufficiently enough to have given time for Hitler's development of his V2 rocket programme. The Americans dropped airborne troops to reinforce defences, but were rapidly surrounded by

German Panzers, and held under siege. On Dec 22 German officers paraded a flag of truce, and demanded American surrender which was rejected. Dependent on air drops for survival, the defenders of Bastogne were in dire straits during the period before and after Christmas, when severe weather halted air activity. They were eventually relieved by the arrival of General 'Blood and Guts' Patton's Third Army.

On Dec. 30 the Americans took the offensive in a two-pronged attack, calculated to corner the whole German force. Their Third Army pushed to the north, their First Army to the south, with the village of Houffalize their meeting point. On the midpoint between Bastogne and Manhay, it was but ten miles from the sites we had occupied. German resistance was dogged and determined. All involved were aware that crisis point had been reached. Hitler now played his last card.

On New Year's Day at eight o'clock in the morning, German fighter planes were deployed over Belgium, Holland, and N. France. Within two hours, they destroyed 206 Allied aircraft and seriously damaged many airfields. It was a Pyrrhic victory. 300 German planes and 253 fully trained pilots were lost. The gamble had failed. By Jan 16 the American Third and First Armies were united at Houffalize. On Jan 23 St. Vith was recaptured. The Battle of the Bulge was ended officially on Jan. 28.

The numbers involved reflect the supreme importance of the stakes fought for: 600,000 Germans, 500,000 Americans, 55,000 British. The casualties indicate the price paid: 81,000 Americans, of whom 19,000 were killed; 1400 British with a death roll of 200; 100,000 Germans either killed, wounded, or captured.

Most of the action had been concentrated in a circle round Bastogne, with Baraque de Fraiture and Manhay very much involved, as we were to discover when we returned, shortly after the fighting had ceased on Jan 28. Before we could do that, we needed to review our present situation, and ensure that our radar capabilities were in good order to resume activities. This essential business was done at Mons.

— Interlude in Mons —

The enforced stay in Mons created accommodation problems. Our radar unit was safe and available for operational service. It needed constant protection, and we had nowhere to sleep or eat. Temporary solutions to both problems were soon found. In the grounds of a castle on the outskirts, Chateau Jean de Bien, we erected four man tents, in which we spent the first few nights. The bitter weather that was preventing air drops to beleaguered Bastogne also affected Mons, and snow, biting winds, and temperatures at several degrees below freezing were testing conditions for campers. Groundsheets, and the clever folding of three army blankets, so as to create nine layers, and sleeping with six underneath and three on top, with the additional cover of a greatcoat, provided a remarkably cosy night's sleep. Getting up, washing and shaving were more irksome and testing.

Food needs were met courtesy of American 'K' packs, which were vastly superior to their British equivalent. There were three packs per day for breakfast, dinner, and tea. each fitting snugly into a field dressing pocket. Between them these three packets provided a balanced and palatable diet, were ingeniously prepared and packaged, and were most acceptable. I recall Jack Home, Ray Durness and me opening our first breakfast packs. Vitaminised biscuits, a tin of processed cheese, packet of cereal, powdered milk, tea bag, twist of sugar constituted the food and drink. Two tiny packs remained. Intrigued, we opened the first. Hey presto—a packet of half a dozen cigarettes and a book of matches. One pack to go. Ray was the first to get his opened. "I do not believe it," he screamed, hysterically, and held up a folded length of toilet paper. Jack and I, having discovered ours, Ray went on searching his now empty carton. "What are you looking for?" I asked him. He shook his head in mock disappointment. " Trust the Yanks not to complete a job," he said. "I was sure I'd find a collapsible latrine in here." The other two packs contained between them a hard chocolate bar it was advisable to suck rather than chew, a tin of bouillon, spam, sweet biscuits, and peanut butter. They kept us going pending return to normal catering.

Our trailer and mobile diesel engine were kept on site at Chateau Jean de Bien, so that we could keep them in good order, and checked daily. One extremely cold morning, we could not start the diesel, and discovered that, overnight, the water content had settled at the bottom of the tank and frozen solid, the oil floating above it. Using round tin containers, in which fifty cigarettes were usually supplied, we filled half a dozen with oil, placed a wick in each, arranged them at intervals along the fuel lines, lit them, opened up the drain cocks and waited. It was a good

Interlude in Mons – One extremely cold morning.

half hour before water began to drain out, and another ten minutes before we detected the smell of pure diesel. Only then were we able to start the engine and transmit power to the radar trailer. With practice and experience, it was possible to start a diesel on your own. A two handed grip on the handle, a few turns to build up momentum, release the handle, skip round to the side, kick in the compression bar, and nine times out of ten she would fire. On this particular morning, it took four of us, with a rope wrapped round the handle, one man at each end of the rope on either side, the third with a conventional grip on the handle, and the fourth to kick in the compression bar. If nothing else, it warmed us up.

In the course of this operation, an explosion on the far side of the castle grounds attracted attention, and two of the radar operators went to investigate. A ten year old local lad had picked up a grenade lying in the long grass, and had been playing with it when it detonated, blowing off his right hand. An ambulance picked him up. You don't have to wear a uniform to become a war casualty.

Interlude in Mons – Mons in the snow.

One Sunday morning, not having any special commitments, Jack and I decided to walk the half mile or so from the castle grounds to the town centre. There were several inches of snow on the ground, and the air was crisp and invigorating. We were wandering aimlessly around the main square, just filling in the time, when a large, executive type limousine purred up and came to a halt alongside. A massively built, very fair man got out and approached us. "Who are you," he demanded in good English with barely a trace of an accent. I answered in French, "Je suis Anglais et mon ami est Canadien Nous sommes Royal Air Force." His face lit up, and placing a brawny arm round each of us, he bawled across the square, "Ils sont Royal Air Force." To our surprise, a ripple of applause greeted his remarks. "You must come with me," he said "We must celebrate." So saying, he led us into a bar. "What will you drink?" he asked. I glanced at Jack who mouthed 'beer'. "Une biere monsieur, merci bien," I answered. Our newfound companion looked shocked, turned to the barman and ordered, "Champagne pour mes amis" and led us to a table. He explained that he was a Swedish glassmaker with a factory on the outskirts of town, and that he always conducted business here on Sundays at about noon.

He would be meeting colleagues over the next hour or so, but we were to stay where we were. We did so, and he ensured that our glasses were topped up regularly. When he rejoined us, he asked where we were staying, and was aghast to hear we were under canvas. "But you must come and stay with me," he protested, "Room to spare in my house." We explained that this was not possible, and that moves were afoot to accommodate the unit in more substantial circumstances. Before we parted, he gave us his personal card with address and telephone number. "You come to dinner one evening," he said, "No need to make arrangements. Just turn up. I see you soon I hope. Au revoir." We thanked him, pocketed his card, and promised we would accept his kind offer of hospitality when next we had a duty free evening.

Events overtook these plans for a while on account of a change in living provision. The authorities having requisitioned a large cazerne in town, we struck camp and moved in. The building had been a school of three storeys, built round a central courtyard. We occupied rooms on the top floor, fitted out with German double bunks of basic timber frames, with strips of metal criss crossing to provide mattress support. Each room had an iron stove, vented through the ceiling. A small room at the end served as a kitchen. It was obviously some time since children had occupied the building. Our welcome was less than effusive. A member of another unit, housed in adjacent premises, opened the fridge in the kitchen, and was killed by the explosion that followed. The previous German occupiers had left their calling card. The buildings had obviously not been inspected before handing over to us.

We were taken aback to learn that the unit was to be officially welcomed by a high ranking officer, flown in specially from England. We mustered in the quadrangle on his arrival. His address was astonishing. We had anticipated a commendation on our contribution to recent events, and best wishes for the future. What we got was short, simple, and to the point. "You are here to represent the best traditions of the Royal Air Force. Don't shit and piss all over the place." With that he quit and flew back to England. Churchillian he was not.

While we were still assembled, and in shock, a sergeant appeared from within the building and shouted, "Anyone here play the piano?" The old hands grinned, as three arms were raised aloft. "Right," beamed the sergeant. "I've a bloody big one on the ground floor here. It's wanted on the top floor. So come on lads, let's be having you. You can give us a tune when the job's finished." As they say, the old ones are the best.

The weather continued to worsen, with heavy snow, accompanied by sharp overnight frost. When the sun shone, which it did most days, it beautified the scene, but barely raised the temperature. On Christmas Eve, Jack and I agreed to sally forth once more into the town centre. Black out regulations were strictly in force, and no lights appeared in windows, but from house after house, the merry sounds of

Christmas wafted across the still air. There was much music, and the sounds of children excited by the anticipation of full stockings in the morning. We retraced our steps to the cazerne, trudged up those flights of stairs, undressed, and crawled between the blankets. What, we wondered, would tomorrow bring for us, conscious as never before of the severed bonds of family fellowship? Christmas Day prospects were bleak. Our unit was attached to no organisation responsible for our daily sustenance. The by now palling 'K' rations would be a poor substitute for a traditional Christmas dinner. It appeared that, for us, there really was no room at the inn.

Interlude in Mons – Heavy snow, the weather continued to worsen.

On Christmas Day morning, Jack and I wandered down to the centre of town once more. Youngsters were out, parading their brand new presents. Behind the house windows, through now opened curtains, were glimpses of decorated trees, holly wreaths, and paper chains. We made our way to a café to celebrate with a festive glass, and to find a quiet corner, where we could sit and eat our Christmas 'K' pack, nestling snugly in the field-dressing pocket of our trousers. Inside the place, a group of American GI's were enjoying a pre Christmas drink. We got chatting, in the course of which we disclosed our celebratory plans for dinner. They were both spontaneous and instantaneous in their reaction. "To hell with that, buddy. You come alonga us. We"ll find a coupla seats with our outfit." And so it turned out. Their mess was just around the corner, and they treated us like guests of honour, feting us with turkey and all the trimmings, Christmas pudding, glass of wine, glass of brandy, and a spanking big cigar. Of all my Christmases, that in Mons in 1944 stands very high. We were strangers -and they took us in.

A day or two later, after consulting with F.O. Armitage, Jack and I decided to accept our Swedish friend's kind offer of hospitality. We felt it advisable to clear it with the C.O., in case he had any qualms on security grounds. He gave us his blessing, but advised us to be non-communicative about our roles, where we had been, or, indeed, about anything to do with the war. "This man is in business on a European scale, and will have wide contacts," he said. "He was more than likely on good terms with the Germans, so be on your guard. His hospitality may well be genuine, but we can never afford to let our guard down. Enjoy your evening."

So briefed, we presented ourselves on the doorstep, without any prior notice. Our host greeted us effusively, introduced us to his wife and son, and to two other guests, whom he had invited to a special dinner that very evening. His wife was a tiny woman, quite plain, but most attractive in manner. She was dressed elegantly, and complemented the décor, which was in exquisite taste. Her son, aged about ten, gave all the indications of being thoroughly spoilt, as is often the case with an only child. The guests were a local furrier and his wife, who was in the later stages of pregnancy. They were a charming couple.

In no time at all, Jack and I were made to feel at ease. Aperitifs were served in the lounge, before dinner was announced and our hosts escorted us to the dining room. This was a magnificent chamber. To call it a room would be to do it a disservice. Valuable pictures graced the walls, curtains and carpets were impeccably co-ordinated, and the ceiling resembled the decorated top of a wedding cake. From its centre hung a truly spectacular chandelier. The ethos created was one of exquisite taste stopping short of opulence, controlled refinement, and gracious living. The overall impression of relaxed elegance was complemented by the dining table, the centrepiece par excellence. Of solid glass, about eighteen feet by eight, it was offset by matching glass chairs. Inset into the surface, at the head of the table, was a control console from which the host could choose an array of lighting effects to suit the mood of the moment. I had seen nothing like it before. I have seen nothing like it since. To soften the glass seating, which was unexpectedly comfortable, fur drapes had been made to measure, courtesy of the furrier. We started eating at 8pm. We finished about 1am. Between courses, we retired either to an adjoining annexe for dancing on a ballroom floor, or to the lounge, just to relax. Choice wines accompanied each course, and such was the excellence of the cooking that, in spite of generous helpings, I felt less distended than had I eaten one American 'K' pack. It was an evening to savour, and one I shall always remember. Though we were pressed to stay the night, we declined gracefully, reaching our cazerne well after two in the morning. We had glimpsed a life style totally at variance with that of our current way of life. It had been a marvellous few hours of escapism.

Meanwhile, conditions in our top floor accommodation had taken a serious turn for the worse. Fuel for the stoves, drawn from a central storage pile, ran out. The weather was still bitterly cold, and we were in dire straits, Desperate situations call for desperate remedies. We had noticed that a Belgian unit, based on the ground floor, exercised and drilled in the quadrangle every morning between 8 am and 8-30. Having located the precise position of the two rooms they occupied, we planned a raid, to relieve them of four German beds, two from each room. This required meticulous timing. We held dummy runs on two consecutive mornings, until we were absolutely confident that we could pull it off. Look out men were posted on every corridor, and at every corner along the route, up and down, between ground and top floors. Sixteen men were deployed as carriers, four to each bed. Two further teams of eight each were assigned, one team to each room. We calculated that, if we began as soon as the Belgians started their drill, we could complete the operation before they returned.

On the signal to commence, everyone raced into position, the bed carriers stripping and making off with the bunks, the teams attached to them reorganising the bunks that were left, so that no gaps were immediately detectable. Since there were some thirty bunks in each room, speed was essential. It all went according to plan, in twenty minutes of frantic activity, as four double bunks made rapid progress along ground floor corridors, up flights of stone stairs to second floor level, along more corridors, and up a final flight of stairs to our third floor rooms. Breathless, but already warmer than we had been, we started dismantling our booty, in readiness for burning. This job was well in hand when our lookouts reported that the Belgian session was finishing. It would have been interesting, and doubtless amusing, to have been present when four bunks, accommodating eight men, were found to have disappeared. We would, I am sure, have been prepared to execute another raid had the need arisen. As it turned out, in less than a week, we were on the way back to the Ardennes.

During that period, I witnessed two incidents typical of the prevailing attitudes. The first was the sight of a voluble crowd, assembled in the main square. Seated on a wooden chair, surrounded by jeering onlookers, was a local woman being shorn of her hair, the recognised punishment for suspected collaborators. There was genuine hatred and detestation in the air. Racial feelings ran very high, and the climate was ripe for exploitation by any politically motivated rabble rouser.

The other occasion was at the opposite end of the scale. A classical pianist, whose name and appearance proclaimed his Jewishness, gave a public performance in a church hall one Sunday afternoon. Hearing part of it while passing by, I was attracted by it, and curious enough to interrupt my schedule to step inside. His audience was very small. I remember neither his name nor his repertoire, but I do recall the peace, contentment, and rapture of his listeners, as he created an hour of peace and harmony in a world still taut and edgy in the midst of sometimes unbearable tensions.

Somewhere between these two extremes of human behaviour, a civilised balance had to be found in the aftermath of a war now rapidly approaching a conclusion. The conflict had been long and bloody, with appalling atrocities on all sides. Would the essential lessons be learned by those charged to broker the peace? I hoped to live long enough to find out. Meanwhile, we were still at war, and there was work yet to be done.

—— Advance into Germany ——

The Battle of the Bulge ended officially on Jan. 28. By the end of the month, we were en route to resume operations at Baraque de Fraiture. It was in a different frame of mind that we journeyed. This time, the sweet smell of victory was in our nostrils. Return to the technical site was both practical and feasible. Within hours of arrival, we could set up, ready to resume operations. We understood that the domestic site was a different proposition. Time would tell.

As we approached Baraque de Fraiture, increasing evidence of savage fighting became apparent, with tanks, both American and German, littering the roadside at intervals. At the log bridge across to the technical site, something in the ditch caught our eye, and we stopped to investigate. Lying face down was a figure, some six feet four inches tall, dressed in the uniform of a German S.S. officer. His boots and socks were missing. In the middle of his back was a huge, gaping hole. A few feet away lay a bloodstained, discarded pickaxe. After some conjecture, consensus favoured a local Belgian as having been the perpetrator. The boots and socks would have been of scant value to an American. Nor, one would imagine, would a GI have felt the need to butcher so violently. Belgium had suffered German incursions over three successive generations. It seemed likely that retribution was being exacted here. How long the corpse had lain there it was not possible to tell. Nobody had thought to give it decent burial. Rightly or wrongly, we left the body undisturbed.

The once familiar run from technical to domestic site was a revelation. The forest scenery that had so often enchanted me in its various guises had been raped. Almost every tree bore the marks of sustained assault, with bark stripped or chipped by bullet and shell. What had once been virgin white snow was now a grey blanket, besmirched and spattered with the detritus of battle. At every corner, crippled tanks and armoured vehicles lay abandoned. American and German insignia bore witness to skirmishes engaged in, to take or defend successive stretches of road. This was the scene of attack and counter attack between forces who knew that the outcome would be crucial. A war that began in Sept 1939 was being fiercely, tenaciously, and violently concluded here.

We arrived at the Manhay chateau. Troops on the move need shelter, especially in the severe winter conditions in which this battle had been waged. The outer fabric of the building bore witness to changes of ownership, with chunks of masonry dislodged and littering the ground where they had fallen. The front door was missing, and the entrance porch was strewn with debris. I raked my boot through a mound in the corner, to reveal, among other rubbish, a French Grammar that had been my travelling companion. A thick volume, of nigh on four hundred pages, the first seventy were missing, probably to wipe someone's backside I presumed. Only just decipherable on the front cover was the name of the author, 'Dondo'.

We stepped across the threshold to find vandalism and carnage. Not a single room had its original door in place. All were off their hinges, and propped up haphazardly. There was evidence of hand to hand combat everywhere, with bullet holes and bloodstains on walls, ceilings, and floors. Bodies, American and German, lay where they had fallen. It was difficult to equate this scene with the memories I had of peaceful weeks of relaxation spent here. Two future courses of action resulted from this initial return visit. First, we needed new accommodation. Second, the appalling mess here would have to be cleared, and bodies disposed of. What we would find in the grounds was a matter, for the moment, of conjecture.

Our new domestic base was several miles to the north towards Liege, in a picturesque village called Durbuy, where a castle had been requisitioned. The journeys to and from the technical site were now much longer, but always took us past the Manhay chateau. The conditions in Durbuy were spartan. No central heating here. At the very top of the castle were three turrets, and in one of these eight of us slept on the concrete floor. The tiny room was octagonal, with vertical slits in the wall, from which archers used to fire arrows when besieged. The wind whistled through these, turning the interior into a fridge. A low lintelled wooden door gave access to a walkway that ran round the outside, with a waist high protective wall. The views were far reaching, panoramic, and magnificent.

The kitchen and mess rooms being on the ground floor, and access to our turret being via narrow stone steps, which in later stages became a spiral staircase, we ought to have become very fit. Unfortunately, our cook saw to it that we weren't. What that man could do to perfectly good food was monstrous, and most of us succumbed to recurrent bouts of dysentery.

The toilets also being on the ground floor, I seemed to spend my off duty hours tearing down the best part of a hundred steps for yet another uncontrollable movement of the bowels, toiling all the way back up, only to have to repeat the process. We were eating out of mess tins, and the root of the trouble was a lack of clean, hot water in which to wash them after use. There was a permanent film of grease on them. After vigorous complaints, the C.O. got rid of the cook, a competent replacement took over, and we all began to recover. It left me with the permanent legacy of an easily upset digestive system.

Advance into Germany – Our new domestic base in Durbuy.

We kept our turret penthouse above freezing point, courtesy of a paraffin burning Valour stove. A rota was established for trimming the wick and topping up with paraffin every morning. It was customary for whoever was on duty to discharge his obligations after breakfast. One morning, the chap concerned did it before breakfast; The fuel was kept in a barrel in the courtyard at ground level. Having done the job, he joined us for breakfast, making the valid point that, by the time we returned to the turret, the room would be well warmed up. We had finished the meal, and were about half way up the stairs, when a loud explosion rocked the upper building, and acrid fumes came swirling down the staircase. Grabbing fire extinguishers, we crept cautiously upstairs, and eventually brought the blaze under control. The Valour stove had disintegrated. Our man had filled it with petrol from a barrel alongside the one

Advance into Germany – Our turret penthouse in the castle.

clearly labelled 'Paraffin' Had he done so at the usual time, we'd have all been in the room when the stove exploded. Just for once, we were glad of the constant draughts that whistled through those arrow slits. Even so, it was days before the smell dissipated.

One morning in the middle of February 1945, we awoke to a glorious Spring day. The views from our turret eyrie were panoramic and breathtaking. At first, we were so taken aback by the beauty stretching out all around us that we failed to notice what was missing. For the first time in weeks, there was no snow. It being our watch's day off, Jack, Ray, and I decided that a stroll along the river bank, flanked by sweet smelling meadows, was an appropriate way in which to welcome Nature's change of dress. Anticipation of the pleasure to come was rewarded by complete fulfilment, at the height of which we stripped to the waist and sunbathed.

On redonning our vests and shirts, we glimpsed an opening in the face of an adjoining cliff, and went to investigate. It was a small cave. We entered and, immediately, the temperature plummeted. Ever the curious, venturesome one, Jack began to edge carefully forward. Ray and I followed tentatively. Within a few paces, it

Advance into Germany – A glorious spring day.

was pitch black, the cave orifice being too low to catch the angled rays of the sun. "Either of you got any matches?" enquired Jack. Ray passed a box to me. I handed it on to Jack. Striking a match, and guided by its flickering light, Jack shuffled forwards, halting when the ends of his fingers were singeing. Another match, a step or two more, a loud yell, a splash, complete silence, and utter darkness followed. I was petrified. A second or two later, Jack's shaky voice echoed round the cave from somewhere just below my feet, "Gee, you guys, give me a hand here," Dropping to my knees, and then flat on my stomach, I began thrashing my arms about, below a gap in the floor immediately in front of me. Another hand swept across mine, slipped past, and returned to grab mine in a vice like grip. Then both Jack's hands were engaged in mine. Meanwhile, Ray was out of his depth. I shouted to him in the darkness behind. "Ray, get between my legs, grab me round the thighs, wheelbarrow fashion, and pull me backwards. Jack's down a hole. I've got him by the hands. For God's sake be quick." I felt Ray get into position and begin to heave. "Hang on Jack," I implored, breathlessly, "just hang on." Gradually, I sensed I was being dragged backwards, and that Jack was coming with me. "O.K." came his voice, hoarsely. "I'm O.K." We released our grips and lay there, in the dark, panting. Eventually, we crawled towards the cave mouth, reached the sunlight beyond, and collapsed on the grass, glad of the warmth.

Ray was the first to break silence. "Quite apart from anything else," he observed, "you're a greedy sod." He was apparently addressing Jack, to whom I directed my attention. Still clasped tightly under his right arm was his folded tunic, from the epaulette of which protruded his forage cap. "How on earth did you manage to hang on to that lot?" I asked, mindful of the recently flailing arms that had met mine in the darkness. Ray answered for him. "Sheer bloody instinct," he said, "He loves his bloody wallet more than his life. Like I say, he's a greedy sod." Jack grinned sheepishly, and withdrew his wallet from its pocket. "Not too greedy to stand you two a drink," he chuckled, "I reckon we all deserve one."

In discussing the incident afterwards, Jack explained that the first thing he realised was that he was in icy water, and could feel a strong downward pull. Had the current been horizontal, he would have been swept away. I made the point that, had the level of the water been a few inches lower, our hands would not have been able to meet. Ray's comment was the most deductive. Had all the snow above ground not melted over the previous twenty four hours, the water table would have been very much lower, and the current would have carried Jack through a labyrinth of caves, passages, and pot holes, never to be seen again. A beautiful Spring day could have ended in tragedy.

Advance into Germany – An off duty spell.

The conditions we had found in the chateau at Manhay having needed urgent attention, F.O.Armitage had taken the necessary steps, as dictated by protocol. We were in an American controlled sector, and it was their responsibility to clear the building of the corpses lying there. This sad duty had been attended to, and I presume decent burial arrangements had been accorded to both American and German war dead. They had not thought to check the gardens around the chateau, where some few feet of snow had collected during the blizzard conditions of the past few weeks.

We have noted the big thaw that occurred at Durbuy, and similar developments happened at Manhay, with dramatic results. More dead bodies were revealed on the ground, as the snow melted and disappeared. One of our watches, during an off duty spell, was deputed to see what steps needed to be taken. Two of them ventured into the rear garden to count the number of corpses. One of them, presumably out of curiosity, turned an American body over to get a glimpse of the face. The body exploded, killing him outright. It had been booby-trapped This led to an immediate suspension of the exercise, which resumed the following day, when our watch was on the rota. Preliminary sighting through binoculars had revealed not only bodies, some American, some German, but German Teller mines. These were known to be extremely dangerous. About the size of a large dinner plate, an initial detonation threw the canister about six feet into the air. A second detonation dispersed the contents of the canister radially, over a wide area. These contents were small ball bearings, metal nails etc. which could inflict nasty wounds. Closer examination revealed the possibility that the mines were linked by trip wires, one explosion triggering a series. Bearing in mind the booby-trapped body, we could not rule out the possibility that others were not linked into the minefield

F.O.Armitage, acting on his own initiative, issued four of us with rifles, and placed us at first floor rear windows, with orders to fire at any mines sighted from there. It was an unforgettable experience that lasted but a minute or two. After a few near misses, one of us struck a mine. In quick succession, the whole field exploded, until silence reigned again. None of the bodies had been violated. Our colleague's death the day before had been a matter of chance. He had chosen to turn the one body over that had been used as a last defiant weapon by some malevolent German. Once again, we handed over the burial rites of the remaining bodies to the American authorities. A final comment on this harrowing episode. Every serviceman carries on him, suspended from a cord around his neck, two dog tags, one impervious to fire, the other to water. By such means, it is possible to establish identity when a corpse is otherwise unrecognisable. Maybe our lost comrade was looking for dog tags when he turned the body over.

The turmoil of events from our retreat from the Ardennes to our return had played havoc with our inward post. I had written regularly to Ann, but her replies had dried up during this period, and I had begun to wonder if perhaps she was trying gently to withdraw. Then, just as Spring broke through, three letters all arrived at once, though written over a six week stretch. All were very affectionate, confessing concern over my situation throughout the volatile happenings to which I'd been exposed. For the first time, I began to cherish real expectations that what we had experienced during those few months at Rodel would come to fruition in due course. It would be up to me to make the first move. I would need to choose a propitious time. Meanwhile, there was a definite spring in my step.

Since returning to Baraque de Fraiture, we had conducted bombing raids almost nightly, and targets were stretching right across Germany, whose air defences were now shattered. It could only be a question of time before the war in Europe was over. None of us had contemplated our own advance into enemy territory, believing we could strike effectively from where we were. Someone in high places thought otherwise, and by the end of February, we were on the move again.

We left Durbuy in convoy, a few three ton Bedfords, 15 cwt. Fordsons, and a couple of Jeeps, adding the Matador and technical trailer on arrival at Baraque de Fraiture. No running westwards for our lives this time. We were heading east, final destination unknown. Only F.O. Armitage was privy to the plans, and even he was involved on a 'need to know' basis. He led the way in a Jeep (he loved that Jeep) and the convoy followed, Matador and trailer in the middle for security reasons. The route took us south of Bonn to Remagen on the Rhine. The great bridge over the river was being rebuilt under adverse conditions. A German tank, sited high on the opposite bank, had been shelling for days relentlessly, causing continual damage and casualties, before being knocked out by aerial attack. Close to one of the piers of the bridge, a memorial listed the names of those whose lives had been lost. We approached

Advance into Germany – Convoy leaving Durbuy.

the river down a sloping embankment that gave access to a floating wooden roadway supported by barges. What followed was one of life's richest experiences.

Driving my three tonner on to the single track road, I was conscious that the other bank was a long, long way away. What would happen if the truck broke down? Would the flimsy looking structure support the truck's weight? Why had I not learned to swim? Before any answers emerged, I was off dry land and driving on water. It was the oddest sensation. Directly below the water, the road was buoyant. Seen through the windscreen, it was level with the bonnet. In the rear view side mirrors, it was at a similar height. The impression gained was that your own piece of road was being moved along with you. It was like being in a dream world. The thought struck me that, with a current running downstream, I was possibly driving forwards and sideways at the same time.

Eventually, we reached the far bank, and the relief of hearing the reassuring sound of crunching gravel under the wheels, as we climbed a makeshift surface leading to familiar tarmacadam. A series of sharp bends took us to the summit and the autobahn beyond. En route, we passed the predatory German tank, and glanced back at its erstwhile target, the Remagen Bridge, now tiny in perspective, its skeleton structure etched into the placid surface of the Rhine and the landscape beyond. Across the river bobbed our narrow floating road. Though we had been in Germany proper for some time now, this was the defining moment. The very heart of the country lay before us. A tyrant was on the very brink of defeat.

Advance into Germany – Steady progress.

We travelled for the next three days at a steady pace through countryside that seemed to stretch forever. It was Jack, the Canadian who had crossed the entire breadth of his own country and the wide Atlantic to enlist in the cause of freedom, who remarked, "Lebensraum. He went to war in search of lebensraum. Have you ever seen so much goddam open space as this?" I could understand his feelings. What we had here was not just acres of space, but lush, fertile, productive, agrarian acres. It certainly wasn't overcrowded either. We observed very few people as we passed through mile after mile. They had all the living room they needed.

Night stops were taken on suitable ground, just off the road, well away from habitation. We slept as we chose to, either in the trucks, or alongside them. The weather was co-operative, and the country air was scented by abundantly emerging Spring growth. For food, we were back on those familiar 'K' packs. On the whole, it was enjoyable.

Venturing ever deeper into enemy territory, we could never relax vigilance, but in truth all around was so idyllically peaceful we progressed without much thought of confrontation. By the fourth morning we were well into Bavaria, and F.O. Armitage called an impromptu parade, as we stood by our vehicles. "Right men, I want you to take a good look at yourselves in your driving mirrors. You look more like a defeated rabble than a victorious unit, about to end this war. By this evening, we will resume what we are good at, precision bombing. That's why we've been sent here. Within a couple of hours, we will have reached our destination. I shall then open the last of my sealed orders. We may occupy this new site for some time. I want you to enter the territory looking spick and span. So razors and bullshit materials out. We leave in an hour's time." I was reminded of the "Don't shit and piss all over the place" speech by that high ranking officer, in the cazerne at Mons. We had ignored that as inept and patronising. Armitage was different. An hour later, we were so smart we hardly recognised each other.

Advance into Germany – Venturing ever deeper into enemy territory.

—— Bad Mergentheim ——

About noon we drove into Bad Mergentheim, a tiny little community of a few hundred, and came to a halt in the main street. Nobody ventured out to greet us. It was as silent as the grave. We sensed the presence of prying eyes behind curtains that twitched occasionally. The C.O. opened his orders. "Right men," he announced, "the rest of you wait here at ease. I want the following radar mechanics to accompany me. (The list included Jack Home and me.) We are going to place our trailer here (patting AMES 9412 affectionately) precisely on the spot from which tonight we'll spearhead a thousand bomber raid on Berlin."

With Armitage in his Jeep leading the way, we proceeded to one end of the village. After consulting a hand drawn sketch map, he led us up a narrow lane, with hedges

Bad Mergentheim – A broad plateau on the edge of the village, where we placed the AMES 9412.

on both sides, to a five-barred gate, which he opened. We drove the Matador and trailer through. Before us stretched a grassed incline that led to a broad plateau, bordered on three sides by forest. In the ground, precisely where indicated on the sketch map, a stake had been driven. Directly over this, we placed AMES 9412. and began pre-operational procedures. On another site, 200 miles away, a second unit was doing the same. The well tried cat and mouse roles led, as planned by higher echelons back in the U.K., to a concerted, concentrated bombardment of Berlin that night.

I have often speculated as to how that marker stake got there. An agent dropped by parachute? An infiltrator with excellent command of German? I shall never know, but the planning was as precise as the location chosen. The bombing raids we conducted from this site were devastatingly accurate, and helped to speed the German surrender.

The technical site having been established, the domestic arrangements had to be set up. The C.O. decided that an adjacent field was suitable and tents were erected. Their use was to sow seeds of dissension. Similar sized tents were allocated to officers and other ranks, the first housing two to a tent, the second six to a tent, a disparity never likely to go unchallenged by men of the calibre we had. The situation was exacerbated when it was discovered that the C.O.'s Jeep warranted a tent, as did a store of firewood for exclusive use by officers. We had no barrack room lawyers on AMES 9412, but we did have men who knew their worth, and were not afraid to state their case effectively.

When officers awakened after the first night, they found the tents that had sheltered Jeep and firewood from the elements dismantled. It had rained heavily, and both vehicle and kindling were soaked. Propped up against the Jeep's windscreen was a notice which read: 'As long as a building remains standing in Germany, none of my men will sleep under canvas---Dwight Eisenhower.' That afternoon, F.O. Armitage led a small party of men into the village to seek out suitable premises. We chose an avenue of semi-detached houses, sufficient in number to accommodate the whole unit, and to establish an orderly room. Notices were served on all the occupants to vacate their properties, taking with them only essential personal belongings. They would be allowed to visit every day at 10am to collect a bucket of coal from their cellars.

The houses were of a good size, with lounge, dining room, kitchen, and laundry on the ground floor, three large bedrooms, bathroom and toilet on the first floor. There was central heating and coal burning stoves. A small garden at the front, and a large one at the back provided very acceptable outlooks from casement windows. It was certainly an improvement on living in tents. The sanitary arrangements were a revelation. All the usual accessories were installed, with toilet pans on both floors. There was no flush system. You sat in position, did what you had to do, and heard your contribution plummeting down the pipe to the built in covered cesspool in the garden. If you were occupying the downstairs provision at the same time as someone else was performing upstairs, you had the spectacular experience of hearing their deposit whistle past you, to be followed by a splash as it landed, bang on target. Once a week, a horse drawn cart came round to empty all the cesspools. The stench was absolutely appalling.

There was an edict, issued by Eisenhower, prohibiting fraternisation with the civilian population. Though I agreed with this as a general principle, I felt there were instances where it could be waived. I was living in a house we had summarily requisitioned at extremely short notice, permitting the owner access to her own house daily, with entry restricted to the cellar. I made a point of being around each time she called, attempting ordinary pleasantries in my School Certificate German.

Understandably wary at first, she gradually relaxed. She was late thirties, her husband was at war, and she had two daughters. Avoiding any reference to her husband, I asked about the girls. They lived with her. I suggested that she bring them with her when next she came, and the following day I was introduced to two delightful blonde, blue eyed youngsters, aged ten and seven. Ilse was the older, Eva the younger.

We had a little chat, and I offered them a couple of American PX chocolate bars each, which they accepted shyly, but quite naturally. To their mother I gave a bar of toilet soap, at which her eyes lit up. This routine continued as long as I was there. Little did I realise at the time that this would prove to be highly significant as events unfolded.

Whether this relationship had any bearing on that between the unit and the local population as a whole is difficult to ascertain, but, a few days after my contacts with this family began, the C.O. sent for me. He had heard I could speak German, and had a problem, to deal with which he would be glad of my help. A heavily pregnant woman was in the orderly room. Would I speak with her? I went along. It appeared she was registered to give birth in Wurzburg, about twenty miles away, was very close to her time, but lacked transport. I relayed the news to F.O. Armitage. "I suppose we should help, as far as we are able," was his observation. "It will relax attitudes towards us. I'll run her over in the Jeep." I'm sure he didn't spot the double meaning in what he'd said. So AMES 9412 became a maternity outpost. Over the next fortnight, some six or seven young women came out of the woodwork, all in varying stages of pregnancy, and all eager for a ride in the C.O.'s Jeep. As far as we could tell, there were no men about below the age of seventy, and there was much conjecture about how our clientele had achieved their current condition. Logically, it pointed to remarkably virile and obliging seventy year olds, which said something for the country life.

Our public display of willingness to be of service to the community was interrupted one day when rumours spread about a man in SS Officer's uniform having been sighted on the edge of nearby woods. The rumours were given some credence when one of our men, going into the cellar of a house but a few doors from ours, found evidence of someone having been sleeping rough there. That night, shortly after midnight, we raided every house in the village. I vividly recall hammering one front door with my rifle butt, and yelling at the top of my voice, "Machen Sie die Tur auf." Upstairs windows opened, and bed capped heads peered fearfully out. I repeated the order, and bolts were heard being drawn back. We pushed the door open and stormed in. There were women and children everywhere, several sleeping on floorboards. Two old men stood in the background, nightshirts wrapped tightly around them. Of younger men there was no sign. For the next few nights, patrols walked round the streets as an extra precaution. During the height of the search, a Russian Pole had deserted his cookhouse duties, armed with a butcher's cleaver, and had disappeared into the woods, intent on settling old scores. He emerged several hours later, disappointed not to have found his quarry.

We knew, from the continuing aerial assaults we were conducting nightly, that German resistance was crumbling fast, and that Russian advances from the east were moving unstoppably, increasing the probability of an imminent end to the war. Further indication was the appearance on Daily Routine Orders of an invitation to those with the required standards to apply for the government's proposed Emergency Training Scheme for teachers. This followed hard on the 1944 Education Act. David Stanley approached me and urged me to apply. "You're a natural," he said. I had a high regard for David's judgement, and valued his assessment. I had no worthwhile job to go back to, and nothing specifically planned. There would be opportunities in the radar industry, particularly in the United States, which had been drawn to my attention. The Civil Service, for which I'd had aspirations before the war, which had brought a temporary halt to examinations, remained a possibility. The more I thought about it, the more attractive teaching became. Within the week, my application was on its way to London, David kindly writing a letter of support.

Correspondence between Ann and me had settled into a regular exchange, which reflected our growing commitment. With definite prospects of a professional career, with the security that teaching offered, I decided the time had come to propose. Almost by return came the reply, accepting the proposal, enclosing information on her correct ring size, and looking forward to my next leave. I'd better pass the Ministry of Education's interview now. Meanwhile, I was a very happy man. That canny old Scot, Jemima, had said that a period of separation would reveal whether or not Ann and I were truly in love or merely infatuated. Well, we knew now. Thank you Jemima, and God bless.

War is full of contradictions. Having spent several hours inside AMES 9412 one night, helping to reduce yet another of Germany's large industrial centres to rubble, I retired to the nearby rest trailer, and fell asleep instantly. It was one of those recuperative slumbers, when you don't move about much, are undisturbed by dreams, and wake naturally, fully refreshed. The life style we led promoted habitual awareness, and whenever I woke I knew instantly where I was, Why I was there, and what day it was. On this occasion, something registered as being unusual. A few seconds of quiet concentration and I'd pinned it down. There was a rhythmic swishing sound just outside the trailer. Gently, I eased the curtain back. It was a glorious Spring day, with clear blue skies. Some ten yards or so away, a German woman, aged in her late forties at a guess, was scything the long grass. She was a handsome woman, sturdy of build, and ruddy of cheek. She posed an idyllic picture of a peasant at peace, in surroundings so tranquil, they exemplified the centuries old rural way of life. It clashed starkly with the violence in which I had just participated. Should I step outside and greet her? Better perhaps, and more honest, to leave her to her work undisturbed.

The air in Bad Mergentheim was heavy, and most of us felt drowsy and lethargic. We were 700 miles from the sea, and to those of us accustomed to a bracing climate, adjusting was an effort. Then there were the changes in fauna and flora. The Spring flowers were beautiful, but a trial to sufferers from hay fever. A new encounter was that with June bugs, a variety the size of a bee, perfectly harmless, but extremely invasive. By now, it was mid-April, but early swarms were about. Just before dusk, they emerged from the forest in swarms so dense that, if you waved your arms about violently, you could kill them by the dozen. Our worst exposure was on a very warm, close evening when all our windows were open. As dusk fell, and we switched on our lights, they invaded, forcing us to close all openings to prevent further incursion. We were left with the problem of walls, ceilings, and floors covered with bugs. As we walked, we crushed dozens to death. With rolled up newspapers, we despatched hundreds more. After twenty minutes, we packed it in, and opened a bottle of German Schnappes.

What followed was a revelation. As usual, not every drop of spirit poured reached a glass. There were occasional spillages. Around each little pool on the table, the remnants of the routed bug invading army congregated, their feelers probing the liquid. We were engrossed as each bug reached its demonstrable alcohol capacity, and tried to take off. Dozens of them were careering drunkenly in bemused circles, their wings whirring at maximum revs without effect. One by one, they reached the stage when they turned over on their backs, legs thrashing wildly, then progressively more sedately, until by degrees they ceased to work at all. We were surrounded by June bugs either dead drunk, or just plain dead. Whichever, they all succumbed to a brush and shovel send off, and the business of a wholesale clean up began. I awarded the accolade for the most spectacular performance to the toper who gyrated to the table's edge, and plummeted to the floor below. Had it had a face, I'm sure it would have been wreathed in contented smiles.

On April 30 1945 news of the suicide of Adolf Hitler and his mistress Eva Braun, whom he had married the day before, was broadcast. We heard it in our requisitioned house on the American AFN radio station. Throughout our time in the American sector, this station had been a constant companion, and many a night watch had been enlivened by the programme 'Midnight in Munich' Shortly after we heard the news, our 'landlady' arrived to collect her daily bucket of coal. She was unaccompanied by her two daughters, and looked out of sorts. I asked her if she had heard the news. She asked what news. I told her. She put on a defiant, unbelieving face. "Propaganda," she said, but didn't mean it. We both knew that the war was as good as over.

The celebrations on May 8, VE Day, were spectacular. We abandoned our British reserve, and went completely over the top. It began with an address by F.O. Armitage. "Gentlemen," he announced, "on the back of AMES 9412 is a large carboy of full strength Navy rum, which we have transported from the landing beaches at Arromanches to its present location, for use in cases of emergency. In my view, such an emergency has now arisen, and I have a strong premonition that the said carboy will fall off the back of the trailer at precisely 18-00 hours today. I am sure you will agree with me that it would be a tragic waste of good spirit were it to drain away into

*Bad Mergentheim – VE Day, we abandoned our British reserve,
and enjoyed spectacular celebrations.*

the parched earth, and German soil at that. I would therefore urge you to prevent such a calamity, by presenting yourselves, suitably armed with regulation issued mugs, outside the orderly room at the appointed hour."

To a man, we responded to this invitation, and returned to our billets, transferring the contents of our mugs to any receptacles we could find, for future use. An inch in the bottom of the mug was enough to see most of us off, and so potent was the brew, that every time we filled our mugs with hot tea, for a day or so afterwards, we were quite merry again. In the meanwhile, uninhibited celebrations erupted. In the vicinity was a castle, rumoured to house a collection of mediaeval theatrical costumes. Some of the men paid it a visit, returning with an assortment of outfits which they proceeded to don. An oxcart was then purloined, and the newly established strolling players toured the village, giving an impromptu, inebriated performance at every street corner. There was no audience. The villagers remained indoors throughout, doubtless unable to come to terms with events.

I was not involved in this revelry, having found another diversion. Just beyond our back garden, the village church graced the skyline, its spire sporting a weather vane.

Four of us, using the bedroom window sills as supports, started firing single rifle shots at the vane, the aim being to send it spinning. After rather patchy success, we resorted to full magazines in a Sten gun, which really sent the vane revolving. A Canadian corporal excelled at this, becoming as drunk as a lord as he celebrated each successful volley. He stopped only when he began to feel really queasy, and staggered to the toilet to be sick. When he returned, he was looking extremely wan, and much thinner round the mouth. "Not feeling too good, mate?" someone asked him. The corporal concurred, but his words were unintelligible. "For God's sake put your teeth in," he was told. He clasped his hand over his mouth. "Oh, no," he groaned. "I've spewed them down the toilet." When the ox cart emptied the cesspool later that week, he sieved through every shovel full, before it was deposited in the container. He was ecstatic when he recovered them. Personally, I wouldn't have bothered looking. All in all, VE Day was one to remember.

The operational need for AMES 9412 was now much diminished, and several of us were granted leave. I had my travel warrants made out to Stornoway, with additional travelling time allowance on both outward and return journeys. It took me three days to reach Calais, travelling by road and rail. The rail journey was in rolling stock that bore all the marks of war damage, with holes in the roof and sides. To make conditions more comfortable, we were issued with an Army blanket, to be handed in at Calais. The company in my compartment was convivial. We were all going home, some for the first time in months. The only exception was a wizened little Army private, huddled in a corner seat, who spoke only once during the trip. We had stopped at a major station and a loudspeaker began blaring. The voice was female, the language English, the accent impeccable. "All officers above the rank of Captain and Squadron Leader----disembark now." Calls were repeated at intervals, the order of rank decreasing each time. The dulcet tones arrived at "All Senior NCO's----disembark now." Our wizened private, who had the appearance of a very long serving soldier, stuck his head through an adjacent hole by his head, put both hands to his mouth, and bawled, "Wogs and f-----g Arabs this way." Apparently much relieved to have got that off his chest, he drew his blanket around himself and retired to oblivion again.

On the platforms at the main stations where we halted, women were offering to buy army blankets for anything up to 500 francs, the top price for blue serge material. Quite a number went this way, apparently to be made into coats, costumes and the like. I retained mine, anticipating repercussions if I arrived at Calais without. I was unduly apprehensive. As we embarked on the cross Channel ferry, very few blankets were thrown into the receptacles provided, and no checks were made. Neither were there customs checks on the other side. Senior NCO's manned the gangways with stentorian shouts of "Hurry along lads. Double up. Your wives are waiting for you." Back packs were full of booty. My abiding memory is of a Regimental Sergeant Major guardsman, erect as a ramrod, wheeling a Silver Cross type perambulator along the platform at Waterloo Station, and exiting into London's busy traffic to successive rounds of congratulatory applause from an amused public.

I was on another mission. With plenty of time before catching the 19-30 train from Euston to Inverness, I made for Bond Street. Here, with the help of a young lady assistant, I chose a solitaire diamond engagement ring, which she wrapped in its presentation box. With it safely tucked away in an inside pocket, I headed for my train. I had forgotten how long this particular journey was, fifteen hours overnight. Having secured a corner seat, I took in the scenery till darkness fell, somewhere over the Scottish border, and dosed throughout the hours of darkness. We arrived at Inverness with time for a leisurely breakfast, before catching the train to Kyle of Lochalsh.

When we entered Stornoway harbour, the familiar sounds, sights , and smells greeted me. Among the usual crowds thronging the quayside was Ann, looking radiant. The reunion was quietly emotional. After eighteen months of separation, we were together again. She had booked me into a private bed and breakfast establishment, and here I slipped the ring on her finger. It was a tender moment, beyond the power of words to describe.

Ann was now in charge of the large canteen close to the airport, so we had to make the most of her off duty hours. It didn't matter. I spent my days there. It was like Rodel all over again, except that this time the relationship was one of commitment. All too soon, the days slipped by, and we were on the quayside again, about to part again for a while. As we stood holding hands, she suddenly broke away and crossed the road to approach a sailor in Royal Navy uniform. I saw them greet each other affectionately, after which she brought him over and introduced him. "This is my brother Donald," she said. "He's crossing tonight as well, so you'll have company." Donald had obviously had a drink or two, but sobered immediately, saying all the right things. Having dispensed with protocol, he suggested a celebratory drink was called for. Ann was having none of that. "You've had enough," she said, and Donald decided that this was not the time to be obstreperous. Together, my newly introduced, future brother-in-law and I went on board. Ann waved from the quayside, and melted slowly away into the darkness. It was hard to part, but there was now a future to look forward to.

Donald installed me in the comfort of the saloon, and went off in search of a drink. I dozed off, and slept until we were approaching Kyle. Up a slope from the platform there was a little café. Here we snatched a quick breakfast, before catching the train to Inverness. By now, I had cottoned on that Donald had a permanent thirst that required regular assuaging, and was not, therefore, surprised when, having placed our luggage on seats on the Inverness to London train, he suggested there was time for a quick one in the adjoining buffet. Not wishing to appear unsociable, I joined him. We returned to the platform to find it empty. The train had left. Not only that. It had left for Glasgow. Our London train was standing at another platform.

We each had a separate problem. He was bound for Chatham to be demobbed, and had left a small attache case on the carriage seat. I was returning to Germany, and had left a Gladstone bag on my seat, and my greatcoat on the luggage rack. Inside the pockets were all my travel documents, and 200 cigarettes that Ann had given me. My wallet, with all my money, I had in my tunic pocket. We had a choice to make: take the London train, or catch the next train to Glasgow. Without documentation, my decision was easy. I had to get to Glasgow and hope that I could recover it. Donald could catch the London train, proceed to Chatham, and try to trace his case later. He opted to accompany me, feeling responsible for our predicament.

Surprisingly we arrived at Glasgow Queen Street station without any ticket inspection en route, and jumped the barrier on noticing a collector on duty. Enquiries revealed that the train we were looking for had terminated at Glasgow Central. We took a taxi there, arriving to find it closed for the night. We rang the door bell and a porter answered it. We explained our situation, and taking pity on us, he admitted us, escorting us to the siding where our objective was standing. "The cleaners will have gone through it," he explained. "Anything picked up will have been locked in the Left Luggage office, which doesn't open till 6am. You can sleep on the train. I'll bring you a brew about 5-30."

Before we settled down, I decided to check the coach where we'd left our gear. My Gladstone bag was there. Donald's case and my greatcoat were not. We slept only fitfully. As promised, our brew arrived on time, hot strong tea, no milk, no sugar, but most welcome nevertheless. We entered the Left Luggage office. Awaiting us was Donald's case and my greatcoat, travel documents and cigarettes intact. I left a generous tip of the latter with the staff. I am unlikely to forget my first meeting with brother-in-law Donald.

Having exceeded my travelling time allowance, I was likely to fall foul of the authorities, if my papers were checked en route. It didn't matter when I got back to my unit. The war was over, and our job was over, for the time being at least. The London stations were the danger points. Red Caps always manned the barriers there. As I approached each check point, along with hundreds of others, I timed my arrival to correspond with the moments when both were simultaneously occupied, and passed through unchallenged.

After an uneventful sea crossing, and a long overland trek by rail and road, I was reinstalled in Bad Mergentheim It had been a memorable leave. It was now June, and our presence on the present site was superfluous. We were not surprised, therefore, when orders arrived for the return of AMES 9412 to the U.K. We were still in the American sector, the land flowing with milk and honey, and set about stocking the trailer with all the food and drink we could muster. It was at this point that I was introduced to the concept of tessellation, and we packed every available nook and cranny, from floor to ceiling, before our mass exodus to Bonn, where the vehicle was made thoroughly watertight for the sea crossing, and sealed with instructions not to be opened until arrival in Britain. It had immunity from inspection by Customs officials. We anticipated high living from now on.

We stayed in Bonn for some three weeks, living in requisitioned villas on Siebengebirge Strasse, the street of the seven mountains. All were visible from my bedroom window. The balcony beyond gave access to ripe peaches, there for the picking, and we took advantage. They were heady days, providing time for reflection.

Among many memories of Bad Mergentheim was one of Ft.Lt. Burnham. Having completed a full tour of bombing raids, he had been seconded to the unit in an advisory capacity, and sat in on many of our operations. He always arrived in full flying gear, and occupied a seat from which he could monitor the screens. For his benefit, we had installed a replica of the radar equipment carried in bomber aircraft, so he was in fact reliving the experience of those thirty plus bombing raids. It was instructive to observe his reactions.

At first, he sat quite placidly until radar contact had been established, and visual corroboration appeared on the screens. As the action developed, his demeanour went through ever heightening hyperactive involvement. He was no longer with us. He was back in that plane, feeling the tensions, exhibiting the fears. Twitching and shuddering, sweat breaking out in large drops, he reached a crescendo of convulsions as the bombs were released, the target struck, and the long flight home begun. There was a swift decline from this to complete relaxation, leaving him slumped in his chair, utterly spent, mentally and physically. The nearest phenomenon I can equate to this is watching someone experiencing an epileptic fit. It gave me an insight into what our aircrews were exposed to, and it remains in the mind, sixty years on, as token of what we all owe to such men

From those early days at Swanage, the members of AMES 9412 had endured much together, and the technical personnel in particular had become closely knit. We all expected repatriation, along with our trailer. We had forgotten the sometimes inscrutable processes of the official mind. The trailer was to be shipped unaccompanied. The unit was to be disbanded. Individual postings would be notified. I have often tried to imagine the reaction of the lucky sod who opened up our trailer back in blighty. All his Christmases came at once.

As for postings, we were scattered far and wide. Mine was to La Capelle, in the north of France, just over the Belgian border. It could have been worse. Thus were colleagues, with whom I had served through some of the most significant months of the war, consigned to new assignments, destined ere long to resume lives they had left, to begin the challenging task of carving out a career for the security of which we had all fought so hard.

── La Capelle, France ──

In some respects, this posting was a new experience. The domestic arrangements were entirely novel. A former children's orphanage at the entrance to the village, approaching it from the Belgian border, housed a unit of about forty men. A substantial villa standing in its own grounds, it had obviously been purpose built. A spacious approach, running at right angles to the frontage, was gravel surfaced for easy maintenance. Entrance to the villa was via a short flight of broad stone steps, leading to substantial doors, flanked by glass panels.

On the ground floor, all the rooms were spacious, having been designed for communal living. There was a commodious refectory with good quality tiled floor, windows along one side admitting generous levels of light, and serving hatches on the opposite wall giving access to kitchen and storage rooms beyond. At the other end, smaller rooms formed administrative offices, adequately sized to serve their purpose. All rooms had unusually high ceilings, some of which were ornately decorated. The tiling of the refectory floor was continued throughout. A central staircase gave access, via an intermezzine landing, to the first floor. Accessible by a door on the left of the staircase was a large cloakroom.

La Capelle, France – Entrance to the villa.

The upstairs accommodation comprised a huge dormitory area and a few individual rooms at one end. It was here that most of the men were allocated living space, occupied by a single bed, table, chair and locker. These arrangements ran round the periphery, the centre of the room being used for recreational activities such as table tennis. Large windows catered for maximum lighting by day. Ceiling and wall lights, powered by the electric main supply, ensured adequate night-time lighting standards. The flooring was timber. Rafters and a pitched roof created lots of headroom. All in all, it was an adaptable environment, warm and comfortable. At the rear of the building was a grassed area big enough to house a fair sized football pitch.

The technical site was at the other end of the village, some three-quarters of a mile away. One followed the main road, turned into a narrow lane on the left after half a mile, emerging on to an open area on which stood a 105 ft. mast, a Nissen hut housing the radar equipment at one end a workshop at the other, and a barbed wire fenced compound for fuel storage. Conventionally enclosed fields in which cattle grazed surrounded this site. Nearby was the La Capelle racecourse. The village itself was quite small, just a few side streets, all of them short. It was set in an agricultural area, the only industry being of the cottage kind. A few shops, cafes, and a large RC church, with convent attached more or less sums it up.

As ever, I obeyed the golden rule on joining a new unit. Let the others make the first move. Initial contacts were with colleagues on the technical site. Thankfully, a four-watch system operated. There were new things to learn. Petrol electric engines generated power to the site. These were basically two stroke motor bike engines and had to work in pairs to generate the power required. With a stock of eight machines to generate electricity around the clock continuously, the maintenance schedule was hectic. Each engine needed servicing at 50, 100, 200 and 300 hrs. The last one was a complete strip down and decoke. Never having worked on these before, I learnt by rolling my sleeves up and getting my hands dirty. I developed great satisfaction in taking an engine apart, cleaning it thoroughly, grinding valve seating and facings, reassembling it, and hearing it fire and start with one swing of the starting handle. The radar part of the work was still there, but maintaining the power supply occupied the bulk of watch time.

Our technical overseer was Sgt. Jim Bray, a Tynesider by birth, and a gas fitter to trade. Homespun, down to earth, married and missing his wife and family, he had his eye on imminent demobilisation, and was filling in time. In joint leadership was Arnold Beattie, a grounded aircrew Warrant Officer navigator, whose peacetime job had been as a Post Office engineer. He had very small feet, a very long tongue, and a disinclination to work second to none. Our C.O., FO Drummond, was affable, non-decisive, ever looking for compromise. The ethos of the unit was neither positive nor negative. It was splendidly neutral. The war was over. Inertia was creeping in.

After the heady days with AMES 9412, this laid back way of life took some getting used to. I was aware of the need to resist the temptation to be sucked into this newfound life of Reilly and formed no close alliances of the kind that had been the hallmark of previous experience. It was a useful period of retrospection, perhaps necessary after the momentous adventures of the previous few months.

A few days after I arrived, I heard a booming voice engaged in conversation with the C.O. on the steps outside. It reverberated in my memory, and I went outside to satisfy my curiosity. It was my old friend the Swedish glassmaker from Mons, en route to the Pyrenees, and having picked up a puncture. Could we help? On seeing me, he enveloped me in an enthusiastic bear hug, explaining to FO Drummond how we came to be acquainted. We ended up drinking together while one of our motor mechanics fixed his vehicle. Life is full of inexplicable coincidences.

Every village has its characters. Two of La Capelle's came early to my notice. One was Marcel, a shifty little man, shy and furtive in manner and approach. He visited us frequently on the look out for cigarettes, and anything else he could scrounge. Nothing was for himself. He was a black market go between. The other, Bernard, was an altogether more intriguing personality. A ladies' hairdresser with premises on the main street, he had a wide clientele, including ladies who travelled miles to patronise his salon. What was most intriguing about Bernard was his sexuality. He was a transvestite. Dressed as a woman, he was astonishingly alluring, and rumour had it that he was himself much attracted to men. On Saturday evenings, a well-established dance was held in our refectory, the tiled floor being admirably suited to such entertainment. Young ladies, attended always by chaperones, attended in fair numbers. Bernard was a regular patron, partnering any airman so disposed. He was a consummate dancer and did not lack support. I did not dance but spoke good French, and was thus the recipient of his ever roving eye and truly witty badinage. He was one to watch was our Bernard.

One of the girls, a regular Saturday night attender, overheard Bernard and me exchanging good natured insults. She was studying a correspondence course in English and was finding it difficult. She mentioned to her mother that there was an Englishman on the unit who spoke French. This led to an approach. Would I consider coaching her daughter? I said I would be happy to oblige, and was invited to call round the following Monday afternoon.

They lived at the far end of the village in one of the short side streets. The house adjoined a blacksmith's smithy, and contained a small public bar in the far corner of the front room. Beyond this was a dining room with stove and cooking range. Off this room was a bedroom. A door in the dining room gave access to a closed attic staircase and another bedroom. The main bedroom was off the front room, and was sumptuously furnished, the centrepiece being a four-poster curtained bed. There were no gardens. Access to the smithy was directly from the street and from the dining room. In a very restricted area there were thus two businesses and a house.

It was characteristic of the way of life that I should be introduced to the family's domesticity at the outset, as if these were essential indications of their social standing. The mother was quick to point out that, though the bar was public, she never opened in the evenings or at weekends. It was more a hobby than a business.

Credentials having been established introductions could begin. The mother, Janine, performed these. She was a stunningly attractive woman, about five feet seven inches tall. She exhibited evidence of a former voluptuous figure, now thickening, wore her luxurious raven black hair swept up on top of her head, had flawless skin and intense violet eyes. Her carriage was imperious, and there was about her an aura of the aristocracy. I learned later that she was the daughter of a wealthy landowner, against whose will she had married Jean, her blacksmith husband, when she was but twenty, and still subject to her father's will. Father and daughter had been estranged for years, but had begun to heal the breach Since the daughter whom I was to coach was seventeen, it seemed possible that she had been conceived before marriage. This probability hardened when I learned that Janine was thirty seven.

Jean was a year or two older, of medium height, spare of frame, but strong and sinewy. He was a prodigious worker, beginning at seven thirty in the morning and working through the day till folk stopped bringing horses to his smithy. He was also a wheelwright and usually had something in this line on the go. He ate sparingly during the day but drank copiously. Dinner was taken en famille at eight o'clock, after which he went straight to bed. Sundays were free and he joined friends for a game of boules on the village green. It can't have been easy for this couple. Apart from the circumstances of their marriage having created a family rift, for the past six years they had endured German occupation during their daughter's childhood years. They seemed to have survived well.

My student, Marie, had just left school and was looking for a career, as yet unspecified. Jeanette, her sister, was three years younger and still at school. They had very different personalities, and relationships were occasionally emotionally explosive. Throughout my time with the family, I found this sibling friction fascinating. Controlling it was Janine's responsibility. Jean worked such long hours he was probably unaware of it. The younger daughter, having been named after him, could twist him round her little finger.

Though the bar in the living room was open to the public, I never saw a drink served there. That Janine knew the trade was obvious, but it must have been a long time since she had practised it. The coaching sessions took place in the living room, always with maman in attendance. We fitted the hours around my duty periods, but they soon became afternoon or early evening assignments. At the outset, when the question of remuneration arose, I refused payment. Janine proceeded to set the ground rules. I was to join the family every evening for dinner. The meals were superb. An instinctive cook, Janine never used a recipe book, and almost certainly could not have written one. A pinch of this, a soupcon of that, and always a contribution from those bottles behind the bar, created dishes to die for. I have yet to meet anyone who could do more different things with an egg than Janine. Though the shops in the village were invariably empty, and strict food rationing was in force, best steak appeared on the menu every night, never cooked or presented in the same way twice. The family kept a cow that grazed in a meadow close to the technical site. Hens ran free in a small area behind the smithy. Milk and eggs were therefore plentiful.

Every Sunday evening. Janine and the two girls visited the local cinema and, after a few weeks, Janine insisted that I join them. It was the highlight of the week for the villagers, with never an empty seat. The films were in French, which enhanced my knowledge considerably. In terms of preference, the cinema took second place to the Saturday dance, as far as the girls were concerned. Preparations began in mid-afternoon, the sisters vying with each other as to who would attract the greater attention. I had not attended these functions previously, never having been remotely interested. Given my now firmly established relationship with the family, I began to keep Janine company as she sat around the refectory perimeter, along with the other chaperones. They seemed quite happy sitting there from seven till eleven, gossiping and knitting while their daughters danced under their watchful eyes. When I told Janine that I had a sister, three years younger than I, who was allowed to attend all sorts of events unchaperoned, she threw her hands into the air. I asked her if she didn't trust her daughters to behave responsibly. Her reply was straight and to the point, "There are not thirty seven different kinds of youth." I found the choice of age intriguing. She herself was thirty seven. Was there here a flashback to her own youthful indiscretions?

To have these guardians of morality imprisoned for four hours without some refreshment struck me as inhospitable. In order to rectify our shortcomings, I set about finding a remedy. Borrowing a huge aluminium mixing bowl from the kitchen, I mashed up the contents of a seven pound tin of corned beef, poured in a bottle of HP sauce, and churned it all up with a large fork. With a few loaves of white sliced bread, I soon had a pile of sandwiches. They were far from neat. They were substantial. We brewed an urn of tea and served it in pint glasses, placing a large tablespoon in each glass before pouring to disperse the heat. The hitherto four hours uninterrupted vigil now had a ten-minute interval for refreshments. The matrons loved it. During the second half, the traffic to the toilets was non-stop, and chaperone duties had to be delegated. Week by week the number of chaperones increased, as word spread about this novel English cuisine.

One Saturday afternoon, while the girls were preparing their outfits, Janine said, "Let me teach you to dance. I can show you the basic steps. The girls will be happy to partner you." Not waiting for a response she proceeded to do just that. She was a good teacher. I was a willing pupil. Like many matronly figures she was amazingly light on her feet. I'd much rather have taken her to the ball than her daughters. The upshot was that I took to the floor, partnered mainly by Marie, and acquired a new social skill. I have not subsequently used it, but enjoyed it at the time. Janine's motives in this regard were not entirely selfless, in that I suspect she hoped a relationship would develop between pupil and teacher. My heart was securely in someone else's keeping, so this Gallic play at matchmaking was a non-starter. In cryptic terms : Gaelic 1 Gallic 0.

Since our engagement, correspondence between Ann and me had been frequent, with the future ever in our thoughts. All in all, we wanted to be together sooner rather than later. I still had no firm prospects, but a teaching career was there for the taking. The seven year age gap bothered her. It didn't worry me, though I could see it was another reason to marry soon. Since she was in a better position to investigate, she undertook to explore the possibilities, and to keep me informed.

Out of the blue, the unit acquired a change of leadership. FO Drummond had become embroiled with Bernard, the latter having pursued the CO assiduously for weeks. Their assignations became public knowledge, arousing doubts as to the propriety of the officer's position. He was open to blackmail for whatever reasons Bernard might have to resort to such tactics. Whether Drummond was pushed, or whether he jumped, we shall never know. The fact is he went, and precipitously at that. In his stead came FO Whittaker, of whom we shall learn more later.

The end of hostilities brought contrasting fortunes to visitor and vanquished. The Allies were demobilising their troops at a rate determined by age, length of service, and trade classification. My demobilisation group was 40. Had I been in the General Duties category, I would have been released by now. As a radar mechanic, it could be anything up to a year to eighteen months before I could expect discharge.

Former enemy troops were consigned to prisoner of war camps, uncertain of the date and conditions of their repatriation. One such camp was in Laon, some forty miles south of La Capelle, and we received orders one day to collect a POW for attachment to the unit. I drove down with the newly appointed FO Whittaker. There was an almost pathological hatred between the French and the Germans, and the conditions in this particular camp were spartan. Hundreds of incarcerated men were shuffling around inside a compound when we arrived, and the French Commandant invited us to select one. Whittaker left the choice to me. "You've been there," he said, "and speak the lingo." I ran my eye over the motley crowd on view, before focussing on a man of about my own height, but twice as broad. I observed the way he moved.

There was an underlying athleticism I liked. Also discernible was still some vestige of personal pride. This man's spirit remained unbroken. He turned round and I had a frontal view. A broad, open face, strong bone structure, and slate grey eyes that caught mine and held them. "That's our man," I said. "Let's see to the documentation." So did Hans come to La Capelle, freed from a prisoner of war camp on the whim of a British airman.

I laid down the ground rules. He would earn his keep. He would be treated fairly. He would enjoy as much freedom as was judged compatible with his status. As far as I was concerned, he was a human being first, a prisoner second. He was put to work in the cookhouse, and accommodated in the attic, with sufficient blankets to make a comfortable bed. He slept on the floorboards. I asked him his name, rank, and number. He told me he'd been a sergeant in a parachute unit. He displayed remarkable physical strength within minutes of his arrival. A heavy Hay box, a device for keeping food hot, had been delivered in my absence and needed shifting across the kitchen. I called a couple of the men to do the job. They struggled but were unable to lift it. "Bitte," said Hans, taking up a crouch position in front of it. Extending arms unusually long for his body, he got a secure grip on both ends, came slowly up from the crouch, using his thigh muscles, and the box cleared the ground. Grunting, he waddled across the kitchen, and lowered it gently into the required position. "Danke," I said. We had made a good start. We never looked back.

One afternoon shortly afterwards, a group of us were kicking a football about on the field at the rear of the villa, when it bounced towards the touchline where Hans was standing. He flicked it up, juggled it with feet, head, and thighs, before kicking it back. I signalled him to come and join in. He was no novice. "We are playing the local village team tomorrow evening," I said. "You are in at centre-half." His face lit up. "Say one word during the game," I warned, "and you'll be driven straight back to Laon." He grinned and held his fingers over his mouth. We murdered the opposition and nobody suspected that the star performer in our ranks was a German POW.

La Capelle burst into life when the racing calendar reached the village. The programme comprised trotting races, with jockeys seated in two-wheeled buggies drawn by highly trained horses. It required skill to trot a horse at top speed whilst preventing it from breaking into a gallop, and the competitive element of a race situation provided an exciting spectacle, full of incident.

Janine invited me to attend as her guest. Her father was one of the jockeys. He was nudging seventy and had raced as an amateur all over France, though he farmed locally. A big man, he had a ferocious appearance, and, according to his son-in-law Jean, an evil temper and sharp tongue. "He is naughty, very naughty." was Jean's verdict, probably from first hand experience. The old man seemed to take to me and said, "You'll be placing a bet." I said that I might but didn't know which rider to back. He showed me the bookies' lists. I said I supposed the favourite was a safe bet. He looked around furtively and whispered, "He won't finish today." "Who do you fancy?" I asked, at which he guffawed. "Moi," he boomed, slapping his thigh. "Moi, certainement." I asked Janine where her money was going. "Papa," she replied. "Papa will win. He grew up on this course." I followed suit and backed Papa.

The track was circular, and the far side was scarcely visible from the stands. They took off, some thirty aspirants, each sporting distinctive colours, all jockeying for position. Papa seemed well placed as they reached the bend going into the far side. As they were negotiating a long stretch, not visible from where we stood, a groan went up, and travelled round the course. The favourite had taken a tumble. Coming into the final two hundred metres, Papa's colours could be seen coming through the field fast. His sprint finish was expertly timed, and he crossed the finishing line with one arm raised in triumph. At the celebrations that followed, I said to him, "You were right about the favourite. He didn't finish." "No," he agreed. "He jumped out of his buggy on a blind bend. It wasn't his turn to win. It was mine." He winked and went to get changed. I was joined by Jean. "A very naughty man," he said, patting a bulging wallet, "very, very naughty." I congratulated Janine on her father's success. "He handles horses extremely well," was her comment, "but you should have seen him with the women when he was younger."

Regular Saturday night dances, attended by chaperones with one eye on the protection of their daughters' virtue, the other on the prospects of marrying them off, provide fertile ground for romantic dalliance. Several examples merit mention. Dan Dewar, an excellent motor mechanic, was adopted by a local family whose daughter, a pretty but rather vacuous only child, evinced early aspirations of wedded bliss. These were intensified when she was found to be pregnant. Being staunch Roman Catholics, the parents urged immediate marriage and Dan moved in. Early demobilisation enabled him to find a job in a local garage, and entry into the Roman Catholic faith, insisted upon by his in-laws, was followed quickly by a shop steward's role, and active membership of the Communist Party. None of these had been in his mind on arrival at La Capelle, but the integration seemed to his liking.

Cyril Swift, a radar operator, was another to succumb to Saturday night fever. He was thirty six, physically unathletic, mentally uninspiring, personally non-charismatic. I doubt if any girl would have looked upon him romantically. He found it difficult to attract a dance partner. Among the array on offer weekly were two sisters, Yvonne and Yvette. Yvonne was engaged to a local man, a liaison encouraged by both sets of parents, as it would consolidate two large land owning enterprises. Yvonne obviously went along with this, but did not let it restrict her natural social exuberance. She was never without dancing partners and flirted outrageously.

Yvette was different. Some illness in infancy had left a legacy. She was almost expressionless, with no visible signs of any emotion. Her conversation was stilted. It was rumoured that she was subject to occasional fits. At thirty, she seemed destined for the shelf. Then fate took a hand. Yvonne got married, and a sumptuous affair it was, with celebrations stretching through the night till dawn. The venue was the family farm. Tables laden with food and drink, and continuous live music to encourage lively dancing, catered for over three hundred guests, among whom were most of our unit. Though the centre of activity was in the farmhouse proper, as the night wore on, couples could be seen slipping away in search of quieter, more private amenities. About 3am, Yvette's father, allegedly checking the well-being of his stock, stumbled upon her and Cyril in what is sometimes discreetly described as a compromising situation. How this had come about is not known, but Cyril, confronted by an angry French father, incensed at the besmirching of his daughter's honour, was persuaded to make of her an honest woman. So a second wedding took place shortly afterwards. He spoke little French. She spoke no English. How the marriage fared I know not, but Maman had no need to chaperone her daughters any more.

The third example is perhaps the most revealing. FO Whittaker had got off to a bad start. Fresh to command, he had been keen to make his mark. Discipline was admittedly slack, the war being over, and almost everyone looking forward to demobilisation. The newly promoted officer, noticing that nobody was wearing collars and ties at breakfast, posted an order, 'Collars and ties will be worn at mealtimes.' The following morning, seated at the table specially reserved for him, he was treated to the spectacle of twelve men, lined up at the serving hatch, wearing collars and ties----nothing else----just collars and ties. It put him off his grub for the rest of the day, and the notice was quietly rescinded.

After this unpromising start, he proved to be a decent sort, and was soon accepted and respected. A regular attender at the Saturday dances, his rank and uniform attracted one of the village's acknowledged upper class families. Once again, there were two daughters, one beautiful and vivacious, the other reticent and almost childlike in disposition. Both were in their thirties and as yet unmarried. The chase was on.

Giselle, the elder, was the centre of attraction, men flocking around her, but never with any sign of lasting commitment. Denise, the younger, attracted FO Whittaker from the outset, who responded to her childlike simplicity and baby blue eyes that gazed on him adoringly. Her enterprising parents seized the initiative, and Whittaker became a nightly visitor to their well appointed home. Janine gave me some background information that the parents had reached the point of considering entry to a convent for Denise, marriage appearing to be a forlorn prospect. Then along came this handsome young English officer. In a remarkably short time, he proposed marriage and was accepted, subject to conditions. He would have to embrace the Catholic faith. So infatuated was he that he agreed, and a course of instruction, lasting several weeks, was drawn up. With but a smattering of French, he asked if I would accompany him, and in due course be his best man. Thus, by proxy, I became initiated into the mysteries, beliefs, and practices of the Roman Catholic Church.

The wedding was held in the local church, which was packed for the occasion. The bride looked as radiant as I had ever seen her. The groom's demeanour was that of a man not fully understanding the processes being undergone. The best man contented himself with reflecting on the mysterious ways God has of accomplishing the apparently unthinkable. The bride's parents were ecstatic. The shadow of the convent had receded.

Christmas crept silently upon us, so different from the last, when there'd been no room at the inn, and the Battle of the Bulge was raging. This year peace reigned and I had two places in which to celebrate one with the unit, the other with my French family. On Christmas Day I helped in the kitchen, preparing the traditional dinner, Hans by my side. As is the custom FO Whittaker and the NCO's served the men. Being the official go-between for Hans, I asked him to take a seat with the men. He declined. I asked him again. He demurred. I confronted him and said, "Hans, I am no longer inviting you. I am ordering you. You will sit with the men and I shall sit beside you." He responded to this and we took our seats. As the CO set our plates before us, and glasses of beer were served, I raised my glass and drank to his very good health. Slowly, he raised his own, clinked mine, and sipped silently. As he plied his knife and fork, a tear formed and trickled down his cheek, to be brushed away on the back of his hand. It was Christmas. He was separated from his family, wherever they might be. I was separated from mine. We found solace in the spirit of the season. Later in the day, the ever-hospitable Janine welcomed me to her family celebrations. I was twice blessed.

Throughout the previous weeks Ann had been actively arranging our wedding plans, and I had been pursuing a leave to coincide with them. We had fixed on Jan 31 1946 in Inverness, So at this particular Christmas, I was thrice blessed. In just over a month's time, the chance meeting of two people, posted to a remote outpost in the Outer Hebrides, would culminate in a ceremony and celebration that would commit each to the other for life.

The build up to the wedding was my principal activity from Christmas onward. Courtesy of the CO I was the recipient of a few bottles of his spirit ration. Janine contributed a bottle of her finest champagne, and some vintage white wines. In the nearby village of Hirson, a short train journey away, I bought a portable radio set, and paid for it in cigarettes. My backpack was full when the time came to travel. This time

Calais was much nearer, but the weather much colder. January is not the best time to cross the Channel.

The Customs procedures had reverted to normal and I was prepared for a substantial levy on my goods over the permitted allowances. With three officers on duty, it was a lottery as to which I drew. Judging by appearance, the one I got was very experienced. I could expect a thoroughly rigorous examination. "Anything to declare?" he asked, noncommittally. "A radio set, several bottles of spirits, and a few cartons of cigarettes." I stated. "Radio set," he commented. "Let's have a look." I opened up the carton it was in. "Make a habit of bringing these in?" he queried. "No," I replied. "I'm going on leave to get married. The radio is a present for my wife. It will be company for her while I'm away." "And the drink?" he pressed. I opened my backpack with its impressive contents, augmented in the duty free shop on board ship by a bottle of DOM Benedictine. He went away and attended to somebody else. On returning, he resumed the inquisition. "How much did you pay for the radio, and how long have you had it?" I reflected for a moment or two before replying. "Six thousand francs, and a month," I replied. He departed again. Rejoining me he said, "If you'd paid a thousand francs less, and had had it a couple of months longer, it would have been to your advantage." He wandered off, yet again, leaving me in a quandary. Back again, and looking me straight in the eye, he asked, "How much did you say you'd paid for this radio?" I took a deep breath, held his gaze, and answered, "Five thousand francs." He nodded. "And how long have you had it?" he continued. "Three months," I replied. "Right," he said, "Nothing to pay there, then. There is of course that bottle of whisky, which amounts to (quoting a derisory amount). My kind regards to your wife and my best wishes for your future."

This pleasant episode concluded, I headed for the railway platform and caught the London train. The capital was as bustling as ever, reviving memories of my days in Battersea. Before me lay that fifteen hour run to Inverness. This time, I was not bound for Bunchrew House. Ann had arranged the wedding for five o'clock in the afternoon, in the lounge of a centrally situated hotel, and had booked accommodation for the small party. Brother Donald was to be my best man, Cathy from Rodel Ann's bridesmaid, and Sgt. Smith, of the Inverness police force, was to give the bride away, deputising for Ann's father. The officiating minister, Rev. William Fraser of the Free Church of Scotland, had a parish nearby. My parents had travelled up by train, and completed the party. Respecting tradition, we did not meet, on the day of the wedding until the appointed hour.

I experienced a hairy moment as Donald and I were rehearsing our roles in the hotel bedroom. I handed him the ring to put in his pocket for safekeeping. He dropped it and it rolled under the wardrobe. This piece of furniture had been built to last, being both solid and heavy, We couldn't budge it. It took two brawny members of staff to shift it enough to retrieve the ring. It was beginning to look as though Donald and I were best kept apart. A simple ceremony, an excellent meal, appropriate speeches, a visit to a photographic studio, and we were ready to catch the night train, en route to Harrogate, our honeymoon venue. Donald had not yet finished. He insisted on supervising our luggage, telling me to look after Ann. We had taken our seats on the train, and were bidding our farewells, when a distraught looking gentleman came tearing along the platform. "Are you the wedding party from (naming our hotel)?" We said we were. "Do you have an extra case?" he asked. I checked. We had. Donald had picked up one too many. But then, he'd had one too many.

We spent a week in a private guesthouse in Belmont Road. The weather was marvellous for early February, and we managed a walk in the Valley Gardens every day. To have each other exclusively to ourselves was a foretaste of what was to come, and we made the most of every minute. At the end of an idyllic week, we parted once again, Ann returning to Lewis, myself to La Capelle. We held fast to the thought that my demobilisation could not be far away.

A surprise belated wedding present awaited my return. In my absence, I had been promoted to corporal. As the demobilisation process developed, vacancies were being created in the non-commissioned ranks, and I was the recipient of one. The move was marked by my quitting the main dormitory to occupy a room of my own along the corridor. More good news followed. Along with a colleague, Roland Oakham, I was invited to attend for interview in Hanover, in connection with my application for Emergency Teacher Training. It was likely to be a long journey, and I was glad of the company. FO Whittaker was most helpful in arranging transport and overnight stops, so we took a leisurely three days travelling in each direction.

*La Capelle, France –
A surprise belated wedding present, I had been promoted to corporal.*

Yet again I marvelled at the vast expanse of Germany and the beauty of its countryside. I also witnessed the devastation of some of the major cities, with Cologne in particular creating an impression. Even now, with the peace in its eighth month, a huge programme of reconstruction awaited implementation. The badly damaged cathedral was a poignant sight.

Though some of our route took us along minor roads, we made good use of those marvellous autobahns, which enabled us to gobble up the miles. We arrived in Hanover in the late afternoon, and were billeted in an old airfield camp. Exploring the immediate vicinity, we discovered a hangar stacked high with brand new toolkits, containing stainless steel instruments with adjustable mirrors on every tool, to facilitate working under vehicles without having to crawl under them. German efficiency personified.

Our interviews were scheduled for the following day, commencing at 9 am. Feeling that a good night's sleep was advisable, I planned for an early bed, but Roland and I went for a stroll beforehand. The change in the street scene was startling. Earlier, people had been bustling about their business. From 7 pm onwards, families began to stake their places for the night, spreading blankets on the pavements. By 9 pm we couldn't walk there, every inch being occupied by people still homeless after the devastation in which I had played a part. It was a salutary lesson. I salved my conscience by recalling London, Liverpool, Coventry, and my own north east, but still retired to bed with images of young children out on the streets while I enjoyed warmth, cleanliness, and comfort.

The day of destiny dawned and we reported on time. A long list was posted on the notice board. It was in alphabetical order, and I was down for late afternoon. We were advised not to leave the premises, since changes in proceedings were always possible. I spent the morning and most of the afternoon watching candidates come and go, some quite happy, others deflated, most just relieved. Eventually, my name was called. I approached the door to which I was directed, knocked and entered.

It was a surprisingly large room, perhaps thirty feet long. At the far end was a table, behind which four men were seated. In the centre of the room, conspicuously isolated, was a single chair. I waited for some movement from those behind the table. None came. Advancing quietly, I reached the chair and stood beside it. A bald headed gentleman looked up, feigned surprise, beamed, and said, "Ah, Cpl. Watson, please do take a seat." Momentarily, I thought about asking him where he wanted me to take it, thought better of it, and sat down. The next quarter of an hour was conducted at a lively tempo. The bald headed man introduced himself and his colleagues, and the questioning began. Each interviewer had papers in front of him, on which he made observations. There was no discernible order of precedence, questions coming from each in random, rapid order. Though these appeared to be unconnected, I sensed there was a structure to the process. These people knew what they were looking for, and how to elicit it. As if by the direction of an unseen controller, the interrogation ceased abruptly. The Chairman regarded me benevolently, from over his glasses, and said, "Thank you, corporal. That was most helpful. I wonder if you will assist us further by retiring to the room next door, and leaving us a sample of your creative writing. A page will suffice. You will be notified of the result of your application in due course. Thank you for attending." I thanked him and withdrew. As far as I can recall, my written piece went something like this:

'It was a pleasant evening as the vessel pulled out of Kyle of Loch Alsh. The sun cast a golden glow on the shimmering surface of the inner harbour, auguring well for the crossing to come. Beyond the piers, the breeze rippling the ocean swell, the scene was transformed into scintillating pinpoints of light on the water, glistening like diamonds. As she plunged her bows into the rolling billows of the open sea, a creamy wake was sliced and turned over, to run frothily along the vessel's sides. Behind her, an ever-broadening wash left evidence of her passage momentarily on the surface of the sea, soon to dissipate and disappear. The views from the deck were panoramic, embracing the Scottish mainland and the Isle of Skye, with bays, headlands and mountain peaks successively catching the angled rays of the sun. It continued thus till daylight began to wane, and I sought the comfort of the passenger saloon, now full of people. Almost all were reading, some with heads in books, others perusing magazines, several skimming an assortment of newspapers. Though I had, as was my wont, a book to hand, I settled to studying the people. Where were they going? Where were they from? What was their lifestyle? One can learn much from books. One can learn more from people. They write books.'

I left my contribution at the desk and took my leave. It was a sobering thought that the last hour would have a profound effect on the rest of my life. All I could do now was wait.

The chaperones at the Saturday dances continuing to clamour for our corned beef and HP sauce sandwiches, we thought we would see if they had wider appeal. Stacking a 15 cwt truck with sliced white bread, bottles of sauce, tins of pilchards, cans of peanut butter and an assortment of chocolate bars, I called on some of the outlying farms with encouraging results, returning with chickens, fresh cream, eggs, butter, and stone ground flour. The unit menu took on a more varied aspect. One farm in particular stands out in retrospect. The house was long and low, and built on a hill, with commanding views to the east. I had some fascinating conversations with the owner and his wife who, in their lifetimes, had seen their home fall into the hands of German invaders three times. I asked them why they stayed. "We are tied to the land by the blood line of centuries." they explained. "They can destroy our home. The land they will never annexe. We will hold it in perpetuity." Such indomitable spirit was reflected in their faces, proud, strong-boned, and weather beaten.

It was about this time that Mike Walker joined the unit. A giant of a man, six feet four inches tall, broad in the shoulder, slim in the waist, and with a head like a Viking warrior, he was an immediate hit with the ladies. Mike wasn't all he seemed. The virile appearance masked an indolence that influenced his approach to life. Beyond doubt, he was the biggest skiver I have ever met. His story spans three generations. His father had worked as a builder's labourer in Birmingham, shovelling soil unearthed in digging out foundations, and loading it into trucks for disposal. At the weekend, he worked for a chemical company that delivered fertiliser to market gardeners. An astute man, he spotted an opening for himself, hired a lorry, filled it with unwanted soil from the building site, mixed in some fertiliser, and sold it to market gardeners as top quality top soil. Ere long, he had bought the lorry he'd been renting.

Within a year or two, he had established a thriving business, serving a suburb of Birmingham. In due course, his son came into the business, and his drive and initiative expanded it into a limited company doing business across Birmingham and beyond. Then Mike, the third generation, was recruited. Spoilt throughout his childhood, never needing to work, not appreciating the value of money, or his inheritance, he was the prodigal grandson. Life for Mike was self-gratification, particularly where women were concerned. With his looks, he'd probably had many.

At the Saturday dances, he could have had his way with any of the girls, notwithstanding the chaperoning. It wasn't a girl who caught his eye. It was Janine. As we were making our way back to the smithy after the dance one Saturday, Mike attached himself to the family group. What transpired was a revelation. Married life for this most handsome and attractive woman was by now a low octane partnership. Jean was probably too tired, after his hard day's work, to even feel the need to rekindle old fires. There was in Janine a slumbering sexuality that, given the right circumstances, and the right man, could have erupted into tempestuous passion. Mike might well have been the catalyst had the circumstances been different. He persisted in the pursuit for several weeks, Janine thoroughly enjoying the headiness of the situation, ever leading him on, never allowing him in. In the end, his indolence succumbed to indifference. Why pursue this unattainable woman when there were so many around who were available, and younger too? I watched Janine throughout this fascinating episode and admired her resilience, and ultimately her loyalty. She relished the sexual power she still possessed, rejoiced that it attracted a man of Mike Walker's unquestioned attraction, but knew that her real supremacy was to know when and where to stop, on her terms. Like her father, she was strong, 'une femme tres forte'. She was not 'une femme fatale'.

Though the relationship between the unit and the locals was cordial, there was an element that resented our presence, and occasionally showed it. When one of the watches came off duty at 8 am one morning, they discovered that the fuel compound had been raided during the night. Lorry tracks were found in the approach lane, but none around the compound itself. A stretcher had been abandoned in a nearby hedge, and it bore unmistakable signs of having supported oil drums. The barbed wire had not been cut, but had plainly been flattened, then straightened out again. The perpetrators were never traced. It had been a well-planned job, timed to take place between the hourly inspections of the power supplies.

On a more individual note, one of our men was quite badly assaulted in a café brawl one evening. He had committed the basic mistake of drinking alone. The first we knew of the incident was a call from the local gendarmerie. Would we go and collect him? He had been hit in the face with a broken chair leg, causing a broken nose, one eye completely closed, and some damage to his teeth. Later examination disclosed broken ribs. Enquiries led to the arrest of those involved, but the CO decided not to press charges. We heard later that the local magistrate meted out his own justice. Whittaker ensured that our man was similarly dealt with. Relationships continued amicably thereafter.

This prevailing excellent rapport was reinforced a day or two later. I went down with a nasty virus that completely felled me, to the extent that FO Whittaker decided hospital was advisable, and began making arrangements for my admission to a military establishment in Reims. Before he did, I asked him to telephone Janine to tell her I would not be joining the family that evening, and for an unspecified number of evenings to follow. On hearing why, she offered to take me in, summon her own family doctor, and look after me until fit to resume duties. Whittaker accepted like a shot, I presumed with my best interests at heart. There is almost always another agenda. "It will save a hell of a lot of paper work," he commented.

I have no recollection of the transfer. I fell asleep in my bed on the unit and woke in feather-mattressed luxury in the spare bedroom up that closed staircase to the attic, the sounds of the smithy underneath. being clearly audible. The doctor was a young man, up to date with recent developments, and prescribed an only recently available drug. "C'est magnifique," he told Janine. It certainly was. Within twenty four hours, fever that had caused delirium had abated, and convalescence had begun. A day or two later, nasty white spots erupted in my throat and mouth, my tongue swelled to the extent that indentations of my teeth were clearly evident in it, and mouth ulcers broke out. Penicillin is a wonderful drug, unless you are allergic to it, which I was and am. The convalescence was longer than expected, and I was comprehensively spoilt.

I have often pondered on Janine's motives in regard to myself. In her eyes, I believe I was the son she never had. I also believe I was the son-in-law she never got. This second possibility vanished with my marriage. Yet, her very real attachment to me strengthened after that event, as her response to my illness epitomises. Relationships are not unilateral. What of mine with her? As I have indicated, she was a remarkable woman, old enough to be my mother, but only just. I certainly didn't think of her in that role. Though sixteen years my senior, I was attracted like others to her comprehensive array of feminine qualities. She was my ideal template of womanhood. Being unattainable, she became an icon to be idealised and fantasised about. We all yearn for the impossible at key moments in our lives. Janine taught me so much about life, and especially about people, but most specifically about women. I am the wiser for our lives having crossed for a year and a half, over six decades ago, when our French and English cultures met and intertwined.

My return to duty coincided with a noteworthy delivery of mail. Sifting through the pile on the refectory table, Roland Oakham spotted two official looking envelopes, a small one addressed to him, a foolscap to me. Handing mine over he said, "I reckon I'm out, you're in." So it proved. I had been accepted for teacher training, and would be notified in due course as to when and where the programme would begin. Knowing that Ann had concluded her term of service, and was living at home, I decided to telephone that evening. There was no domestic connection, but the public phone for the village was housed in the storm porch of the croft house opposite. It was used mainly for outgoing calls, but whenever it rang the resident owner-occupier usually took a message. On the off chance that she was in, I rang about 9pm Lewis time. After a few rings, a voice asked if it could help. "Could you please take a message for Annabella at number 24?" I asked, politely. "I can do better than that," came the reply, "She's in my sitting room having a cup of tea. Who shall I say is calling?" "Tell her it's her husband calling from France," I told her. "Oo, my goodness," was the excited response, followed by a stentorian yell, "Annabella, it's your man on the line." We had a good chat. She was overjoyed at my news. We could now plan firmly for the future. I was glad I'd phoned. It was lovely to hear her voice again.

La Capelle, France –
Could you please take a message for Annabella at number 24.

Ever since Christmas, Hans had been working away in the kitchen and elsewhere, apparently filling in his time philosophically, retiring to his attic retreat in the evening. I saw to it that he had a radio for company, and normally left him undisturbed.

For no specific reason, I invaded his privacy one evening, and asked him if there was anything I could do to improve his lot. He thought a bit and said he would like to go to church on Sunday mornings, if that was possible. He was a Catholic. I said that I would look into it. I reported the conversation to the CO who gave me permission to approach the church authorities. On the following afternoon, it being a glorious day, I walked down to the convent attached to the church, and pressed the bell push at the main entrance. No response resulting, I was about to ring again, when sounds from within stayed my hand. The door swung open silently, and an elderly nun signalled to me to enter. I felt the ethos of the place immediately. Silence held sway over a spacious interior that basked in a sort of half light. I asked if I might have a word with the Mother Superior. The nun inclined her head,

La Capelle, France – Croft house, Lewis.

said nothing, glided smoothly into a nearby recess, and disappeared. It was several minutes before anything happened, the continuing peace and tranquillity prevailing. I took a seat and basked in the balm.

From out of the shadows emerged a slim figure, moving noiselessly as though on well lubricated ball bearings. No feet were visible beneath a long robe as the apparition made silent progress towards me, stopping where a filtered ray of light fell across its face. I suppressed a gasp. The face reflected the ethos of the surroundings. Pale, placid, unlined, almost porcelain in its texture, it was breathtaking in its own right. But the eyes. Oh, those eyes, a deep, fathomless violet that seemed to probe my inner being, while being themselves impenetrable. What in heaven's name was a woman like this doing sequestered in a nunnery? She introduced herself and asked my business. I told her who I was and explained that I had a German POW of her faith who wished to attend Mass on Sunday mornings. If I brought him, was she prepared to guarantee his safe return? She said she was. I took one last, lingering look at that incomparable face, and drank deeply from those limpid violet pools. "Merci bien," I said, taking my leave. "A bientot." I never saw her again. I delivered Hans every Sunday morning from then on and he was always there for collection. The Mother Superior was as good as her word. What a role for such a vision. Mother she would never be. Superior she most certainly was.

Meanwhile, a welcome innovation at the technical site was the acquisition of two diesel engines, each mounted on three-ton Bedford trucks. Working 24 hrs each, in successive sessions, they supplied power to the radar equipment, making the petrol electric sets redundant. The watch workload was considerably reduced. After a few weeks, it was decided to house the diesels in purpose built Nissen huts. From this we inferred that the site had a long-term future. One of the diesels was duly installed on a concrete base, which would require at least three days to set hard enough to support the thrust of the engine in motion. Once this was commissioned, the other diesel could be similarly housed.

I had been working on the first diesel's housing all morning, and it was satisfactorily installed on its bed of concrete before I went off for dinner. Half way through my meal, I was summoned to the telephone. There was a problem on the technical site. The second diesel, still in its Bedford truck, was on fire. I dashed upstairs to my bedroom window, from where I knew I could see in the direction of the technical site. Beyond a small copse black smoke was billowing. I sped back downstairs, collected three off duty men, jumped into a Jeep, and broke all the local speed limits. When I reached the site, things didn't look too good. The station was still on the air, but the heat and flames prevented access to the back of the truck, where I had planned to shut the diesel down, and disconnect the power line to the radar station inside the adjacent Nissen. Another factor made the situation much worse. The tar coating on the Nissen exterior was alight. We could lose the lot—diesel, Bedford, and a complete radar station.

There was only one course of action open to me, and that required immediate implementation. Donning heavy rubber gloves, and grabbing an axe from the workshop, I attacked the heavy seven-cored power cable, warning others to stand well clear. There could be a lethal display of fireworks, and that part of the cable still attached to the diesel would be live. It was surprisingly easy to hack through the cable. That done, I climbed into the Bedford driving seat, crossed absolutely everything, and pressed the starter. She fired first time. I remember thinking she wouldn't be cold for sure. Slipping into first gear, I eased her foot by foot until she had real purchase, went into second, and drove like a bat out of hell. When I judged she was far enough away from the radar equipment to pose little problem, I flung the door open and raced back to where the truck had been. The rest of the crew had extinguished the blaze on the Nissen hut roof and sides.

All eyes were on the blazing Bedford and diesel. A second or two later, they went up with a colossal roar. The radar mast, some thirty yards distant, stood 105 feet tall. The pall of thick black smoke from the ruptured diesel tank had rocketed almost as high. I assessed the situation. I had no power. The only available diesel was standing on a bed of setting concrete. I still had a transmitter, a receiver, and an aerial mast. I also had a massive operation due about midnight, involving a few hundred aircraft. To cap it all, FO Whittaker had taken off for the weekend on an unofficial visit to Paris with his recently acquired wife. I had real problems and little time in which to solve them.

The unit had been off the air since I had cut the power supply some ten minutes previously. The normal time allowed for the resumption of operational efficiency after a breakdown was two minutes. I entered the radar hut and asked for a connection to the highest-ranking officer available at Wing HQ. A Wing Commander came on and asked to speak to the CO. I told him that FO Whittaker was currently fully occupied (not untrue) and that I was handling this very serious emergency. I summarised the situation and provided the only partial solution. "I need power, sir," I said. "In the workshop I have what is left of petrol electric engines that supplied power before we switched to diesels. I've had a quick check, and I can have two running in time to perform normal checks on the radar equipment, preparatory to tonight's operation. If need be, I could run them through the night, but two more engines as standby would be advisable. I may be able to cannibalise parts from others we still have on site, but I cannot be sure of that. There must be old petrol electric sets on stations elsewhere. It would be a great help if they could be located and brought here as soon as possible." "Go ahead with tonight's operation, corporal," came the reply. "I'll have spares up there as soon as possible. Good luck." Within the hour, I had the station back on air, powered by two petrol electric engines. The rest of that day, and the whole night was spent in creating another pair of engines from spares we had lying around.

We started the big operation with enough cover to feel safe, should either of the two engines in commission break down. Extra spares began to arrive in staggered deliveries, and were added to the pool. With our commitment to the night operation met, we were not yet out of the woods. It would be another two days before our only diesel could be brought into service, and the petrol engines were used in pairs in eight-hour shifts. I spent the next day and night meeting these requirements. FO Whittaker returned late in the evening of the second day, aghast at what had happened, but relieved to know that I'd covered his absence.

I was still at work, nursing my petrol electric engines on the afternoon of the third day when someone entered the workshop. "I'm looking for Cpl. Watson," said a cultured voice. I was dead tired, unshaven, scruffy, grimy, and fed up. Without rising or saluting I said, "You've found him----sir." "Ah, don't get up, man. I can see you've got your hands full," said the Wing Commander. "Get my spares did you?" "I did sir. Couldn't have managed without them." "Excellent. Excellent," purred the Wing Commander. "Is FO Whittaker about?" "I think you'll find him at the domestic site," I answered."He's had rather a rough few days." With that he took his leave. Within a week, two promotions were announced. I became Sgt. Ken Watson. The CO became Ft. Lt. Whittaker. All's well that ends well as they say.

Possibly feeling sheepish, on his next trip to Paris the CO left his wife behind, and invited me to accompany him. This time, it was just a day trip and we took a Fordson. Though my driving skills had developed since acquiring my licence, Parisian traffic was a new experience, not helped by the fact that my vehicle had celluloid side windows, excellent for keeping out wind and rain, lethal for not being able to see through. I drove round the Place de la Concorde with both front windows down. The draught was fierce, the views excellent. I dropped the CO off at the officers' mess, arranging to pick him up at 8 pm. What his business was he didn't say, but I had a few hours to myself. My first call was to the sergeant's mess, my initial experience of life at this level. I decided I liked it.

I thought it advisable to check the petrol level in the Fordson before starting the return journey. It's as well I did. The gauge registered empty. No problem. This was a twin-tanked vehicle. I went to check that the second tank supply line was open, to find that the feed cock had jammed in the closed position. All the gunge in the bottom of the other tank had been sucked into the engine. I checked the fuel level in the second tank.

It was full to the brim. In the glove compartment was a round tin containing fifty cigarettes. I emptied it, fed a clean rag into the neck of the petrol tank, and wrung it out into the tin. A few repetitions and the tin was full. I then opened the cock on the full fuel tank, poured the tinful of newly won petrol into the air intake, and closed the empty fuel tank feeder line. I hoped that the flow from the full tank, backed up by the supply in the air intake, would blast the blockage through. With fingers crossed, I started her up, giving the accelerator a gentle touch or two. She was a little reluctant at first, then began to splutter spasmodically, until, with a sudden full-throated roar, black smoke belched out of the exhaust to disperse in the Parisian air. I drove to the depot, filled the empty tank, and went to get cleaned up. Of Paris I had seen very little.

It was already dark when we left, and once the centre of the city was behind us street lighting became less frequent and, ere long, we were on unlit country roads. Whittaker had dosed off beside me and I was maintaining a steady 50 mph. For several miles there was no traffic in either direction, and the monotonous whine of the engine, along with the thrumm, thrumm, thrumm. of the tyres, made concentration difficult. Straight level roads asked for no gear changes which would have broken the hypnotic rhythms. Focussing on the probing headlamp beams exacerbated the feeling of lethargy and drowsiness. A red taillight up ahead registered. How long before I overtook him? I continued, still at 50 mph. The distance between the red taillight and me was decreasing rapidly. Must be stationary. I'll pull out, ready to pass him. Hold on. He's in the middle of the road. Something's wrong. I changed down from fourth gear to second, omitting third, applying the brakes in regular depressions of the pedal. I was about twenty yards away when I realised I was approaching a closed level crossing gate, its red warning light centrally mounted. I threw the steering wheel round and applied the brakes fully. Slight drizzle had made the cobbled road surface greasy, and the vehicle slewed round to come to a stop broadside on to the gate. There was only just room for me to get out. When I did I vomited.

Whittaker awoke, much bemused, found the driver's seat unoccupied, and clambered out. Taking the situation in very quickly he enquired, "Are you OK?" Wiping my mouth I nodded. The train for which the gate had been closed passed through, and the road ahead opened up. "You'd better take over sir," I said. "Get back in the driver's seat right now," ordered Whittaker. "If you don't you may never want to drive again. You've had a nasty shock. What you need is the hair of the dog that's just bitten you." He was right. Within a few minutes I was myself again. In retrospect, it had been a narrow squeak.

A rather less dramatic driving experience occurred a few days later, when an RAF padre visited the unit. In the evening he expressed a desire to meet the men on duty at the technical site, whom he would otherwise have missed. The CO gave him directions as to how to get there, but he seemed unsure of himself. "I'll tell you what," suggested Whittaker, "Why not let the sergeant here drive you there? He knows the way, and he's a very capable driver in night time conditions." Here he shot me a conspiratorial glance. "Well that's very good of you, " said the padre. "My car's just outside." I occupied the driver's seat and sat there bewildered. Trucks I understood. I'd never driven a saloon car. Anyway, I managed to start it. Steering it was another matter. The slightest deviation of the steering wheel produced alarming changes of direction. By the time we reached the technical site, I had just about mastered it. Not sufficiently it seemed for the padre's peace of mind. He insisted on driving on the way back.

La Capelle, France – Rededication Procession.

One of the abiding memories of La Capelle is of taking part in a rededication ceremony. At the end of the 1914-18 war, the Allied victory had been commemorated by the erection of an obelisk on the roadside at the outskirts of the village. In 1940 German tanks had deliberately desecrated it as they roared back into France as invaders. A newly commissioned replacement, suitably inscribed, was now installed.

La Capelle, France – Rededication ceremony.

We were invited to provide half a dozen men in full dress uniform to join the dedication parade and ceremony. It was an honour to lead our contingent as the procession marched down the village main street and on to the site. Crowds lined the route and we were warmly applauded as we marched along. Our presence in the community was fully confirmed that day, marching as we did with various units of the French armed forces.

My unexpected promotion to sergeant had increased significantly my rate of pay, with knock on effects regarding plans for dealing with demobilisation.

At the rate at which radar mechanics were being released I had expected a date around June or July 1946. This promotion had probably pushed that period further on. The big imponderable in planning for the future was when I could expect to start teacher training. Ideally, being demobbed one month and starting preparation for a new profession a couple of months latter would fit the bill nicely. What I was hoping for was as short a break as possible between the two. I had nothing to return to save the job as an accounts clerk I had held before enlisting. I wasn't keen on that, even as a stopgap, and the pay would be derisory. The longer I could continue as a Sergeant Radar Mechanic the better from a financial point of view. On the other hand, Ann and I wanted to be together. Having discussed it over a period, we decided to wait and see how things worked out.

Events gave further food for thought when it was announced that plans were afoot to hand over our radar site to the French air force, and some of their personnel were attached to us for training on the job. The CO delegated responsibility for this programme to me and I devised wall charts, written in French, designed to impose rigour into faultfinding procedures. Over a period of six weeks several new mechanics were successfully inducted. For me the complicating question was whether I was doing myself out of a job. What would my position be after the takeover? The CO asked questions higher up the chain of command, and came back with an intriguing answer. My position as sergeant was secure, but a specific posting could not be promised at this stage. Were I, however, to sign on as a regular for nine years, a permanent Warrant Officership was on offer. This really put the cat among the pigeons. I now had to balance a further nine years of life in the RAF, in a rank many would die for, against a teaching career, always presuming I passed the training course. The former would mean married quarters, or long spells of married life apart, and the search for a new career nine years on. The latter would provide a career for life with a pension at the end. I settled for teaching and decided to take demobilisation whenever it came along. I told Ann, who was in full agreement. All we needed now was my ticket to Civvy Street.

The handover to the French had meant that for me leave was out of the question for several weeks, and I reached the stage about August when I thought I might as well forget all about leaves and await my demob. One by one, colleagues were departing, not to be replaced. Being busy on the technical site kept me fully occupied and the weeks slipped by. Before I knew it another Christmas had crept upon us. It was a relatively low key affair. There were few of us left, the unit was running down, and the French were to take over completely imminently. Hans accepted his seat at the table without demur and we toasted each other's good health. Over our time together we had built up a good relationship based on mutual respect. He continued his regular Sunday morning attendance at church.

A day or two after Christmas the CO took the unusual step of visiting me in my room. "I've got news for you, Sergeant," he beamed. "We're getting rid of you at last. Your demob's come through." I bounded off the bed where I'd been stretched out listening to the radio. "Great," I exulted. "When do I leave?" "You're to report in Paris on Jan 3," he advised, adding, "Happy New Year." "And a Happy New Year to you too, sir," I reciprocated.

Now that it had arrived, I found myself experiencing unexpected mixed feelings. It wasn't that I didn't relish the thoughts of a new life, especially with Ann, but the past six years had imposed a pattern it would not be easy to discount. Those years had been good to me, had shaped my view of the world, had been enriched by firm friendships and studded with momentous events. All fell into perspective that night when I phoned Lewis with my news. Ann was not available but my message was passed on. "Join me at home. Expected time of arrival January 4." I reckoned that arrival in Paris on the third should see me home on the fourth

My farewells to Janine, Jean, and the daughters were said at an evening meal at which Maman excelled herself, and a bottle of champagne was opened. As a special concession, she invited me to open the bottle. My only previous experience had been at the CO's wedding reception when I had performed the function with some aplomb before a huge crowd of guests. On that occasion, Janine had given me expert coaching. Sad to say, I proved to be a poor student on this final evening. As we all know, the slow easing of the cork, allowing the pressure to be released in its own good time, achieves the highly satisfactory conclusion of a spectacular explosion, accompanied by a catapulted cork. This time the cork split and a thin stream of pressurised champagne sprayed the length of the table with Janine in pursuit, glasses at the ready. On this note, my French family and I took leave of one another.

When the time arrived, Cpl Tom Goodacre, who was being demobbed at the same time, and I were to be given transport to Wing HQ at Reims, where further arrangements would be notified. Late in the evening before departure, I climbed the stairs to the attic to say farewell to Hans. He was noticeably low in spirits, probably wondering what the immediate future held for him following my departure. "It will not be long before you too will go home," I said, in an effort to cheer him up. "It's a long, long time since I saw home," he remarked ruefully. "Do you have family?" I asked him. He took some time to answer, obviously struggling to control his emotions. "A wife and two daughters, " he replied, huskily, and began rummaging in a battered wallet. "Here, I show you." He handed over a rather old, well-thumbed snapshot. I gazed on it in mounting disbelief. I was looking at the woman whose house we had taken over in Bad Mergentheim. Beside her stood the two flaxen-haired girls to whom I had given chocolate bars. "Hans," I said in a voice just above a whisper, "where in Germany is your home?" "I am in Bad Mergentheim" he replied. Another long pause followed. "And your daughters' names," I said, "are Ilsa and Eva." He regarded me in silence as the bizarre truth sank in. "You are the kind Englishman my wife has told me about," he mused. Then, stretching out his hand for the return of his photograph, he said, "Danke. Danke schon." adding, and I write it in English, "And now I can tell her that you were good to me too." Still stunned by the revelation of this remarkable coincidence, I held out my hand. Hans took it. "Tomorrow morning I shall be leaving," I said. "I hope with all my heart that you will soon be returned to your family. Do please remember me to them." Hans smiled enigmatically. "Herr Ken leave tomorrow. Hans leave day after." I advised him to do nothing rash. Again he smiled. "Auf wiedersehen," he said, "und wieder danke schon." We parted. He was not to be seen the following morning.

Tom Goodacre and I took a last look at the villa and the main street of La Capelle as we headed for Reims mid-morning. We'd been advised that the onward journey to Paris would be by bus, and so it proved. We were treated to a rural route that seemed to take in every village between Reims and Paris, where we arrived in the early evening. Luckily there was a regular stopping place quite near the camp to which we were to report. We booked in, to be told that bad weather in the Channel had caused cancellation of several ferry crossings, that there were none tomorrow, when we would need to report in again. Meanwhile, they had overnight accommodation but had no objection to our sleeping out. We opted for the latter and travelled into the city, where we booked into a cheap bed and breakfast place in Montmartre. I asked the concierge the price. "With or without a woman?" he asked. "Without," I replied and Tom and I occupied adjacent rooms at the front of the building. The women were without, i.e. outside all night, and we heard a succession of them bedding clients until we fell asleep.

I'd had the foresight to take note of the telephone number of the transit camp office, and rang first thing the following morning. No crossing for us today. I persuaded them to accept similar daily calls until there was a crossing. We had all the relevant documentation. All we needed was the go ahead.

Since neither of us had been impressed with our Montmartre experience, we decided to move up market. Our departure railway station being the Gare du Nord, we went into the hotel of the same name, which was directly opposite. Speaking French, I asked at the desk if they had two rooms available for the night, with the possibility of an extended stay of a further night or two. They had, a porter was called, and he led us to the lift, stepping out on the top floor. The rooms were small, at the rear of the building, and had no view, but what odds—we were going home soon. As he put our bags down, the porter enquired surreptitiously, "Have you any cigarettes?" "Yes," I replied, "plenty of cigarettes." On a whim, I asked him how many cigarettes would secure a larger room at the front and with a view. He quoted a figure. "Dirt cheap," I thought and started haggling. We finished up in the honeymoon suite (no demand in early January) with full maid service for three nights. As Tom tucked into a Continental breakfast, served by a frilly aproned French maid, and looked out of the wide bay windows at the Parisian scene beyond, he sighed contentedly and said, "I've never done anything remotely like this before." "Nor me," I observed, "but I could definitely get used to it."

A telephone call on the fourth morning confirmed that the honeymoon was over. We booked out, crossed the road, and boarded the train for Boulogne. Two memorable observations filter back through the memory. First, The Channel looked very rough. Second, vendors were selling bunches of bananas.

Almost every passenger bought a large hand, intent I'm sure on taking them home, where bananas hadn't been seen for years. That was my intention too. I could not resist tasting one to recapture the long forgotten flavour. It was delicious. A second confirmed my initial judgement. Within ten minutes, I'd persuaded myself that I could scarcely take home the paltry few that were left, so I scoffed them as well. The crossing was really rough, and I thoroughly deserved to be seasick, but wasn't. All around me people were retching, and I couldn't help but notice that bananas figured prominently in their vomit.

Our final destination was RAF Kirkham in Lancashire, where we arrived about 6pm. The meal on offer was unappealing so we decided to eat out, boarding a double decker bus bound for the town centre. One or two stops along the way, a delicious smell wafted up the stairs to the upper deck. Tom and I exchanged glances, said not a word, rose, belted down the stairs, and on to the pavement. Directly in front of us was a fish and chip shop. It had tables set out. The counter was extremely high, and I stood there like a ten year old, eyes glazed, as a huge portion of cod, chips done to a turn, and lashings of mushy peas were heaped on to an enormous platter. Salt cellar, pepper pot, and vinegar bottle were on the table. Tea was served in huge mugs. To cap it all, slices of white bread were available. I'd forgotten the special flavour white bread and butter has when eaten with fish and chips. We returned to camp thoroughly satisfied.

Within the hour we'd become civilians again, clothed in a paper –thin grey suit with chalk stripes, shirt, collar and tie, underclothes, socks, pair of shoes, light fawn macintosh and trilby hat. It felt very strange. "That's your lot," said the sergeant in charge of the transformation. "You can go back to the missus now." "I'm all for that," said Tom, who lived nearby. So saying, he wished me well and departed. "Where are you bound for?" asked the sergeant. "T'other side of the country," I replied. "North east coast to be precise No chance this time of night." He consulted some timetables. "If you can get to Preston for eight o'clock, you'll catch the express to Scotland. Change at Penrith and you'll get a connection to Darlington. The last train from there to your place is 00-15 hrs. I reckon you can make it." he said. "You'll need a taxi to Preston. If you like, I'll order one." I jumped at the chance.

The subsequent journey was one of the coldest I have ever experienced. The train over the Pennines was unheated, and the difference between the civilian clothing just acquired and my recently discarded RAF uniform was made increasingly evident. I awoke the family unexpectedly about 01-30. The cold was soon forgotten in the warmth of the welcome. My wartime days were over. A new life awaited.

Epilogue

A month later a package arrived from the RAF containing a Certificate of Good Service, awarded for devotion to duty. An accompanying letter, signed by an Air Commodore, explained that, had I still been in the Service the award would have been presented at a full muster parade. A week or two after that a letter arrived bearing a German postmark. It was from Hans. As he had said he would, he'd disappeared from La Capelle the day after I'd left, eventually arriving at Bad Mergentheim. How had he done it? His Sunday morning visits to church had provided more than spiritual nourishment. The unfathomable depths of that Mother Superior's strikingly violet eyes held the secret confessions of many souls, and sought to minister to their needs. In Hans' case she had arranged his safe passage across Europe, from convent to convent. It had taken weeks but his prayers had been answered. It speaks volumes for the respect we had for each other that he felt it safe to confide in me. Perhaps this is a fitting way to end these memoirs, with an Englishman on the one hand, and a German on the other, reconciling the differences that had driven their nations into bitter conflict, and saluting each other as fellow human beings.